Spiritual, Moral, Social and Cultural Education

Exploring Values in the Curriculum

Edited by
Stephen Bigger
and Erica Brown

David Fulton Publishers
London

David Fulton Publishers Ltd
Ormond House, 26–27 Boswell Street, London WC1N 3JD

First published in Great Britain by David Fulton Publishers 1999

Note: The right of Stephen Bigger and Erica Brown to be identified as the editors of this work has been asserted by them in accordance with the Copyright, Designs and Patents Act 1988.

Copyright © David Fulton Publishers Ltd 1999

British Library Cataloguing in Publication Data
A catalogue record for this book is available from the British Library

ISBN 1–85346–593–3

Typeset by FSH Print & Production Ltd
Printed by The Cromwell Press Ltd, Trowbridge, Wilts.

Contents

Contributors

Dr Stephen Bigger, editor, freelance writer and M.Ed. tutor at Westminster College, Oxford.

Alan Brown, Deputy General Secretary of the National Society (Church of England).

Erica Brown, editor, Head of Research and Development, Special Educational Needs at Westminster College, Oxford.

Jackie Chapman, senior lecturer in Art Education, Westminster College, Oxford.

David Coates, senior lecturer in Science and Technology Education, Westminster College, Oxford.

Ann Disney, senior lecturer in Primary English and Children's Literature, Westminster College, Oxford.

Shirley Dobson, lecturer in German, Westminster College, Oxford.

Jennifer Gray, senior lecturer in Physical Education, Westminster College, Oxford.

Dr Chris Higgins, senior lecturer in Mathematics and Information Technology, Westminster College, Oxford.

Margaret Jones, senior lecturer in Mathematics and Mathematics Education, Westminster College, Oxford.

Ann Jordan, senior lecturer in Primary Education, University College, Worcester.

Dr Avril Maddrell, senior lecturer and research fellow in Geography, Westminster College, Oxford.

Paul Maiteny, consultant and researcher, Grubb Institute of Behavioural Studies, London; tutor, MSc in Environmental and Development Education, South Bank University; associate lecturer, Open University; and consultant to Global Vision Network, Elstree Film Studios.

Stuart May, lecturer in Geography, Westminster College, Oxford.

Jennie McFadden, senior lecturer in Science, Westminster College, Oxford.

Philip Meadows, Assistant Professor of Historical Theology and Wesley Studies, Garrett-Evangelical Theological Seminary, Evanston, Illinois.

Dr Tim Pound, senior lecturer in English, Westminster College, Oxford.

Nick Rose, Oxfordshire LEA Advisory Teacher in Technology and Head of Design and Technology in St Augustine of Canterbury Upper School, Oxford.

David Smith, researcher, Stapleford Centre, and assistant editor of the *Journal of Education and Christian Belief*.

Peter Stead, senior lecturer in Music Education, Westminster College, Oxford.

Dr Paul Taylor, senior lecturer in History Education, Westminster College, Oxford.

David Thomas, tutor in Drama, Westminster College, Oxford; chair of examiners for Drama with SEG, and former Drama Adviser for Oxfordshire.

Ros Wade, OXFAM Educational (United Kingdom); and course director, M.Sc. in Environmental and Development Education, South Bank University.

Preface

This book is for all teachers in primary and secondary education, whatever their subject specialism. The state school curriculum is now tightly specified in terms of subject content; but education is also about pupils' learning – so their total set of experiences in school are important, stemming as much from how they are taught as what they are taught. Pupils do imbibe information; but more importantly they grow as individuals and develop values and a stance for living out their lives. This is influenced by many things – home, family, the media, friends as well as school. But school can be a place where experiences and values are integrated, discussed and shaped into a meaningful philosophy of life. All curriculum subjects can contribute to this, within a whole-school ethos which promotes personal and social development.

This book, by a range of teachers and teacher trainers, explores whole curriculum issues (Part 1) including religious education, drama, citizenship and vocational education; and (Part 2) the National Curriculum subjects. Some readers will want to read through this book in its entirety as a way of reflecting on the pupils' whole experience; others may wish to focus on their specialist subjects but will get a fuller insight into spiritual, moral, social and cultural issues, and the development of values in general, by reading Part 1 in addition to their specialist chapter in Part 2.

We hope that spiritual, moral, social and cultural issues, being promoted by OFSTED and others following the 1988 Education Reform Act, can be viewed as opportunities to help pupils to learn and develop rather than additional impositions on an already overburdened teaching force. Good teachers actively develop an environment and ethos in school in which all pupils can flourish, intellectually, emotionally, physically, creatively, morally, socially, culturally. Education engages each pupil as a whole person: how to integrate a segmented subject-based curriculum should be planned and not left to chance. This is not a new concept, but it is easy to lose sight of it where syllabuses are imposed in detail and taught by different people. This concern for pupils' welfare, well-being and wholeness has been described as promoting their 'spiritual health'[1] through caring personal concern, respect for the individual, and avoidance of hypocrisy, rigidity, negative pressures and conflict. This powerful agenda sees education as developing the individual within the group rather than an exercise in handling information.

Spiritual, moral, social and cultural education is a huge controversial area, without general consensus on many key points. A book of this sort has therefore to be introductory, pointing to sources of further reading and providing signposts through the issues. In a sense, each chapter justifies a volume to itself. To shape a book within these constraints, the editorial hand has been heavy and we would like to thank contributors for their patience and forbearance; their ideas are their own, and there has been no 'party-line'. The writers have produced stimulatingly different approaches to their task; but it is interesting how common ground has emerged.

Stephen Bigger and Erica Brown
Oxford, October 1998

Note
[1] John W. Fisher, 'Helps and Hindrances to Fostering Students' Spiritual Health'. Paper at the conference on 'Where are we going with SMSC', Fifth Annual Conference on Education, Spirituality and the Whole Child, Roehampton Institute, 1998.

Part One

The Whole Curriculum

Chapter 1

Spiritual, moral, social and cultural education

Stephen Bigger

What kind of young people are being turned out by the education system? Youngsters who know facts about academic subjects? Or motivated responsible young adults with a thirst for understanding, a curiosity about life, a concern to contribute to the communities in which they find themselves, and to build relationships with other people? The compulsion to 'reform' education has focused on systems and curriculum, but should not lose sight of how education affects pupils and fits them for the tasks ahead. Which vision of education we choose helps us to create policies and priorities on teaching and learning. There is a tension in British education between many different voices, debating teaching and assessment methods, accountability, relationships between schools and parents, and values.

Schools have been turned upside down by developments stemming from the 1988 Education Reform Act which brought in a National Curriculum of traditional subjects, choosing a vision that pupils should be aware of and interested in these. 'It is quite common for people to excel at subjects yet not have benefited as persons' (Newby 1997, p. 292): this raises the question of the extent to which education should focus on understanding life and the world and our place and role within it – educating the whole person (Erricker *et al.* 1997). As a response, cross-curricular perspectives and themes were put in place, demonstrating how social, personal, environmental, vocational and citizenship perspectives could be introduced. These are of low priority in a crowded school curriculum.

The 1988 Education Reform Act had higher aspirations as is revealed by its opening statement, that the school curriculum should promote the spiritual, moral, cultural, mental and physical development of pupils and to prepare pupils for the opportunities, responsibilities and experiences of adult life. The National Curriculum Council (NCC 1993) produced a discussion paper with a broad secular view of spirituality, and with moral values 'which contain moral absolutes' sounding like a behaviour policy. The Schools Curriculum and Assessment Authority (SCAA) reported on a national conference regarding the place of spiritual and moral development in education for adult life (SCAA 1996). From this came a national forum to advance discussion. The focus on spiritual, moral, social and cultural aspects of education recognises the importance of human experience – of life, of how we think about ourselves, our responsibilities, our place in the world, and our responses to others who are different. Whatever else it does, education should help children understand themselves and their world and enable them to make an informed and responsible contribution to their community and to society. Academic subjects have a part to play, contributing to a school's positive ethos. The Office for Standards in Education (OFSTED) are required to monitor this.

In this book we examine the human side of the school curriculum – both in the formal curriculum which is planned and taught, and the informal curriculum of hidden messages that pupils pick up. If pupils are *taught* justice but experience unfairness in the school system, the informal learning from experience may be the more powerful. The legally prescribed daily act of collective worship can provide a focus for a caring, sharing ethos: but we need a substantial redefinition of 'worship' (usually used in the context of believers) to have an *educational* rather than confessional purpose, for groups of pupils from a range of religious backgrounds or with secular life-stances. A focus on the values discussed here provide a starting point.

Values

The main aim of education is a matter of political debate, but answers revolve around the following:

• knowledge and understanding;

• preparing children for later life and wider society;

• the development of responsible attitudes.

In a sense education sets out to teach students to become informed and functioning members of society with the skills to contribute to work and to the community. These different aims present dilemmas as to how balance is best achieved. The traditional curriculum packaged knowledge into named subjects, each with a body of skills and an implicit 'canon' of preferred subject content. Assessment ensured that the material has been understood. The structure of the National Curriculum encourages this, although skills, attitudes and values can, and are encouraged to be explored in relation to the topics covered by appropriate teaching and learning methods.

OFSTED distinguishes between good and bad schools, according to its own set criteria, in which attainment in academic subjects predominate. A school might be getting excellent academic results but not developing responsible young adults ready to play a part in the wider world. This has been expressed sharply by deschooling arguments, such as by Ivan Illich (1971) who argued that, if the educational focus is inappropriate, schools are not preparing young people for life but are damaging their abilities to become responsible and creative members of society. Schools, on this view, are bad for pupils, however good their academic results.

Our task is to enable schools to become good for children by encouraging participation in learning which includes responsible problem-solving, critical management of information, informing choices and developing skills. That this can be done through the curriculum orders is implicit in government statements. The emphasis on spiritual, moral, social and cultural aspects of learning can help to transform teaching and learning strategies and address wider and deeper issues. Watson and Ashton (1995, p. 73) stressed the usefulness of the concept of *openness* – openness to fresh evidence; to the experience of others; to appreciating real needs and situations, especially relating to other people; and to critical assessment. Values are highlighted in the cross-curricular perspectives and themes which begin to address environmental, multicultural, vocational, economic and political values. These are not assessed, so not all schools will give them high priority (let alone a budget). Teachers need the support of other adults in the community – parents, the business community, the police, medical, social and youth services. Partnership strategies have flourished over the past decade and are a potent underused strategy towards a more socially integrated education system.

Schools deliberately promote their core values – generally expressed as tolerance, respect, responsibility, fairness, caring, sharing, cooperation, and commitment. They try, not always successfully, to put these values into practice in daily routines. We will now explore the parameters of the terms spiritual, moral, social and cultural, widely used today as a guide to organisation and planning. We will then examine, in later chapters, how curriculum areas can respond positively to this agenda.

Spiritual aspects

The word 'spiritual' tends to evoke religious feelings of prayer, meditation, mystical vision and relationship with the divine. This stems from a time when sacred and secular were scarcely divided: the 'spiritual' was embedded in story, of deities, of divine actions in the world, of Jesus, or Krishna, or Shiva, of personal relationships with deities, and of faith. Inner feelings of trust, commitment and aspiration were seen naturally as part of this domain. True there was tension between mystical spirituality and orthodox religion which felt threatened by the lack of doctrinal boundaries. And as a result, some paid with their lives, accused of being heterodox (i.e. not orthodox, or as the authorities would say, heretical). A religion can nevertheless be big enough to encompass spiritual growth and insight, and many religious leaders were spiritual innovators.

The word 'spiritual' has a curious history, deriving from the Latin *spirare* 'to breathe'. 'Spirit' was commonly the same word as 'breath' and 'wind'. The Greek *pneuma* (which gives us our word pneumatic) can mean breath, wind or Holy Spirit. Observation noted that breath is evidence of life, so it was used as a metaphor for the inner life, the self, the life force. Wind then mythically symbolises

God's breath, evidence of a Creator's existence. 'Spirit' is primarily a metaphor for that which animates us, which includes intellect, emotions, personality and personal commitments. That it was customary to operate within current frameworks of religious doctrine should not restrict us today at a time when secular life-stances are also common. The spiritual focuses on contemplation about ourselves, our place in the cosmos, our responsibilities and the meaning we give to our lives and experiences. We seek inner peace. The insights, flashes of deeper understanding and awareness, can be life transforming. Issues of life and meaning are often mundane as we struggle to work things out the hard way. Today these are by no means, and need not be, tied to religious doctrine.[1]

What we mean by 'self' involves both physical and inner dimensions: we have an inner picture of ourselves which is not necessarily accurate. People under-esteem or over-esteem their abilities and personalities. In a sense 'self' is our image of the inner consciousness, the word we use to describe our personal together-ness. However, personality can dramatically change after brain damage, and emotions can be stimulated by electrical brain stimulation, so our inner being is influenced by outer stimuli. Are we a body filled with personality which departs elsewhere at death? Traditional Christianity talks of *body, soul* and *spirit*, dividing our inner consciousness from our enduring spiritual essence. The belief, that when we die, we survive, we are not annihilated, is the root of religious hope. The alternative is that when the body dies, the whole being dies with it, because our 'self' is only the accumulated experiences and perceptions processed by our brains. On this secular view, there are no ghosts and no immortality. To die is to cease to be. Either view is properly possible as an expression of spirituality.

Schools are religiously neutral educational institutions: we need to tread a careful path between assumptions and beliefs about spirituality found in a society that includes a variety of religions and a strong secular trend. The spiritual, our inner life or self, our non-tangible personality, our self-awareness, cannot be located in a post mortem. We appreciate beauty, reflect on experience and creatively express our personality. We create an holistic understanding of our human lives as a step towards recognising personal meaningfulness. OFSTED commented (1994b): 'Spiritual development is to be judged by how well the school promotes opportunities for pupils to reflect on aspects of their lives and the human condition through, for example, literature, music, art, science, religious education and collective worship, and how well the pupils respond'. In practice however, it has proved difficult to conceptualise and to implement (A. Brown 1996)[2]. OFSTED's *evidence* for spiritual education consists mainly of religious education, despite its declared intention for spirituality to be much broader. E. Brown (1996) focused on opportunities for stillness, for pupils being aware of themselves as individuals, for reflection and sharing, for feeling wonder at beauty, for personal responses, and for working in a secure environment which values, supports and respects them. Stillness is not content free: it can be a medium for religious *expression*, focusing on God; or *ethical*, concentrating on loving kindness; or *personal*, remembering family and friends with affection; or a *rational* calming process, emptying the mind of trivia. *Wonder* is self-constructed, a way of describing an emotional response which itself develops (whether it declines or increases) over time and experience. *Awe* is a particular kind of emotional response, to something vast (the universe) or powerful (a storm, a mountain). Religious people may set these in a particular doctrinal framework (the powerful creator God).

Becoming more aware of who we are causes us to consider our limitations: our *mortality*, coming to terms with the fact that we will die – this impacts on the way we live our lives and manage our relationships; our *shortcomings*, developing strategies to overcome our weaknesses and to use guilt positively; and our *limited understanding* about life, our futures, and about the nature of death, leading to speculation about an afterlife, the nature of the soul as (or *if*) distinct from the body, reincarnation and rebirth, heaven and hell. That we have a soul or spirit which is immortal and will exist even when our body is dead is a widely held religious belief, emphasising the inner awareness of ourselves as persons: 'I' will not cease when my body wears out. However, our concept of self is intellectually constructed through our (somewhat biased) reflection on our feelings, thoughts and actions. The existence of an 'I' behind this often faulty self-image (and the nature and essence of our 'selves') is more than an academic question – but we cannot trust our mental self image; humans are skilled in self-delusion.

In education, spirituality will be expressed in general terms:

• the concepts of self, self-worth, self-esteem;

• the concept of relationship, how we set our own self-worth beside that of others;

• our needs, physical, emotional and psychological;

• our self-understanding and self-realisation;

• questions of the meaning of life and mortality.

Spiritual perspectives can help pupils come to terms with:

• who they are;

• what kind of people they are;

• how we construct meaning and purpose for our lives;

• how we express hope, aspiration and faith;

• personal trustworthiness, honesty, quality and good faith.

Moral aspects

The term 'moral' refers to norms of socially acceptable behaviour – although society tends not to hold a unanimous view, as witnessed by controversies about abortion. Moral education encourages not only the learning about moral rules but also the investigation of moral decision-making. The formal intellectual process of analysing moral situations is called *ethics*, which examines underlying issues and principles in personal choices. A moral rule would not necessarily be accepted. We are looking in a sense at:

- what ethical dilemmas need discussing;
- the validity of moral norms;
- how behaviour lives up to moral expectations and ethical principles.

An ethical analysis does not have a fore-ordained right answer. Each situation is unique; general principles need balancing against each other. Some commonly used concepts are not always easy to define – justice, exploitation, discrimination, good faith, honesty, reliability, trustworthiness, malice. Legal decisions can be unjust, as Jews under Nazi rule attest, as the laws were discriminatory. In not too distant times, the law supported slavery and racial discrimination. 'Exploitation' assumes that an imposition is 'unfair', that those with an unfair advantage have used their power against the interests of the weaker. But there is room for debate: whether a low wage-earner is 'exploited' is not clear-cut. Examples of discrimination are often subtle and capable of being explained away when challenged. 'In good faith' and 'with malice' have been puzzled over by juries: a malicious witness may be very plausible.

Children need to experience moral debate in action, to be treated with respect, and to develop awareness of ethical issues and dilemmas in practice. Ethical debate involves real world situations seen from different perspectives by people with different agendas. They experience the use and abuse of power not only in governments but also in their own lives, in school. Bullies cause unhappiness in those they encounter: those who assume power – Hitler, Stalin, Idi Amin, Pol Pot – can cause absolute desolation to millions. This raises issues of how young people can resolve conflict. A school's ethos can help pupils' to develop expectations of responsibility and self-reliance, to consult, to be honest about other people's feelings, and to respect each others' needs and desires. It can, in O'Brien's words (1998) promote positive behaviour.

The question of moral absolutes is often raised, that moral rules are laid down by revelation – the Ten Commandments, the 613 laws of the Torah for Jews, the golden rule for Christians, the Qur'an for Muslims. For some these will be important guidelines – but often need interpreting for current use. Revelation uses a different moral process, not logical deduction but the application of externally given rules which may be contradictory and need interpreting. Morality here is derived from obeying the scriptures and following the example of significant religious leaders. Terms like 'evil' and 'wickedness' refer to actions as well as people. A miscreant can repent; but some, like Hitler, committed evil acts deliberately, persistently, with pleasure and without remorse. At what point can we label *people* as evil? And what as a society do we do about them? Human rights abuses are unfortunately common even today. Can we reshape our future in terms of a global respect for human rights? And to what extent should we consider the rights of other animals also? For those without authoritarian morality, there needs to be a baseline.

Policy-makers sometimes become obsessed that pupils should be taught 'right' from 'wrong' (thus OFSTED 1994b). The distinction between externally *imposed* and internally *chosen* morality reappears in the literature of moral education (e.g. Piaget 1932) where children are said to move from an externally imposed set of rules (*heteronomy*, or other people's rules, motivated by fear of sanctions) to a higher stage of working out moral principles for themselves (*autonomy*, within of course social rules by common consent, which can be flouted). There is a conflict here between individualism and communalism – independence being asserted as a higher value than remaining within a particular doctrinal framework. Social conformity however is valued by religions which regard an 'anything goes' autonomy as undisciplined and self-centred. Saint Augustine reputedly said 'Love God and do as you wish': that is, our fundamental attitudes affect what we are, what we do and what we wish. Rather than having to obey a set of rules, it is possible to become the sort of person who naturally wishes to act in line with certain standards. Lawrence Kohlberg (1984) spoke of *Pre-conventional* (characterised by reward and punishment), *Conventional* (good boys/nice girls with respect for authority), and *Post Conventional* (forming values and principles). Carol Gilligan (1982) emphasised caring relationships and emotional ties. Our own moral paths will be shaped by others and perhaps by a tradition (a handing down from parents to children). Choices are not made in a vacuum. Autonomy is not the same as self-centredness. Moral education focuses on our relationships and responsibilities, how positively we contribute to our community, and how we moderate our wishes by considering the needs of others.

Virtue, says Aristotle, is a disposition to autonomous and responsible right action motivated by human happiness in its broadest sense (Thomson 1953). It cannot be achieved without laws and education. Matt Ridley (1996) relates this to evolution: reciprocity gave humans a distinct evolutionary advantage by relying on goodwill and trust, ostracising those who are not team players. There is a difference however between teamwork and moral action: the cooperative activity may involve the domination of weaker groups whose inclusion in the team is not viewed as needed. 'Virtue' (the desire for reciprocity) may be in the genes – but so are contrary pressures, for sex, for power, for affluence. Skillen (1997) argues that teaching virtue implies anti-authoritarian schools, democratic classrooms, children given responsibility, and pedagogy involving discussion and group activities. Wringe (1998) defines virtues in terms of an 'ethic of respect for equal freedom'.

Social aspects

Humans are social animals who 'come into the world equipped with pre-dispositions to learn how to cooperate, to discriminate the trustworthy from the treacherous, to commit themselves to be trustworthy, to earn good reputations, to exchange goods and information, and to divide labour' (Ridley 1996, p. 249). Through rendering and receiving mutual aid, humans have evolved both complex societies and passed on important discoveries such as language, tool making and agriculture. Language enabled traditions and stories to be passed on, although language variations encouraged insularity. Non-verbal language, and in particular the smile, crossed linguistic, social and cultural boundaries, encouraging a wider reciprocity; yet in general the potential for non-verbal communication has never really been developed. Social cohesion has enabled the development of skills and culture, yet continuing cooperation cannot be taken for granted: altruism is weaker than the instinct for personal survival. Given a choice between giving aid and being killed, most prefer to stay alive. Vicious authoritarian regimes have showed how threats to life can focus people in their millions on staying alive at the expense of social conscience: yet many steered the dangerous course of risking their lives rendering covert aid. Cooperation, whether an instinct or learned behaviour, needs to be made explicit and supported if it is to survive the vicissitudes of power politics, conflict and war and if it is to play a part in everyday conflict resolution. Collaborative work boosts social skills; and on a wider level, the corporate life of the school community can add a sense of belonging.

In the school curriculum we link social education to 'moral' and 'personal' education (Tattum and Tattum 1992). OFSTED (discussion paper 4/1994) stress the importance of personal relationships and an environment of good behaviour and respect, pointing to teachers' expectations, welfare, personal responsibility and pride in achievement, commitment to school values, consistency and the promotion of self-esteem. Social education has particular points to make about relationships in family, community, national and global settings. Humanity has had a history of exclusivity, a concern to promote one's own family and community at the expense of others, even with violence. There is a growing movement today to transcend national boundaries and look to the health of the whole planet; but there is more rhetoric than reality. Aid budgets become skewed by national interests, decisions impacting on developing countries are made (by for example the World Bank, or by multinationals, or by the United Nations) without adequate consultation either of governments or people. We have only just begun on the path towards global planning.

Identity

Our sense of identity may be linked with family, locality, nationhood, language and religion. Identity is an important marker of meaning, defining our place in the world and determining the way we look at ourselves. It may create deep bonds within the community we identify with (albeit there will also be pressures and tensions). Matters of identity become more complex when families are widely spread, when various languages are spoken at home, and when there are different religious affiliations. Other groups may play an increasing role – friendship groups, professional colleagues and so on. A person might evolve a sense of identity in which the close family play little part, and in which the location of friends is global rather than regional or local. Through the Internet, the group might be virtual, with individuals never meeting face to face. Our sense of kinship and friendship helps us to organise our relationships and establish a position in society. Our sense of identity is affected by the judgements other people make and the descriptions they use. Children described as 'stupid' will feel stupid. Children with multiple disabilities can be helped to appreciate their uniqueness and the contribution which they make.

Power

Society is organised, which means that some people lead and others are led. Those that lead hold power and can thereby affect the lives of others. The values issues here focus on the responsible use of that power, to benefit the community and to support individuals within it. The powerful might be politicians, industrialists, managers or aristocracy. Wealth can buy privilege; the wealthy tend to produce social structures and strategies which maintain and increase their advantage. The poor, with few bargaining counters, cannot easily compete.

Power and wealth combine in international relations also. Many multinational companies have greater wealth than some developing economies. Their commercial decisions can break a country, particularly where commercial crops and products are restricted in range. We hear about corrupt rulers of developing states, and there are serious issues here; but chief executives and managers of multinationals are accountable not to society but to shareholders interested mainly in profit. This opens the gates to exploitation.

Education can explore the proper use of power in various ways. More is learnt from actions than from words, so power-sharing and responsible use of power need to be experienced as well as discussed. Through democratic organisation in school, pupils can learn to live as a self-regulating community used to being responsible for their own actions. This works differently with different ages, but responsible problem-solving strategies are appropriate from infant classes to sixth forms. Clearly the best results come when pupils experience continuity throughout schooling: creating democratic approaches with classes not used to them takes time and sensitivity. Teachers have to balance the need for organisation involving a degree of authority, with the need for the development of self-discipline, for its own sake and not because it is externally imposed. Yet some external rules can become socially agreed for the good of the group. Such guidelines come more naturally from a motivated community, so actions to develop motivation through involvement and participation are crucial.

Status

Society is divided into a series of parallel communities. Some revolve around ethnic origins and provide support mechanisms for people who originate from the same place, speak the same language and share the same religion and culture. We call these ethnic minority cultures, sometimes forgetting that the majority group may also have an ethnic character (e.g. white Anglo-Saxon Protestants). Another form of social stratification produces class distinctions. These have been traditionally described in terms of upper, middle and working classes: other social analyses refer to socio-economic groups based on jobs and earning power. Our place in the stratified order is likely to determine educational experience and achievement, income level, housing, nutrition and even life expectancy.

Social justice

The curriculum needs to take an interest in how society legislates and organises itself in ways which allow for fairer distribution of opportunities. Children can be actively involved in working towards more socially just conditions. This is more than political correctness, which the advantaged on occasions attack by maligning extremes presented as absurd: it is about showing respect for all and creating a fairer world in which people are not written off as victims. This involves an understanding of people as interdependent, needing each other in many different ways.

Cultural aspects

Culture is an ambiguous term, but gains some strength from the ambiguity. For the person in the street, culture means the arts (theatre, art galleries, dance and music) and heritage industries (museums, castles and stately homes). But culture is also an anthropological term for the whole attitude, belief system and world view which produced these artefacts and ceremonies. Thus we speak of monocultural and multicultural perspectives (from one cultural point of view or from many). The 'culture' of 'multicultural' involves beliefs, the arts (dance, story, song), and the characteristic ways in which particular sets of people view their world, including their language and identity. Brown and Brown (1997) see cultural development as involving values, beliefs, attitudes and customs which form the basis of identity and cohesion in social groups.

Culture is thus wider than the arts. We need both accurate information (and preferably examples and experience) and sympathetic understanding of other cultures, their attitudes, expectations, modesty codes and food preferences. Stereotypes about ethnic groups persist and need challenging. Each ethnic group has its own settlement history and current socio-economic factors may be a consequence of this – poor housing, high unemployment and so on. But there will be great variety within ethnic groups – educated and poorly educated, well off and poor, professional and working classes, different religious affiliations and so on. Teachers need to be sensitised and well-informed to help children develop respect and learn accurately, and to discourage prejudice and discrimination.

Intercultural understanding is important as children grow up in a world community with opportunities to travel and with world news entering their homes through television. They need to understand what they are seeing and to begin to see issues through the eyes of others. They become aware of global issues if only through famines and environmental concerns. Concerns such as fair trade, sound economies, personal freedoms, and social responsibility may help us all to be less parochial in our attitudes and look beyond personal prosperity and advantage. This is more than giving pupils knowledge about other cultures – their attitudes towards others need exploring, challenging and enriching. This is the strength of the antiracist agenda which gives clear guidelines about what is unacceptable in attitudes, prejudices and actions in our responses to people from other cultures (Griffiths and Troyna 1995, Kincheloe and Steinberg 1997). This provides a moral baseline, using *respect*, *friendship* and *social justice* as yardsticks.

Religion, festivals, food observances, ethical expectations are part of culture and cross national boundaries. A Muslim might be Arab, or African, Pakistani, Indian, or from the Far East – or indeed British. There may be variations, but also common ground. There are many more Jews in America than in Israel, and there is a variety of Jewish traditions, such as Hasidic, Orthodox, Reform (or Progressive) and secular Jews. There are Jewish African tribes (stemming from Jewish traders) and Jewish Arab tribes, such as in Yemen. North European Jews (or Ashkenazis) are distinct from Sephardic Jews from Spain and the wider world. Such diversity is found in all faiths and cultures and needs to be recognised and celebrated if children are to see through crude stereotypes.

Sympathy, empathy and respect are important educational outcomes: teaching tends to focus on critical and analytical skills (answering the question 'prove it'). This is often referred to as 'modernism': but there are many things that are not susceptible to quasi-scientific 'proof'. Indeed, to some, 'modernism' becomes dangerous if it obscures vital perspectives about justice, identity, power relationships and so on: these have become the 'post-modern' agenda. The desire for empathetic understanding of other people has come down a different philosophical line called *phenomenology*. This starts with the notion that the things which appear to be real are actually constructed in our heads: we have to uncover our mental assumptions and stereotypes and lay them aside if we are even to begin to perceive the underlying reality. This is particularly true with our view of other people. We have preconceived ideas based on appearance, accent, clothing – and on the prejudices passed on to us by other people. Laying these aside (or 'bracketing them out') is an important mental discipline; and it helps to build up both empathy and respect in that we can begin, sometimes for the first time, to see people as they really are. There is still room for critical analysis, but at least we can be more certain that what we are analysing is not a prejudice.

Language is an important part of cultural identity. Mother tongue tends to be supported educationally only if the language is dominant, like English. In Wales and Ireland, tensions over language have been resolved by bilingual teaching and the same is true in some Canadian cities (English and French) and in the USA (English and Spanish). There is a brief history in England of mother tongue support for children of ethnic minorities, but all languages cannot be supported (maybe over 40 different languages in a single school) so only dominant minority languages (e.g. Urdu, Bengali) tend to be resourced. For teachers there is a message here to avoid the impression that a mother tongue is worthless or despised, finding ways of allowing children to cherish and celebrate their language. Pride in language and communication tends to enhance ability both in English and in mother tongue. Progress in either will support progress in the other because language will be perceived as important and increase personal motivation.

Conclusion

Schools are concerned with more than the acquisition of knowledge. Knowledge itself tends to be problematic, constantly revised in the light of new data and perspectives. Pupils need the skills to understand the issues, and need to develop a breadth of vision to ask 'why' as well as 'what'. They need to be able to reflect upon the meaning and significance of knowledge – the significance for our understanding of ourselves and our potential, our relationships, our community and our cultural identity and responsibilities.

References

Ainsworth, J. and Brown, A. (1995) *Moral Education*. London: National Society.

Brown, A. (1996) *Spiritual Development in Schools – Invisible to the Eye*. London: National Society.

Brown, E. (1996) *Religious Education for All*. London: David Fulton Publishers.

Brown, A. and Brown, E. (1997) *Religious Education in the Primary School*. London: National Society.

Carr, D. (1996) 'Rival conceptions of spiritual education', *Journal of Philosophy of Education* **30**(2), 159–78.

Day, P. (1997) *Social Development*. London: National Society.

Erricker, C. *et al.* (1997) *The Education of the Whole Child*. London: Cassell.

Gilligan, C. (1982) *In a Different Voice*. Cambridge, Mass.: Harvard University Press.

Griffiths, M. and Troyna, B. (1995) *Anti-racism, Culture and Social Justice in Education*. Stoke-on-Trent: Trentham.

Illich, I. (1971) *Deschooling Society*. London: Calder & Boyars.

Kincheloe, J. L. and Steinberg, S. R. (1997) *Changing Multiculturalism*. Buckingham: Open University Press.

Kohlberg, L. (1984) *The Psychology of Moral Development: The Nature and Validity of Moral Stages* (Essays in Moral Development, vol. 2). San Francisco: Harper & Row.

NCC (1993) *Spiritual and Moral Development* (Discussion paper No. 3). London: School Curriculum and Assessment Authority.

Newby, M. (1997) 'Literary development as spiritual development in the common school', *Journal of Philosophy of Education* **31**(2), 283–94.

O'Brien, T. (1998) *Promoting Positive Behaviour.* London: David Fulton Publishers.

OFSTED (1994a) *The Annual Report of Her Majesty's Chief Inspector for Schools: Standards and Quality in Education.* London: HMSO.

OFSTED (1994b) *Spiritual, Moral, Social and Cultural Development.* London: OFSTED.

Piaget, J. (1932) *The Moral Judgement of the Child.* London: Routledge and Kegan Paul.

Ridley, M. (1997) *The Origin of Virtue.* Harmondsworth, Penguin.

SCAA (1996) *Education for Adult Life: The Spiritual and Moral Development of Young People.* London: School Curriculum and Assessment Authority.

Skillen, T. (1997) 'Can virtue be taught – especially these days', *Journal of Philosophy of Education* **31**(3), 375–93.

Tattum, D. and Tattum, E. (1992) *Social Education and Personal Development.* London: David Fulton Publishers.

Thomson, J. A. K. (1953) *The Ethics of Aristotle.* Harmondsworth: Penguin.

Watson, B. and Ashton, E. (1995) *Education, Assumptions and Values.* London: David Fulton Publishers.

Wringe, C. (1998) 'Reasons, rules and virtues in moral education', *Journal of Philosophy of Education* **32**(2), 225–37.

Further reading

Haydon, G. (1997) *Teaching About Values: A New Approach.* London: Cassell.

Halstead, J. M. and Taylor, M. J. (1996) *Values in Education and Education in Values.* London: Falmer Press.

Watson, B. and Ashton, E (1995) *Education, Assumptions and Values.* London: David Fulton Publishers.

These are helpful introductions to exploring values in school.

Notes
[1] For the view that secular spirituality is a contradiction in terms, see David Carr (1996).
[2] For other views from the National Society (Church of England) see also Ainsworth and Brown (1995); Day (1997).

Chapter 2

Religious Education
Alan and Erica Brown

There is an irony that spiritual, moral, social and cultural education appears to have grown directly out of the words of the 1988 Education Reform Act (Chapter 1, sec. 1, para. 2a) rather than out of any National Curriculum issue. What sharpens the irony is the way in which the intention of the Act has become focused in a manner unintended, certainly unplanned. It was the introduction of the OFSTED inspection process following the Schools' Inspection Act 1992 that raised the profile of Spiritual, Moral, Social and Cultural ('SMSC') education and indeed that profile continues to imprint itself upon the inspector and the inspected.

But the irony does not end there, for the inclusion of those words in the Education Reform Act, and the word 'spiritual' being first, came about through pressure from the churches and other Christian organisations. The 'spiritual education' of pupils remained a prime aim of the Education Reform Act. Even the first version of the National Curriculum used the term 'spiritual' only for it to be omitted from the later slimmed-down version. So, with the inexorable movement of any quango, the Values Forum was created to ensure 'values' – spiritual and other – were very much part of school life. This continued to be reinforced by OFSTED, and inspectors are now required to comment on the opportunities for 'SMSC' in every lesson.

This preamble is of particular relevance to religious education because 'SMSC' is often placed under the umbrella of religious education and the religious education teacher is required to be responsible for its presence in the school on the assumption that religion is about spirituality and morality.

Policy

There are, in England and Wales, about 5,000 state maintained schools with a religious foundation, roughly one third of the total number. Religious education is locally determined through County Agreed Syllabuses for religious education in Community Schools, Voluntary Controlled Schools and some Foundation Schools. In Voluntary Aided schools the religious education is the responsibility of the governing body who approve its content.

To devise a policy that could be equally effective in all schools is problematic. Central government decided not to prepare a curriculum document in RE for all schools but encourage locally based 'agreed' curriculum documents. This would be demanding enough for central government but when religious education in 'county' (soon to be called 'community') schools and some 'foundation' schools as well as voluntary controlled schools is determined locally, it is not easy to ensure coherence across the nation – or even between one LEA and another. Add to this mix the school with a Christian foundation which would regard their religious education policy to be in line with that Christian foundation, and there is a recipe for chaos. Religious education is commonly expected to deliver a substantial amount of each school's commitment to 'SMSC' in less than 5 per cent of curriculum time. In many schools it receives even less, so there is great pressure on the religious education teacher to teach the subject *and* ensure that 'SMSC' is represented to an appropriate degree.

What can religious education contribute?

There is within the professional religious education circuit a lack of agreement about what constitutes RE as a subject. Some regard the subject as a synonym for citizenship or at least providing a framework for a spiritual and moral code which needs to be imprinted on the student. Others regard it as having no direct effect upon the person, preferring to interpret it as a subject discrete in itself. These polarisations are obviously caricatures, but just as the SCAA model syllabuses of 1994 on religious education drew attention to 'Learning About' and 'Learning From' religion, so with religion itself. The question is, 'Is religion a code of conduct, the encapsulation of a moral way of life, to which adherence is required, or is it a means of coping with life, a means of responding to profound questions about the nature of life, the universe and everything?'

Take, for example, a Church of England secondary school where the religious education is very good: i.e. there is ample curriculum time, well-qualified teachers who teach well, and excellent resources. Religious Studies in the curriculum *is* very good *and* the pupils' religious education is enhanced by worship (*both* the statutory *act of worship* and voluntary *services*), by extra-curricular opportunities, by links with churches and clergy and by the religious commitment of the staff. Even in this scenario, the school experience will not constitute the total experience of pupils. The family and the media will also play an important part in exploring a range of social and cultural issues. What should be important is that young people will be able to make connections between their learning in the formal educational context and their life experience. And perhaps even more importantly, that the ethos and mission of the school is demonstrated through the teaching and learning which takes place. Some thought needs to be given to this by the Head of RE. How are the broader implications of religious education to be represented in the non-denominational school where there is no particular religious ethos? Is religion studied? Should it be? Are pupils encouraged to engage with the issues? Or is the divide between Religious Studies (that is, the study of particular religions) and religious education (that is, the development of issues and concepts at a personal level) so wide that the spiritual development of the pupils is affected?

Spiritual development

> Spirituality is like a bird: if you hold it too tightly, it chokes, if you hold it too loosely, it flies away. Fundamental to spirituality is the absence of force. (Rabbi Hugo Gryn 1992)

Self-discipline

Fundamental to all religions is that of self-discipline. Prophets, teachers, founders (or other spiritual leaders) are portrayed as possessing an iron self-discipline which embraces an ability to speak, teach and believe in such a manner that their own vision for society and for the individual is expressed. Those who follow after them strive to follow in their footsteps. This is not, however, a repression of the soul or the person, but a means of finding one's true self. All the great teachers and prophets have, as far as we know, reflected on their position in relation to the vision or revelation they bring.

Self-awareness

Bishop David Konstant, the Roman Catholic Bishop of Leeds, wrote:[1] 'Across the curriculum, spiritual development involves intellectual curiosity, questioning, challenging the perceived values of society, realising that there are often no easy answers to the important questions about life which arise…'. In other words, the accepted order, upon which we all rely, should not be taken for granted. Spiritual insight should have a prophetic aspect whereby there is a continuing analysis of how we live and the way in which we live. We may find our society acceptable but the implication is that we will not. This may lead young people to develop a vision for the future based on understanding rather than on obedience alone for its own sake.

John Hull, in his book, *On Sight and Insight* (1997), writes of two occasions when the senses caused him to reflect on the nature of his blindness and others' ability to see. In 'Bells', the spiritual quality of the bells rung at a wedding lifts him up beyond the mundane. His spirit soars but would those who are sighted and caught up in the beauty of the church and the wedding even have noticed them? Similarly in 'Rain', he notes how his garden is brought to life in the rain because of the different sounds of the grass, leaves and so on. In both cases Professor Hull is fully self-aware, mindful of the world around him, conscious of his relationship with the environment. We can take things for granted; but religious education can open up young people to new understandings of their life experience. Indeed this quest for personal development should also be part of the teacher's experience, and adults generally. School, in a sense, is a preparation for a future in which personal reflection is deemed important.

Self-knowledge

Self-knowledge also lies at the heart of religious awareness and understanding. Brian Keenan's book, *An Evil Cradling*, is hardly a religious book – it is a diary of despair and discernment, hope and friendship; yet one passage becomes as close to that religious self-knowledge as one might ever expect. He experiences what, in another context, could be a religious conversion.

> My own mind was equally restless, seeking out something on which to concentrate and evade the crushing boredom of the coming hours. The room was flushed with the morning's half-light. Birdsong sparked softly outside. Said and I were caught up in our mutual rapture, drifting heedlessly around one another like fish in a tank. Suddenly the dreaming silence was shattered. Said was weeping great shuddering sobs. This was a different kind of weeping from the automatic religious melancholia of his prayers. He walked around the room crying, the whole room seemed to fill up with his anguish. I felt, as I never had before, great pity for this man and felt if I could I would reach out and touch him. I knew instinctively some of the pain and loss and longing that he suddenly found himself overwhelmed by.
>
> The weeping continued. Said became fleshy and human for me. Here was a man truly stressed. His tears now wrenched a great well-spring of compassion. I wanted to nurse and console him. I felt no anger and that defensive laughter that had before cocooned me was no longer in me. I lay on my mattress and looked up over the top of the sheet. Said's shadow, caught, in the sunlight, was immense. It flowed up the wall and across the ceiling. He was now chanting, fleeing from his sadness into recitation. His hands were clasped on the top of his head in the gesture of prayer. His body swayed and turned in a slow chanting circle. The room was filled with his eerie shadow and the slow rhythmic utterances choked with sobs. At times his voice broke and he cried out in desperation for Allah. I felt my own tears. I was transformed with a deep and helpless love for him. I had become what he was calling for.
>
> I woke John. 'Look at this, look at this' I urged quietly. We both stared at the great moving shadow, fascinated and compelled. After a few minutes, John, exasperated, sighed in disgust and turned away. I remained watching. There was something unbearably beautiful about it. At once terrified and intrigued, my loathing for this man began to fall from me. I no longer thought of him as

nothing, and felt guilty for having dismissed him so completely. Said's violence against us was a symptom of his need for us. Here was a man whose mind was forever locked in that desert wilderness that I had known during my worst moments of isolation.

To empathise with a captor is said to be a characteristic of a hostage's mental response, but it gives an unexpected perspective of life which has the potential to be illuminating. School pupils can only gain from exploring step by step such aspects of human existence as the roles we play, our deepest assumptions and prejudices, our friendships and relationships, and our mental image of ourselves. Discussion, literature, drama and the arts can all help pupils see themselves in a different light and all can be used as strategies for teaching religious education. This will encourage pupils to be analytical by applying reason to their experience; but they should also become fully aware of their emotions and inner life, involving their appreciation of the world around them, and their aesthetic awareness. This helps us, as teachers, to develop the whole child: this could offer especial benefit to able, high-achieving pupils who may be caught up in an empirical world where nothing counts if it cannot be seen, measured and proved.

An understanding of the 'sacred'

We have adopted the Polynesian word 'taboo' or 'tabu' into our language. It seems to mean 'forbidden, and in fact in the common English usage it still does, but in fact it carries a greater weight. It has a sacred or special quality about it – rather like the Holy of Holies in the Jewish temple. There is an aura about the 'tabu' – indeed, not unlike the aura that can surround individuals. Perhaps 'set apart' is a better interpretation.

Religious Education should enable pupils to recognise the power of the special place, the special person, the quality of being 'set apart'. It should provide a sense of the numinous whereby pupils can appreciate a greater depth to life. Of course, some will wish to affirm this is not a religious phenomenon – we can experience the 'numinous' or the 'sacred' outside a religious context. This is true, but religion is 'about' sacred or special places and people and while 'sacred' like much English usage reflects a Christian frame of reference, the idea and the concept is applicable to many religions.

The sacred place is about space and as John Hull has written:[1]

Spiritual education inspires young people to live for others. Spirituality exists not inside people but between them…spirituality is to do with solidarity and communion.

If spirituality *involves* the space between people and how we relate (otherwise it would be a self-centred spirituality), then we are immediately led into the contribution religious education can make to moral education. As the Reverend Daishin Morgan put it:[1]

Spiritual development requires us to transcend notions of personal adequacy and inadequacy, complacency and self-doubt. It is the ability to be content with the appearance of ambiguity…it enables one to find stability within the arising of doubt and fear…it gives one a basis for forming relationships.

A very common topic in the RE curriculum is places of worship and there are many books and support materials which help teachers engage pupils. The essence of a place of worship, however, is less about the furniture and its uses and more about what goes on in that place. Some places of worship are awesome architectural structures, others ooze serenity and peacefulness, others again have a strong social base creating an environment in which people meet, worship and eat. The 'spiritual' is more than the 'holy' or the 'sacred', otherwise all spiritual people would be hermits; in religion the spiritual encompasses the search for God (or whatever the goal of the quest is) by including the range of activities that make human beings what they are. If the spiritual is right then the moral, social and cultural aspects fall into place. A place can be 'set apart', can be 'tabu' but it has no spiritual resonance unless its importance is reflected in the moral, social and cultural life of that particular community. It is not possible for the 'spiritual' to stand alone, it has to have a social and cultural context to give it meaning and expression.

Moral development

One of the interesting features of the tension between religion and morality is the way in which some religious leaders and teachers have challenged society's traditional values. In religious education terms it is at least a possibility that pupils would be more interested in the *Dis*agreed Syllabus than in any Agreed Syllabus, for the process of agreement encourages compromise among selected representatives and discourages the controversial and unconventional.

Religions are usually quoted as providing a framework for morality but it is up for debate whether that is truly the case. Politicians tend to object to the clergy criticising a political statement or action, and advise them to leave politics to the politicians. Religious education should help pupils realise that morality and religion may have a symbiotic but often confusing relationship. Students need to understand the issues, both ethical and religious, to help them develop their own informed opinions. If this is regarded as important it will help them to understand how religious people try to reconcile conflicting beliefs and principles.

What often lies at the heart of religious behaviour, and indeed conviction, is not morality but duty. It is the person's responsibility to respond in certain ways; to do their duty, to God, to another person, to society, to their community. Morality, in religious terms, is less connected with conventional actions and more with a developing sense of responsibility and commitment. Religions may of course embody ethical principles which are not unhelpful to moral understanding and they may equally demonstrate actions and attitudes which are not ethically defensible. It is not unknown for religious duty to be used as a rationale for killing people.

One of the remarkable features of many religions is they recognise failure; there appears to be a sympathy with the morally incompetent person who repents. God is viewed as merciful and compassionate so one's sense of wrongdoing can be resolved or redeemed. This is an interesting but often overlooked feature of religion to which religious education can make a significant contribution. Some prophets of doom teach 'no second chance', but that does not seem to be the actual message within the major religions and philosophies. There are, of course, rules and regulations which determine the state of relationships with other people and other communities, but in the main these appear to encourage responsibility and duty.

Religion is not, and never has been, a set of rules. Rules change. The rules of sport may be different next year from this year. Morality is an attitude of mind occurring within a framework of beliefs and commitments. A person's duty, to God, country, family, or social group is the essential element in moral behaviour and religion teaches that what religious education can do is ensure that pupils recognise that religion has an open dialogue with morality, neither constraining nor substituting it. Understanding the nature of religion's critique of morality, and ethical critiques of religion, is important and best addressed through religious education though not solely, other areas of the curriculum have their responsibilities too; but there is a skill and the skill is how pupils can apply this understanding of ethical issues to their own lives and concerns.

In most religions the search is personal – it is *your* salvation, *your* enlightenment, *your* judgement. The egocentric nature of the religious quest can seem at odds with the ethical concern for others. If others get in the way of my search for salvation, why can't I elbow them out of the way and continue on my way? As one might expect, the answer is complex. One possible response could be that one's own individual concern has no meaning unless contextualised in relation to other people. Each person has, therefore, a responsibility *for* himself but a responsibility to others. In practical terms this is expressed in charitable activities, opinions on social issues, specific responses to the needs of the poor, etc. For many religious people the personal quest for God (or enlightenment) lays upon them the need to express the personalness of their belief in the arena of social welfare whether that be working for a religious organisation, expressing firm views on abortion, or working in a secular occupation which serves the needs of others. There is a creative tension between the duty to oneself and one's duty to the world.

Social development

Schools are individual and unique institutions. Most pupils in Britain (93 per cent) are in state schools with 7 per cent in public and independent schools. Each school has a distinctive ethos and culture, they are an essential part of society's method of socialisation. Good behaviour and success is rewarded; poor behaviour and low achievement is admonished. Pupils aged 5 to 16 are put together – compulsorily – with others with whom they may not in other circumstances wish to meet. Teachers (and parents) enable that process to take place. Though each school has a distinctive ethos and character even if they belong to the same denomination or are community schools, there will be obvious broad similarities between them. Schools, through the creation of agreed rules for pupils and staff, try to ensure respect for others, for if they are unable to do so the life of the school community breaks down.

Religions are also social entities; they exist through and around community behaviour in churches, temples, gurdwaras or mosques. Though there will be some common ground, each will have its own identity, its own idiosyncrasies, hierarchies, ways of working, agreements and arguments. There is a cohesive fragmentation in religion which binds the group together when under criticism or attack, but allows for some internal discussion and debate when appropriate. In many ways, the history of religion is the history of social fragmentation. Many religions teach variants of 'love your neighbour' but this is not always evident in their internal and external relationships. The sociology of religion is a long-established discipline which can help the social development of the student both academically and effectively. It explores what people actually do and actually think, using observation and interview techniques.

Religious education contributes to social development when it points to the essential sociability of human beings while weighing in the balance the schismatic nature of that sociability. It can help pupils to recognise that things ebb and flow, rise and fall. Empires come and pass away, religious practice moves onward. Change abounds. Nothing ever stays the same even though many wish it did. Each school is different each time new pupils or new members of staff join. Religions change, otherwise they die and are usurped by a new prophet or a new message. No religion can afford to be locked into the history of its formation though its formation will have determined history.

Religious education can also address social issues. In the primary school there is often an initial focus on relationships and friendships, people who help us and how we can help others. This addresses issues such as working and living with others, and working towards harmony or conflict. Secondary religious education addresses personal responsibility in contexts such as sexual relationships, family, work, wealth and the environment. Explicit religious teaching and example can illuminate many of today's problems, in ways which encourage pupils to think for themselves and reach their own informed judgements.

Cultural development

The a-cultural aspect of religious belief is often overlooked in religious education. Islam may have embraced the Qu'ran revealed through the prophet Muhammad in Arabia but it has transcended cultural boundaries. Jesus was a Jew but the Christian Church grew from its Jewish origins and is culturally diverse. So too are most world faiths, even those that do not seek converts. 'British Muslims' may have ethnic and cultural roots in South Asia, Africa, the Caribbean, America or Europe.

In America, 'Polish-American', 'African American', 'Native-American' might add Christian (Baptist/Episcopalian/Methodist), Jewish, Muslim, Rastafarian and so on to define religious aspects of their background. In religions, there is a great diversity in cultural background which influences what people believe and how they worship. It is virtually impossible to stereotype a religious view – members of faiths argue, debate and reinterpret as the generations pass. We cannot say (although some do!) 'All Christians do this,' or 'All Jews do that'. Would that we could – teaching would be easier but wouldn't it be dull? The essence of RE is the liveliness and vigour of religion, its internal and external diversity.

What emerges from effective religious education is both this diversity of religion as well as the similarity of religious practice. Marriages are different in and between religions, but those religious people who marry still want a religious ceremony. Humankind across faiths and cultures express their most important feelings similarly. So in a superficial way religious education can help pupils understand cultural diversity and similarity and apply it to their own situation. Every faith is diverse, and teachers should not strive to teach stereotypes but recognise and explore variety. This may entail coming to terms with the strange and exotic; but we also need to explore deeper meaning and avoid the teaching of the exotic for its own sake, when for example religious education is confined to colourful festivals and visits to 'strange' places of worship. In time, those things that at first seemed exotic and strange become familiar. The feeling of strangeness is akin to culture shock. It may pose a problem for us, challenge our attitudes and our responses as we close our minds to new ideas and ways of life. Working through it, however, can offer us a gateway to new understanding of ourselves as well as of others.

It is too easy to confuse 'multi-faith' and 'multicultural'. As we have seen, religions cross cultural boundaries with surprising ease. Britain is a country which, while having a relatively small number of people from non-Christian religions and an even smaller number of people who are other than white Caucasian (together the number is well under 10 per cent) exists in a multicultural, multi-ethnic, multi-faith world. Indeed its history is of global involvement (for good or ill). For the cultural development of students to be properly enhanced not only will they need to learn about religious diversity but also cultural diversity – not least the cultural diversity within the British Isles. How much does the curriculum teach about Wales, Scotland and Ireland? and what diversity exists there?

If religious education is to contribute to cultural development, there is a need to break down xenophobic and ethnocentric attitudes to ensure students have opportunities to look across cultures, to respect other people's beliefs and practices (within reason) and to begin to understand that the great human dilemma is to explain the purpose of life. People do this in different ways which creates a glorious diversity, rich in colour and vitality; but it may mean that the religious education teacher has to break down mental barriers in pupils, their parents and members of the school staff. Exclusive religious attitudes are not uncommon – a belief that those who practice a particular faith are right, and others are wrong.

Teachers have to learn to teach about faiths to which they do not belong, in ways which children brought up in that faith would find affirming. Such openness is also a learning objective: religious education plays an important part in the school's task of exposing prejudice and racist attitudes among pupils. The challenge for teachers is to affirm the value of each faith whilst also developing enquiring minds in the pupils they teach. Religious education should not claim all religions as true in all respects, although it seeks at all times to be respectful, viewing religious views as sincerely held. This is the crux of what is referred to as phenomenology – an open study avoiding personal assumptions and value judgements and allowing the real voice of the believers to be heard. The ultimate aim of religious education is for children to explore, examine and personally evaluate what they encounter, to make up their own minds in an informed way about whether to think religiously, what religious concepts to accept, and how to relate to the various religious people they will meet in life. One of the most important building blocks of values in this process is the affirmation of respect for religious education as a curriculum subject, and for the object of study, the religions themselves. This alone can engender the enthusiasm and motivation for an area of study which has the capacity to transform pupils' attitudes and understanding.

References

Gryn, H. (1992) *Things of the Spirit: Sacred Guidelines for Collective Worship*. London: City of Westminster.
Hull, J. (1997) *On Sight and Insight*. Oxford: Oneworld Publications.
Keenan, B. (1994) *An Evil Cradling*. London: Vantage Books.

Further reading

Cole, O. W. (1997) *Spirituality in Focus*. London: Heinemann.
An excellent resource for teachers wishing to explore how the teaching of world religions embraces a spiritual dimension in their belief and practice.

Jackson, R. (1997) *Religious Education – An Interpretative Approach*. London: Hodder & Stoughton.
A text which discusses the relevance of religious education in schools with particular reference to world religions and how far it is possible to understand someone else's religious position.

Mackley, J. (1997) *Looking Inwards, Looking Outwards*. Derby: Christian Education Movement.
A teachers' handbook, student resource materials and activity sheets which act as a springboard for personal and group reflection.

Note
[1] In an unpublished article for the Values Forum, quoted with permission.

Chapter 3

Drama

Stephen Bigger and David Thomas

Drama has had a chequered recent history in the school curriculum. It was not included as a National Curriculum subject, and yet there still are Heads of Drama, and drama studios, in many secondary schools. Drama and Theatre Studies are popular options at GCSE and A level and there are vocational courses in Performing Arts. There are however no National Curriculum 'orders' which now so dominate the lives of teachers of other subjects; but as a consequence the subject experiences some vulnerability. Valuable guidelines have been prepared by the Arts Council (1992), the Calouste Gulbenkian Foundation (1989, 1992), and the Department of Education and Science (DES 1989, 1990). Helpful books for teachers (e.g. Bolton 1992) include some on drama for special educational needs (Peter 1994, Kempe 1996).

Drama is first and foremost a discipline with its own aims, objectives and rationale. It can also be used to support other subjects and has survived both in this support role and as an extra-curricular activity through school plays. Teachers have found it a helpful medium for exploring and developing values. Being 'in role' creates an empathy with the characters, helping to understand their (and ultimately our own) feelings. The plot enables pupils to explore situations and their outcomes, even to try out a variety of different strategies to see how outcomes are affected. This emphasises that actions have consequences, and that we can influence events by reflecting on how we respond to situations that face us. Drama can develop relationships – friendships, caring relationships and even hostile ones. Pupils can develop their understanding and social skills to come to terms with wherever they find themselves. Relationships bring responsibilities which can raise complex issues and emotions. Drama can unpack attitudes which underlie all of these important aspects of education, uncover prejudices, and help pupils become reflective and responsive members of the community.

Active learning by participation and involvement uses personal experience to help work out problems and develop skills, competence and confidence in all curriculum areas. Drama is centrally based on active personal participation, re-enacting stories and situations, demanding decisions and choices. Yet drama needs to be taught well: a role play can confirm people's prejudices and, worse, give opportunity to the bully and do psychological harm to the victim. How can a teacher turn this into effective learning? How can it help to build confidence? And help people to become more reflective? Drama needs to incorporate response and reflection, through discussion and debate. It is more than a performance reciting someone else's written text. It is an opportunity for self-expression, exploring emotions and experiences. With the very young, it is called 'play', but again effective 'play' has to be carefully structured to provide appropriate opportunities and to incorporate teacher interventions.

Drama should enable people to explore the human dimension of issues in depth. So much of our view of life is based on superficial stereotypes. Our first impressions are affected by what we expect to see, and we may not take a second look. We may be locked into a phoney world view in which views on race, gender, class, occupations, age, and so on are unreflectively fossilised. To break through the stereotype will take more than simply listening to a lecture. Drama can help to humanise or personalise the situation. By developing an imaginary scenario, pupils are asked to put flesh on the bones of the characters. What's his name? How old? Is he married? Children? Hobbies? What are his parents doing? and so on until the character is a real person and not a caricature. This builds up respect for other people and a sense of their worth and value. We have seen the opposite too often – depersonalising people, identifying them as groups and not individuals (Jews, Protestants, Catholics, Muslims, Croats, Serbs, Tutsi, Hutu) to name only a few who as groups have been subject to barbaric inhumanity. The name becomes a number. In the death camps, Jews were deprived of name, clothes, hair, family, hygiene and everything that would otherwise identify them as human. They were depicted as mice, vermin to be exterminated. In Drama, the opposite needs to happen, with people seeing others as real, sometimes for the first time.

Fair key questions for teaching drama will be important in this chapter to help give us a focus.

- *Who am I?* A great deal of drama deals with self-image, self-worth, issues of identity and self-realisation. What kind of person am I? What do I want to become? These are **spiritual** issues.

- *How do I relate?* How can I define and develop my relationships? What value do I give to others and how does this affect my behaviour to them? How should I behave towards others? These are **moral** questions.

- *How do I fit in?* How does my life fit alongside other people's lives? How do I gain approval? What groups do I relate to? What social rules and expectations do I need to take account of? And what kind of response is proper to these? These are **social** facets.

- *How do I live?* How can I define my lifestyle and compare it to others? Can I come to understand my own background and culture better and learn to appreciate the other cultures that touch my life. This gives us a **cultural** dimension.

The Arts Council, introducing drama teaching for teachers, divides its approach into three: making, performing, and responding.

Making

Drama involves creating a dramatic situation, fictional yet meaningful to the people taking part. True, some start with a script (explored in the next section) but more often the plot and characters will stem from an idea communally developed. The teacher of drama will be a facilitator who asks the right questions to develop a depth of thinking: this is a key educational process. Drama making will explore the emotions – the joy of being and relating, the magic of creation and expression, the exploration and resolution of fear and anxiety. It bonds the group together as drama cannot operate without trust and openness. We sometimes have to learn to trust and have confidence in others, and there are drama exercises to encourage this: one in which group members are blindfolded and let themselves fall backwards into the arms of colleagues, trusting them to be there, and being gently passed around a circle in this manner.

Understanding and expressing emotions is an important part of being human which education can easily ignore: drama gives opportunities for this to be based on real experiences, actively explored. The blindfold has other benefits: the feeling of not being seen can break down inhibitions in the self conscious. The lack of sight gives a vulnerability that group members can work through and explore in a safe setting, in a world in which vulnerability is best hidden for fear of intimidation. In feeling vulnerable, it helps to empathise with other people's vulnerability. It gives a particular understanding also of those who are visually impaired. Emotions are powerfully explored through body language: these involve explicit facial expressions of joy, or of disgust and anger; but there are many subtle ways of expressing approval or disapproval which in real life we can get wrong, either conveying the wrong impression or misinterpreting other people's signals, mistaking approval or disapproval and so on. Education through drama can considerably strengthen pupils' non-verbal communication.

Basic ideas for drama can come from anywhere: from a story, a news item, a suggestion from a pupil, a teacher's idea. It might develop from fiction, or follow real life situations. Primary school work based on *Fireman Sam* explores fire risks; secondary school situation drama can involve bullying and drug abuse. It develops through discussion, probably with small groups of pupils discussing the issues and choices involved. This may give some guideline to the plot, but there may be choices still to be made. Then we develop characters, fleshed out, human rather than cardboard, ones we and the audience can fully identify with, whose attempts to deal with problems we can relate to, whose attitudes we can applaud or despise. Both plot and characters will unfold, but there may be many different resolutions as alternative solutions to the evolving fictional circumstances.

Our four questions might help.

Who am I? (spiritual aspects)

Can the plot illustrate, explore and expand understanding of the human condition? Can it present a dilemma to illustrate choices? Can it explore what makes people tick? Can it explore keeping good faith and being true, and in contrast dishonesty, letting people down and apathy? The drama can show how different approaches can have different effects, how changes of attitude and strategy can affect what happens. Pupils throughout this are deepening their own understanding of their own behaviour and attitudes, and seeing how different life strategies can have different results. The question, 'What kind of person am I?' can be complex and uncomfortable to address. It needs a non-threatening context that drama provides, distancing pupils through fictitious characters yet living real personal experiences through these characters.

How do I relate? (moral aspects)

A dramatic plot may not set out to be moralising (it is probably better if it does not) but everything that happens will have implications about relationships, that is about moral choices. Every choice is in a sense a moral one, in that the character will have had to weigh up the pros and cons and considered the ethics of particular actions. No one is an island, but we each live our lives in relationship – to family, friends, colleagues, strangers we affect, people yet unborn who will be affected by the consequences of our actions. Relationship in this widest sense brings responsibility – to respect others, to help and assist, to provide for the helpless, to give as well as take.

How do I fit in? (social aspects)

This may give the impression that we need and want to fit in, but this might not be so. The point may be that it is important not to fit in and we need the skill and strength to do this. Peer pressure may prevent people becoming criminals because they do not want social ostracism; but behaving morally may also cause social disapproval. The Nazi machine not only disapproved of any who helped victims of its terror campaign, but shot them where they could. Soldiers sucked into the machine might face dire consequences for opposing the system: indeed Eichmann warned them that human sympathy was an insidious form of weakness of which they should beware. Peer pressure is relevant to the experience of young people – fashion, playground ostracism, drugs, dares, macho images for boys, victimising any who are different or who show weakness. Drama can help young people come to terms with peer pressure and to stand up for principle if required. They can use peer pressure to influence others not to behave stupidly and unfairly. This social agenda can lead to positive contributions the individual can make to the community and to society as a whole.

How do I live? (cultural aspects)

I have been brought up in a particular way, with particular values, and customs. My culture might be white and middle class, or black, or 'Asian'. Of course there are many different cultures within whatever categories we invent (is Asian culture Hindu, Sikh, Muslim, Buddhist, communist, traditional, liberal, or youth?). We all tend to think that our way is best, but openness to and respect for other lifestyles has been stressed educationally through and since the Swann Report of 1985. Drama can create intercultural situations and dilemmas, or give exposure to performers from cultures other than the dominant one. Drama is dynamic, so we expect our lifestyle not simply to be described and depicted but also questioned and challenged. Television drama has raised issues and concerns in new ways, whilst comedy pokes fun at cultural attitudes. Both have a benefit in encouraging reflection on our lifestyles and can provide models for pupils.

Performing

The process of creation we have just described might lead to a performance or might be done for its own sake. If performed, the spontaneous would need to be crystallised into a 'text' (not necessarily written down) and decisions made on which 'reading' (or set of choices) to follow. (It would be a brave decision to have a different variation each performance, but there is room for spontaneity in a performance, and this would make the point about the fluidity of a drama text.)

Performance also brings in Theatre Studies and performance of written plays. Here the concern is for understanding and interpreting the text. Decisions have to be made on whether to focus on the author's world, or the modern. The main issues of the work may seem to be contemporary issues still and the play, even if written for another age, can be seen as making a contribution to contemporary debate.

Communication of human responses to such issues is not only verbal, but includes body language, tone, interrelationships of characters, and touch. Touch is particularly problematic, since people value their personal space which we do not wish to be inappropriately 'invaded'. Communication by touch outside the family is therefore not easily learnt by young people, and touch can therefore be misinterpreted. Touch which invades, oppresses and is generally deviant is never acceptable and drama must never be allowed to mask this. However, within a context of trust, self-esteem and positive relationships, touch can break down barriers between people and help to express things which cannot be put into words – being consoling, encouraging, showing concern and giving approval. And the more young people understand of touch in this proper and positive sense, the better they will recognise deviance and know what to do about it, since they will experience less confusion.

Again, our four questions will help.

Who am I? (spiritual aspects)

As well as interpreting the play, the actors are interpreting the roles they play, humanising figures sometimes broadly painted in the text. Live performances will vary, with achieving convincing performances only some of the time. Getting inside a character is a skill which needs developing and if theatre is going to be more than a spectator activity, involving pupils in performances is needed to give them these experiences and to allow them to develop. Entering imaginatively into someone else's experience helps to raise questions about our own emotions and attitudes. A performance can bring both performer and audience to tears with a powerful story of love, despair, hope, suffering and anger. The performer has in addition to keep emotions under control and to deliver the right expression of these at the right time. They also explore through rehearsal a range of reactions to and consequences of emotions. Working this through dramatically raises awareness of human behaviour and responses which has a spin-off in personal life. Performance opens up individuals. It is hard to be shy and detached from life when you are thrust into the limelight. Behind a performance lies spontaneous exploration of character in role.

How do I relate? (moral aspects)

Performance also requires exploration of behaviour and relationships, seeing a range of potential consequences and humanising issues. Drama examines relationships which work and which fail, the joy of resolution and the despair of disrupted friendship and partnership, trust and treachery. The performer lives through these emotions, draws on their own memories and resolves conflict not only on stage but in their own minds.

There is however a gap between real and fictional relationships. Some actors are open as individuals, willing to express real emotion publicly. Others are comfortable with fictional emotion but keep private emotions private; and some confuse real emotion with that of stage or screen. So among performers there is potential to encourage reflection on personal style.

A play requires dedication and teamwork, and a sense of fair play. Failure to turn up to rehearsal inconveniences other players; one poor performance is enough to ruin the performance. The play therefore promotes collaboration and consideration.

How do I fit in? (social aspects)

Similarly performance encourages social skills and can bring with it self-confidence and self-esteem. Acting out a role can help to eliminate hang-ups. A failing student teacher who acted out the role of the best teacher she knew found her problems dissolving. The drama troop work as a team, with give and take, support of colleagues and mutual celebration.

Drama also raises social concerns, issues of marriage, family, social esteem, war and conflict. The question *how do I fit in?* sums up many plots. Resolutions involve characters who do fit in, those who can't, and those for whom principles sets them against social expectations, which they wish to transform. It is not a crime not to fit into an unsuitable environment.

How do I live? (cultural aspects)

Drama performances bring to life situations which enable us and young people to enter into other people's lives. Television 'soaps' create communities of which the viewer becomes an honorary member and goes through the range of emotion and experience that the characters encounter. We are not quite at the level of Star Trek's holodeck, in which viewers become participants in the story, but there are ways of treating a performance as interactive, involving the audience as participants and allowing them to influence the choices which are made. By performing in plays, young people can experience a variety of family and social groups, from different national and ethnic backgrounds, with different assumptions, concerns, expressions, vernacular expressions and dialects. In education, we seek to make learning come alive; drama performance can put pupils on the spot in asking 'What would you have done?', and developing empathy for a wide range of characters. History and religious education can benefit from a performance of stories: this might be extensive (and perhaps intrusive) school performances such as the nativity play; but more routinely, performing a story briefly in the classroom can bring a lesson to life, and benefit from good drama practice in expressing and responding to emotion and relationship. Performance might bring alive the classics of other cultures and still relate to life choices. The Indian epic, the *Ramayana* is performed worldwide, not only in India. In south east Asia, Javanese shadow puppet (*wayang*) performances use it as a medium for political comment. The Thai kings named themselves after Rama and their capital, Ayodya, after Rama's capital. In the west, television series follow the story. A recent series in India brought business and traffic to a halt showing its power to captivate a modern audience. Rama's story is linked with the Divali festival familiar to both primary and secondary schools. The story is about husbands and wives, siblings, friends and enemies, humans and animals, power, rescue and revenge – all powerfully emotive today. Such performances can take pupils inside any culture, east or west, north or south, ancient or modern. They can reflect on their own lives using performance as a lens and a filter, focusing on aspects they might otherwise have taken for granted.

Responding

Young people are also consumers of drama, watching it nightly on television, and more occasionally going to live shows. Schools from time to time take pupils to performances either of standard repertoire plays or of special programmes on contemporary issues such as drug abuse. Performances can be interactive, keeping interest by involving pupils in the plot and action. The experience of going to the theatre is important – for some pupils, it will be the first time. There may be a measure of enjoyment and recreation, but 'theatre' should also engage them critically and make them think. They may not only reflect on issues and themes, but consider the style and construction of the play, the viewpoint and the characters. Shakespeare plays try, whilst being true to the text, to be lively, expressive and personalised. It is important to turn history into human beings and consider their motivations, emotions, strengths and weaknesses.

It is particularly important to enable young people to view television intelligently since this is a widespread and common experience for them, from which they soak up points of view on the basis of which they form their own attitudes. The critical process (which later becomes called 'media studies') need not diminish enjoyment by raising awareness but will enable young people to watch at a different level, asking why writers, actors and producers made the choices they did.

Who am I? (spiritual aspects)

The issue of personal identity is pervasive. As we view characters working out their own lives and circumstances, viewers are tacitly invited to consider their own responses to similar issues in their own lives. Possibly their real choices might be influenced by what they have seen – whether to take drugs or not; to have a baby or not; to patch up a friendship or not. There is a difference between copying a favourite star and using a wide variety of points of view to give oneself alternatives. The latter is informed, the former is not. People place themselves through drama, reflect on their own circumstances, use role models to perceive themselves differently. The difference between a failure and a success is probably in the head, as a self-fulfilling prophecy; and this can be changed. Teachers can assist by encouraging real discussion about personal issues raised on television or in other drama, to help children become active rather than passive viewers. They might consider who they identify with (and why), analyse decisions and choices, debate how conflict might have been resolved, and on the basis of asking what kind of people the characters are, reflect on what kind of people they are and would like to become. They might become more aware of fact and fiction as media dramas paint a picture of reality which is an artificial creation. Is a school really like the one depicted? Is Britain like that? Is America? Why has that part of it been selected? Whose voice is missing? 'Spiritual' suggests that drama can help pupils to personal growth, understanding themselves better, expressing themselves more clearly, seeing possibilities that might otherwise have been missed.

How do I relate? (moral aspects)

Drama can also encourage moral growth without being moralising. These are plays which introduce moral dilemmas and choices, which can prompt class discussion. Moral behaviour assumes that we respect other people's rights and concerns and try to meet our own without trampling over theirs. This is to admit a relationship with these others. We recognise closeness through terms such as family, friends, colleagues, neighbours – but recognising every human as 'neighbour', as a 'fellow' member of the human race. Drama explores the whole variety of relationships between these categories. We may, with William Russell's *Blood Brothers* explore how twins relate; or with *Macbeth* (and other Shakespeare histories) how kings and politicians should behave. Television explores relationships between teacher and pupil, police and public, men and women, adults and young people. Moralistic plays suggest easy answers; most situations are however complex, and the drama is heightened by that very complexity. What happens when both sides think they are right? How do we reach compromise? When might principle override compromise? How do we make decisions when each choice is equally attractive or equally problematic? These help pupils develop decision-making strategies, although it would be wrong to suggest it will make choosing easier!

How do I fit in? (social aspects)

Johnny Speight's Alf Garnett graphically explored racism, sexism and bigotry – does that mean Speight was a bigot? No, but we need to be aware that social and political critique can be interpreted in unexpected ways. By criticising anti-heroes the programme moralises; by not, writers may be accused of approving of them. TV drama focuses on marriage, family, power relationships and pupils need to examine the points of view expressed, and to verbalise their responses. Soaps are about communities, about those who fit in, and those who don't. Is fitting in always important? Or are there times when we have to stand up for a principle, even at the cost of unpopularity? Drama is often political, either overtly or tacitly: it is concerned to debate social issues, to expose shortcomings, and to suggest change. Tacit examples would encourage the audience to make up its mind on the evidence presented of weakness in the status quo. What to do about bullying, and how to cope with peer pressure might be examples explored in school.

How do I live? (cultural aspects)

There are many examples of cultural diversity in drama productions, and we have spoken already about the *Ramayana*. Through plays, pupils 'meet' people from many other cultures and learn about their lives. Some may be 'traditional culture' – great literature from the past; but others may be new, modern and contemporary. Issues of racism, bigotry, and intolerance, and inappropriate assumptions and inaccurate information about other cultures, will have to be addressed.

In world cinema and media, the most pervasive 'culture' is the American, carried by satellite, film and music. It is a picture of America which needs deconstructing – Hollywood and Dallas are not typical; poor black Americans are rarely depicted positively; and American Indians have not always had a fair press. In visiting Zambia, this western influence was very strong, which led to a neglect of local cultural forms, either in drama, dance or music. Nevertheless, a very funny play full of political critique crept through, *Joseph, have you got your bicycle yet?*, where

Joseph tries hard to acquire the appropriate documentation for his impounded bicycle, but fails to get through the impossible bureaucracy until, as an old man, his bicycle, still impounded, is a rusty heap. Children can, after reflection on the drama they see, turn the process full circle and make and perform drama around their own concerns.

References

Arts Council (1992) *Drama in Schools.* London: Arts Council of Great Britain.

Bolton, G. (1992) *New Perspectives on Classroom Drama.* Hemel Hempstead: Simon & Schuster.

Calouste Gulbenkian Foundation (1989) *The Arts in Schools: Principles, Practice and Provision.* London: Calouste Gulbenkian Foundation.

Calouste Gulbenkian Foundation (1992) *The Gulbenkian Enquiry into Puppetry.* London: Calouste Gulbenkian Foundation.

DES (1989) *Drama from 5 to 16: HMI Curriculum Matters 17.* London: HMSO.

DES (1990) *Aspects of Primary Education: The Teaching and Learning of Drama.* London: HMSO.

Kempe, A. (ed.) (1996) *Drama Education and Special Needs: A Handbook for Teachers in Mainstream and Special Schools.* Cheltenham: Stanley Thornes.

Peter, M. (1994) *Drama For All: Developing Drama in the Curriculum with Pupils with Special Educational Needs.* London: David Fulton Publishers.

Recommended reading

Peter, M. (1995) *Making Drama Special: Developing Drama Practice to Meet Special Educational Needs.* London: David Fulton Publishers.
A practical discussion of drama as a helpful teaching strategy for pupils with special educational needs.

Somers, J. (1994) *Drama in the Curriculum.* London: Cassell.
An illustrated and practical book for teachers, about drama as a subject and as a cross-curricular strategy.

Winston, J. (1998) *Drama, Narrative and Moral Education.* London: Falmer Press.
A study of the value of story and drama for moral development, with examples of good practice and suggestions for classroom activities in primary schools. Of relevance also to secondary English and drama teachers.

Chapter 4

Citizenship Education
Paul Maiteny and Ros Wade

'Death knell for Britain's sense of civic duty: institutions in decline'. 'Self-help citizenship'. These were the *Daily Telegraph* and *Guardian* headlines announcing the first report by the Foundation for Civil Society (FCS) on 30 October 1996: *The Deficit in Civil Society in the United Kingdom* (Knight and Stokes 1996). It shows how civil relations and social, cultural, religious and moral life are deteriorating in the UK, with membership of community-orientated organisations (churches, trade unions, mutual aid organisations) and participation in politics (especially amongst young people) all in decline. Civil society is today more represented by issue-based concerns such as the environment, human rights and other special interests, including education. Community networks and relations in general are breaking down as people feel less trust or responsibility towards their neighbours, and feel increasingly 'on their own' – powerless, alienated and anxious.

Yet, as Machiavelli once wrote, the success of free, democratic institutions depends on the character of the citizens – their 'civic virtue' (Putnam 1993). Instead, we are living in the 'risk society' (Beck 1992) where values and relations are economic rather than social, and individualism is second nature. The social, moral and spiritual (including psychological and emotional) consequences are now being felt. It remains to be seen whether young people will be able to reconcile this with the amorality of market culture. Morals and values have to be *experienced* as meaningful if they are to be lived. On the other hand, the report shows that some community-based institutions are growing – mostly religious or spiritual. People still value the sense of belonging to a community with shared beliefs, but do not always find traditional institutions providing for this (Reed 1978).

Educational policy and practice

The debate about education for citizenship is relatively recent but concern about moral, personal and social development is not. Since the 1970s schools have raised issues of relationships, family, health, sex, drugs and careers. Experiential learning and 'active tutorial work' encouraged social skills and awareness of rights and responsibilities. However, most of these programmes restricted themselves to personal and social awareness related to school and careers, neglecting broader social, political and cultural contexts. Since teachers responsible for such areas are rarely specialists, there is a temptation to restrict discussion of values to teachers' own views. There are, nevertheless, some excellent materials that address wider issues and concerns, for example John Foster's materials recommended as further reading (see end of chapter). Citizenship education has common strands and shared concerns. Most teachers would agree with Voiels that 'citizenship education is an integral part of the personal, social and moral development of children' (in Holden and Clough 1998, p. 197); but the two are not identical.

The National Curriculum guidance *Education for Citizenship* (NCC 1990, p. 2). describes it as developing 'the knowledge, skills and attitudes necessary for exploring, making informed decisions about and exercising responsibilities and rights in a democratic society'. It expands on earlier models which 'often focused on knowledge of the machinery and processes of government' by emphasising 'positive, participative citizenship' and the socio-cultural 'variety of communities to which people *simultaneously* (our emphasis) belong: family, school, local, national, European and world-wide'. It reinforces the need for an inclusive definition of citizenship that encourages awareness of living in an interconnected world. The National Curriculum stressed the cross-curricular nature of personal and social issues and skills, and developed guidelines for citizenship. Citizenship, as other cross-curricular themes, provided the cement integrating the 'bricks' (the subjects) into a meaningful whole. However, they have rarely been used in this way. The need to reverse this trend has been preoccupying policy-makers, given public concern over breakdown of social norms and values. The New Labour government puts a high priority on these issues, as evidenced by the Advisory Group on Education for Citizenship and the Teaching of Democracy in schools, headed by Bernard Crick.

The framework for school inspection mentions the need for *an understanding of citizenship*. In practice, this has been a low priority, with greater emphasis on literacy, numeracy, and raising standards. Furthermore, the concept of citizenship is problematic: teaching young people about structures and processes is one thing; teaching them to understand what it means to be a citizen, and to develop the skills needed for active citizenship and to exert pressure for change is quite another.

What is citizenship?

No person is an island. We all depend on others, and others depend on us. This implies taking responsibility within this relationship, in the interests of all, including ourselves. There is mutual dependence also between people and their ecological environments. All such systems are much more than the sum of their parts; they are holistic systems where all parts are mutually dependent. The *ability to think holistically* is a key skill for active and responsible citizens. This means developing awareness of our social, economic and ecological impacts (or 'footprints', Wackernagel and Rees 1996) – how our choices, actions and lifestyles relate to other people and to our ecological life-support systems. Awareness of connectedness – or globality (not to be confused with *free-market globalisation*) – needs to become a habit in a world of economic, ecological and social interdependence. For example, low-cost goods in the rich countries depend on low-cost labour and natural resources. Every person is a link in the chain and eventually feels the consequences of their values and actions in their environments. Transportation burns fossil fuels and causes pollution.

Another important consideration in a world of global interdependence is where a person should draw the boundaries of their community and, therefore, their civic responsibility. Around the immediate locality? The city, state, region or the whole world? The answer to this has to be of a 'both-and' nature rather than 'either-or'. We are, necessarily, global citizens. But this means little without also 'walking the talk' at the local level. Robert Putnam (1993), in *Making Democracy Work*, defines civic community according to four essential features:

- *Civic engagement:* citizens participate actively in public affairs, defining and pursuing their own interests in the context of broader public needs. They recognise themselves as community members who serve their own needs through serving the community.

- *Political equality:* citizens have equal rights and obligations. Civic community is held together by reciprocal and cooperative relations. Leaders see themselves as responsible to their fellow citizens. Politics is localised enough for citizens to feel they can be heard.

- *Trust, solidarity and tolerance:* Local social networks are strong, fostering mutual trust, respect and support.

- *Associations: social structures and practices* embody the norms and values of the civic community and contribute to the effectiveness and stability of democracy.

Relations within schools and between schools and government do not, on the whole, exhibit strong civic values in the UK today. The challenge of citizenship education is therefore a tough one. It involves a strongly holistic approach, in terms of interdisciplinarity and the need to draw out emotional and reflective capacities. The challenge is greater still given the short history that citizenship education – and the concept of citizenship – has in the UK.

Bazalgette (1992), of the Grubb Institute of Behavioural Studies, argues that the idea of 'citizenship' has been missing in the UK because British, and especially English, people, within a monarchy, have identified themselves as *subjects*. Psychologically this could imply a greater tendency to see oneself as dependent rather than interdependent and to defer responsibility and leadership to others.

1. Being an effective and responsible citizen entails being able to take an holistic perspective of society, where you see yourself as an active part of a larger integrated whole. From this a sense of responsibility is more likely to emerge, not least because *you* depend on, but also contribute to, society's overall integrity.

2. To change this situation is *not* just a matter of changing external structures and prescriptions but rather enabling young people to develop emotionally.

3. Citizenship requires active awareness of interdependence and the ability to draw on (and develop) one's inner resources (especially the English). It could be argued, then, that consciously or unconsciously, the British have been inhibited from developing a self-image of themselves as citizens.

Towards a concept of 'global citizenship'

Many would also argue that the concept of *national* citizenship is problematic in the UK, comprised of four different countries and a huge diversity of culture. For Lynch (1992) this situation offers the opportunity to abandon a citizenship limited to national boundaries and develop a more global model for a sustainable and equitable world. Lynch describes three levels of citizenship:

1. The local community, including familial, cultural and social groupings, defined by language, religion and ethnicity but not necessarily geographical location.

2. National citizenship, determined by birth or choice but which may not be restricted to one nation.

3. International citizenship, drawing on interdependencies between members of the world community, regardless of the other two levels.

Since citizenship has only recently been emphasised in the UK, the British, and the English in particular, given their historical identification with empire (an international concept), may be less trammelled than others with nationalistic definitions and therefore able to move more readily to conceiving themselves as 'global' citizens. This is, of course, a generalisation. In Scotland, for example, there is a greater tendency for people to identify themselves as Scottish than British. Nevertheless, the recent boost to national identity brought about by devolution is still seen within a wider European and global context.

Oxfam's Education team, with a wide variety of teachers and other educationalists, has developed a definition of global citizenship which incorporates Lynch's levels. A global citizen is someone who:

• is aware of the wider world and has a sense of their own role as a world citizen;

• respects and values diversity;

- has an understanding of how the world works economically, politically, socially, culturally, technologically and environmentally;

- is outraged by social injustice;

- participates in and contributes to the community at a range of levels from the local to the global;

- is willing to act to make the world a more equitable and sustainable place;

- takes responsibility for their actions.

Inner experience and feelings are also important and teachers clearly play a key role in stimulating a sense of citizenship in pupils. Michael Barber (1997), as head of the DfEE Standards and Effectiveness Unit noted, 'If the ethics of teachers do not promote world understanding, whose will? If teachers are not among the first to become, in effect, citizens of the world, who will?'.

Values dimensions of citizenship education

Values and morals are of central importance in education for citizenship, but how they are addressed needs careful consideration. Patrick Tobin, chair of the Headmasters' and Headmistresses' Conference, fears that education for citizenship could lead to indoctrination. This risk should be taken seriously and is most likely if based on values and morals that are defined and prescribed by policy-makers, and if teachers cannot or do not embody those values and morals in their own lives. From a political perspective, citizenship clearly means something very different in a pluralistic, multicultural, democratic society than in authoritarian dictatorships. In authoritarian systems, official policy on values and citizenship do not correspond with majority views and experience. They offer a salutary lesson in the consequences of imposing values that mean little to the people themselves. *The lesson, in a nutshell, is that policy is not enough.* Long-term, sustainable change comes from within people – from convictions, values and priorities. So does 'social and moral responsibility', the first feature of 'citizenship education in a parliamentary democracy' as understood by the government's advisory group (QCA 1998, p. 14).

Education for citizenship, then, requires experiential dimensions to encourage learners to engage with the question of what being a socially and morally responsible citizen means in their own lives. Learners need to be able to reflect on their own roles and impacts, and on the meanings, values and priorities underpinning them. Bazalgette (1992, p. 38) stresses that 'the development of each individual's identity is at the same time part of the development of the society in which that individual lives'. And quoting Erikson (1967, p. 23), 'we cannot separate personal growth and communal change, nor can we separate the identity crises in individual life and contemporary crises in historical development because the two help to define each other and are truly related to each other'.

It is encouraging to note that the final report of the government's advisory group on Education for Citizenship and the teaching of democracy in schools makes reference to the *global* dimensions of citizenship (QCA 1998, p. 18). Many responses to the interim report stressed the need to empower young people 'to make choices and take action which will make a contribution to bringing about changes which will make the world a better place' (Development Education Association 1998). The final report stresses a whole-school, cross-curricular approach: 'Schools need to consider how far their ethos, organisation, and daily practices are consistent with the aim and purpose of citizenship education ... schools should make every effort to engage pupils in discussion and consultation about all aspects of school life on which pupils might reasonably be expected to have a view' (Karen Gold, in *TES* 17 July 1998, p. 18). Citizenship education is still an emerging concept. Teachers, pupils and wider civil society all have contributions to make to its development. 'A main aim for the whole community should be to find or restore a sense of common citizenship, including a national identity that is secure enough to find a place for the plurality of nations, cultures, ethnic identities and religions' (QCA 1998, p. 17).

Much of the debate around education for citizenship has assumed that young people do not participate in democratic processes due to lack of knowledge about the processes. Yet, the experience of young people who do actively participate, albeit unconventionally through road protest for example, is that the structures and processes themselves frustrate genuine participation and a sense of being listened to. This points to the need to recognise informal networks and pressure groups as legitimate aspects of the democratic process and citizenship. Non-government organisations such as the Development Education Association, British Youth Council, Centre for Education on World Citizenship and Oxfam have been heavily involved in the debate and have produced innovative and practical contributions. Such groups reflect public values and concerns that are often under-represented in mainstream party politics: yet, they are increasingly the lifeblood of modern-day civil society. It is logical to involve them centrally in citizenship education.

Democratic structures have to be adaptable to the needs of the time. It would be strange if citizenship education could not nurture young people's participation in terms they could relate to. When pupils say they cannot be bothered to think about societal issues because no one listens to them at school, that they are just told what to do and want to get their GCSEs out of the way, this should cause grave concern. Most schools are hierarchical and increasingly bureaucratic, providing few opportunities for ordinary teachers or pupils to contribute to the organisation or curriculum. Meaningful citizenship education must allow for more pupil involvement in the institutions of greatest relevance to them. Hence, a key stop following Lynch's levels (see above) is to nurture in young people a sense of being a 'school citizen'. If schools are experienced, not as relevant places of shared meaning and purpose, but as fragmentary and divided, we should not be surprised that the society emerging from them also reflects divisive values. This vicious circle is hard to break and requires that citizenship education nurtures the capacity for active, critical, practical engagement and a sense of belonging by young people. Education that does not do this risks taking us down the road of an indoctrinated, compliant and unthinking citizenry, perhaps also cynical and alienated. Such a 'citizen' would seem to be a contradiction in terms. 'Citizenship' is active rather than passive.

Following this logic, citizenship education may be structured into three strands that build on each other:

1. **Education about citizenship** (knowledge of democratic processes and structures in this country and elsewhere; thinking about what being a citizen means).

2. **Education for citizenship** (development of skills, values and attitudes necessary to be an active citizen, of their schools for example).

3. **Education as citizens** (use of 1 and 2 in active participation at a range of levels).

Learning to be a global citizen in practice

Active citizenship integrates moral, social, cultural and, arguably, spiritual awareness and puts it into practice in everyday life. Oxfam's curriculum for Global Citizenship identifies skills, knowledge and values spanning all subjects and age groups that assist in this, particularly in the school context.

> The importance of cross-curricular work is implicit within this outline...[schools need] to provide the opportunities for more flexible, cross-curricular approaches...Above all, the ethos and practice of the school community are all important, as values and attitudes of young people will shape the future world in which we will live. It is of paramount importance that the aims of the school should incorporate a commitment to social justice and equity and that these aims should be reflected in the practice of staff and pupils within the school. (Oxfam 1997a, p. 13).

Several examples of good practice exist. The Eco-school movement and the School Grounds movement, for example, use processes to involve the whole school community in environmental issues. Such models can be extended to encourage willing, democratic 'school citizenship' in staff, pupils and other stakeholders. School Councils, for example, require discussion and decision-making on social, cultural and moral issues. Several schools have also set up 'bully courts' which involve children in judging the behaviour of their peers and working out solutions to negative behaviour. Pupils have also been involved in interviewing and selecting teachers (*Developing Rights*, Oxfam 1997b, p. 19).

The Oxfam outline Curriculum for Global Citizenship

According to David Hicks (Hicks and Holden 1995, p. 112), 'Whilst some pupils feel that they can act on a personal level to help create a better future, many do not. They feel that school has given them an inadequate education in this area. While they often hope for a more just and sustainable future, school provides little opportunity for discussion on such issues'. The Oxfam outline curriculum shows how the knowledge, skills, values and attitudes of global citizenship translate into the curriculum. It indicates differentiation across ages, phases and abilities. (See Figure 4.1). This is not a linear process and elements in Key Stage 1 may be revisited as required.

Key elements

Knowledge and Understanding
Social justice and equity
Peace and conflict
Diversity
Sustainable development
Globalisation thinking

Skills
Critical thinking
Ability to argue effectively
Cooperation and conflict resolution
Ability to challenge injustice and inequalities

Values and Attitudes
Value and respect for diversity
Empathy
Sense of identity and self-esteem
Belief that people can make a difference
Commitment to social justice and equity
Concern for the environment and commitment to sustainable development

---

Figure 4.1 (from *A Curriculum for Global Citizenship*, Oxfam 1997)

Spiritual and moral dimensions of citizenship

Oxfam's ultimate aim is to eradicate poverty and hence its education programme works primarily in the moral, social and cultural dimensions. This reflects difficulties in formulating spiritual dimensions to fit a curriculum context rather than a lack of concern with it. In fact, the Values and Attitudes section is the most important part of the outline curriculum precisely because it emphasises the need for change, as it were, within the person – at the level of feelings, convictions and emotions.

Policies are most effective when they resonate with what people feel is important and consistent with experience – in other words, when they are meaningful to people. Only then can individuals incorporate them into their lives and become *active* citizens. It is therefore essential that citizenship education helps young people reflect on their own roles in society in an emotionally mature and responsible way so that they see that citizenship is a choice rather than a prescription. Behaviour and action that is not rooted in personal conviction but in pretence or obedience to policy will inevitably be ultimately unsustainable. Any eclipse of authoritarian regimes demonstrates the perils of over-reliance on policy prescriptions to bring about genuine change.

Spiritual development is an intimate, personal process. It is difficult to articulate but underpins responsible behaviour in the social (and ecological) sphere. Some describe it as a growing sense of one's own integrity and, simultaneously, of one's responsibility as an essential part of an interconnected web of life and social relations on which one depends in everyday life (Capra 1996). From such awareness is likely to emerge a moral conviction that seeks to care for this web rather than to damage it. A moral outlook based on rules and dogma rather than deep-rooted experience and awareness is likely to be more superficial, brittle and unsustainable. *Living Values* (Brahma Kumaris 1995, see 'Teaching materials') provides helpful guidelines and activities for exploring inner values that influence attitudes and behaviour.

It is this experiential dimension, and how policy-makers can take account of it, that is emphasised in the work of the Grubb Institute.

Examples of practice in the classroom

Many teachers will already be covering aspects of the Oxfam framework. Key Stage 2 Diversity (Knowledge and Understanding), for example, might be partly covered by a history unit on Benin. Or in geography, study of an African city or Indian village offers opportunities to learn respect for other cultures, and raise awareness of socio-economic issues such as inequality (Knowledge and Understanding, Social Justice and Equity). For Tanner (in Holden and Clough 1998, p. 243), study of overseas localities provides 'an excellent context for nurturing young global citizens'. The teaching pack, *Speaking for Ourselves, Listening to Others* (Leeds Development Education Centre) shows how children and teachers in Leeds have linked with pupils in Nairobi, exchanging photos, self-portraits and information about themselves.

At Key Stage 3, (Knowledge and Understanding, Social Justice and Equity) the PSE curriculum can consider rights and responsibilities within the school and wider society. The teaching pack *Developing Rights* by Oxfam, produced with PSE teachers, offers graded activities interrelating personal, local and global experience from around the world. An activity on bullying relates how disaffected and alienated street children in Brazil formed an association and, through representations to parliament, gained respect, rights, and legal protection from violence. Sheffield pupils, through role play and discussion, developed under-standing of social, moral, cultural and political processes in another country.

Engaging and nurturing 'spiritual' capacities

Hampshire Development Education Centre, working with the LEA, has combined drama, RE, music and geography in promoting responsible global citizenship. The Thengapalli project, was inspired by local communities in Orissa, India, working together to reverse the devastating ecological effects of deforestation. Spiritual factors have been important in stimulating both the action in Orissa and the UK children's appreciation of the situation. The latter were encouraged to engage their capacities for wonder, love, empathy and the sense of connectedness in experiencing, 'at a distance', the relationships between nature and the Orissa community.

Local Agenda 21

Many local authorities are involving their communities in envisioning and planning for the future in drawing up Local Agenda 21 – called for by the Earth Summit declaration on the environment and development. Some schools have become involved. In Croydon, the LEA and local businesses have issued 'environmental challenges' to pupils on issues of local relevance. In other projects, children have presented their ideas to local councillors. In the Global Footprint project, run by the Humanities Education Centre, Tower Hamlets, primary children will assess their schools' impacts on local and global environments and make recommendations for change. Social and moral decisions will have to be made about causes and effects of environmental and socio-economic problems. Children could also consider fair trade by analysing the origins of their food and the moral implications of importing cheap food from overseas.

Volunteering

With older pupils, volunteering in charity shops or conservation work might be integrated into the curriculum. Volunteering requires good planning, adequate training, support and debriefing, and care that volunteers are not merely fund-raising. Camden sixth formers took it a step further by setting up a Fair Trade group, and researching and producing a booklet on where to buy fairly-traded products. It was distributed by local Oxfam campaigners.

Conclusion

An active and engaged citizenship education provides a practical and experiential testing ground for spiritual and moral development, the values they inform and the consequent personal and socio-economic decision-making. It provides a *real life* context. Few other areas of the curriculum provide such opportunities.

Citizenship education is about identifying present priorities, values, and working with these to construct a future society in which we would want to live. A MORI poll (January–February 1998) of 11 to 16 year olds shows 70 per cent of young people want to know more about the world and global issues but 54 per cent feel powerless to change anything. As the Foundation for Civil Society has found, young people's political participation is declining in spite of their concern. Is this because society emphasises the wrong type of politics for young people, that it does not reflect what is most important to young people? Or is it the political *processes* that they feel alienated from rather than the politics, *per se?* Or both? How many adults feel alienated for similar reasons? And do young people take their sense of alienation with them into adulthood? These are vital questions for a democratic and civil society.

Citizenship education is about nurturing a sense of personal responsibility to a greater whole, and exercising it. It should show young people that they are valued (thereby experiencing the significance of valuing others), that they can make a difference and make sound moral, social, cultural and spiritual choices. This requires not just telling children about policy and how things 'should be' but helping them to recognise, experience and take responsibility for how their desires and priorities shape their behaviour and the world on which we all depend. It is about creating a future in which we would choose to live.

In his novel, *Stark*, Ben Elton describes a world on the verge of ecological and social collapse which the richest people are planning to abandon. Sly, a billionaire chiefly responsible for this, offers a chilling warning of this kind of future: 'Something could have been done a long time ago, but we didn't do it did we chum? We opted for instant profit and comfort, beer and skittles at the expense of the whole of future history' (Elton 1989). This is a future that no person wants but many fear. Research by Hicks and Holden (1995) indicates that many people share a hope for a future of greater equality, sense of community, justice and peace. Since over 74 per cent of young people surveyed in the MORI poll cited school as an important source of information about global issues, teachers have a powerful influence on the society of the future. As Hicks and Holden (1995, p. 6) state: 'Through education we have the opportunity to help young people understand their right to a future and the responsibility they have to ensure that this right is available to all. We can help young people to feel positive about the future and to believe that through their actions they can make a contribution for a more just and equitable world'.

References

Barber, M. (1997) *The Learning Game: Argument for an Education Revolution.* London: Galleons.

Bazalgette, J. L. (1992) *Clean Different Things – How English Children Learn to be Subjects and Might Learn to be Citizens.* London: Grubb Institute.

Beck, U. (1992) *Risk Society: Towards a New Modernity.* London: Sage.

Capra, F. (1996) *The Web of Life.* London: Harper Collins.

Development Education Association (May 1998) *Response to the initial report from the advisory group on Education for Citizenship and the Teaching of Democracy.* London: DEA.

Elton, Ben (1989) *Stark.* London: Sphere.

Erikson, E. (1967) *Identity: Youth and Crisis.* New York: W.W. Norton and London: Faber.

Hicks, D. and Holden, C. (1995) *Visions of the Future; Why We Need to Teach for Tomorrow.* Stoke-on-Trent: Trentham.

Holden, C. and Clough, N. (eds) (1998) *Children as Citizens: Education for Participation.* London/Philadelphia: Jessica Kingsley Publishers.

Knight, B. and Stokes, P. (1996) *The Deficit in Civil Society in the United Kingdom.* London: Foundation for Civil Society.

Lynch, J. (1992) *Education for Citizenship in a Multi-cultural Society.* London: Cassell.

NCC (1990) *Education for Citizenship. Curriculum Guidance 8.* London: NCC.

Oxfam (1997a) *A Curriculum for Global Citizenship.* London: Oxfam.

Oxfam (1997b) *Developing Rights.* London: Oxfam.

Putnam, R. D. (1993) *Making Democracy Work: Civic Traditions in Modern Italy.* Princeton, NJ: Princeton University Press.

QCA (1998) *Education for citizenship and the teaching of democracy in schools, Final report.* London: Qualifications and Curriculum Authority.

Reed, B. (1978) *Dynamics of Religion.* London: Darton, Longman and Todd.

Wackernagel, M. and Rees, W. (1996) *Our Ecological Footprint: Reducing Human Impact on the Earth.* Gabriola Island, BC, Canada: New Society Publishers.

Teaching materials

Developing Rights, Oxfam, 1997.

Living Values: A Guidebook, Brahma Kumaris, 1995.

Speaking for Ourselves, Listening to Others, Leeds Development Education Centre, 1995.

Thengapalli, Hampshire County Council, 1997.

Useful organisations:

Brahma Kumaris, Global Cooperation House, Pound Lane, London NW10 2HH. 0181 459 1400.

The Bridge Trust – Spirit of Learning Network, Wychwood, 20 The Chase, Reigate, Surrey RH2 7DH. 01737 762261.
Development Education Association, 29-31 Cowper Street, London EC2A 4AP. 0171 490 8108.
Foundation for Civil Society, 200 Banbury Road, Northfield, Birmingham B31 2DL. 0121 476 8707.
Going for Green, Churchcote House, 56 Oxford Street, Manchester M60 7HJ.
The Grubb Institute of Behavioural Studies, Cloudesley Street, London N1 0HU. 0171 278 8061.
Oxfam Education, 4th floor, 4 Bridge Place, London SW1V 1XY. 0171 931 7660.

Further reading

Foster, John (1992–93) *Issues: The Cross-Curricular Course for PSE*, vols 1–5. London: Collins Educational.
These five workbooks provide a PSE course for 11-16 schooling. Each has a separate teacher's book containing helpful photocopiable resources. The course covers economic and industrial understanding, self-awareness, careers, health education, education for citizenship and environmental education.

Foster, John (1994) *Personal, Social and Health Education Answers*. London: Collins Educational.
This pack, which includes posters, offers guidance for personal and social education in primary schools.

Oxfam Education (1997) *A Curriculum for Global Citizenship*.
This free book (see preceding section for address) contains an outline curriculum covering all Key Stages, with practical classroom and whole-school examples of good practice.

Chapter 5

Careers and Vocational Education

Stephen Bigger

The focus in the school curriculum on work as an aspect of adult life comes throughout schooling: two 'cross-curricular themes' require careers education, and economic and industrial understanding (EIU) to be covered (NCC 1990a, 1990b). Whole-school planning is needed to plot in which subjects different aspects of this could be covered; and in secondary schools particularly, a separate focus on careers and work experience is generally found. Some pupils begin to specialise in vocational courses in Key Stage 4 and beyond.

With young pupils from early years to primary age, awareness of work comes through workplace visits, input from various professionals, projects and discussions of parents' employment. These often have outcomes in writing, play, drama and research on a range of local industries and businesses, and certainly not excluding those professionals with whom pupils come into contact within school.

Primary school: possible activities
shops – hospitals – fire-fighting – police – energy – transport

Pupils may aspire to particular careers as a result of people they meet, so it is important that stereotypes do not seem to *exclude* (most notably by avoiding gender stereotypes). This not only involves being careful with language (e.g. police*man*, fire*man* instead of police officer and fire fighter) but also by using role models of both sexes, ensuring that girls realise that they can become doctors (and boys nurses), and so taking these roles in play activities. Equal opportunities can be made explicit in this work, with pupils becoming critically aware of the need to decode and resist stereotypes. Books, and especially book illustrations, need to be the focus of healthy criticism; and pupils should be encouraged to become sharp television critics. The primary school years may not be the time when career decisions are made, but they provide the roots of motivation (or demotivation) for future choices. A full and rich engagement with work related activities is therefore important.

The secondary school is directly engaged in the process of career choices, leading to guidance to help pupils to make appropriate choices for post-16 education. This process is supported by careers guidance, offering input from the local (now privatised) careers service. Schools can use personality tests and job preference questionnaires (Parkinson 1997a, 1997b). Those who choose academic courses may be able to participate in career-focused initiatives such as Understanding Industry. Work experience in Years 10 or 11 is now routine but there are concerns about quality and focus. Vocational courses can be general (for example the General National Vocational Qualification, (GNVQ), or specific (such as in business practice, car maintenance): they operate on three levels – foundation, intermediate and advanced, ensuring that there are appropriate courses for all attainment levels after GCSE. By being practical and project centred, there is a strong emphasis on active learning which some students prefer. Unfortunately, the development of a vocational curriculum has not been without its problems (Tomlinson 1997, Hyland 1997). Schools have generally resisted the replacement of education about work with training for work (Lewis 1997). Winch (1998, p. 377), comparing high skill and low skill vocational models, comments, 'How VET [vocational education and training] is seen is bound up with questions of how people are motivated, what kinds of social conditions are necessary to motivate them and the general relationship between economy and society ... [It] touches on the heart of what any society is about.' White (1997) focuses on how work should be linked with personal well-being.

This emphasis on choice, as a pupil reaches the age of 16, implies values. Some questions are worth asking:

• How do we regard work?

• What values are implied within work and within particular careers?

• What analysis of values can be addressed to work situations?

Work can be viewed as a chore (to be endured for the money), or as a pleasure which brings its own rewards. Our attitudes greatly effect our motivation: we might explore:

• the notion of a worthwhile job (philosophical)

• doing a job as well as we are able (spiritual)

• jobs which help others (ethical)

• working well with others (social)

• jobs which expand people's minds (cultural)

For disabled pupils, and those with severe or moderate learning difficulties, employment is not an easy progression to make. Even work experience placements can be problematic, because of physical difficulties (e.g. access for wheelchairs); or the attitude of employers ('my clients won't want to see disabled people about'); or perceived behavioural problems ('I don't want someone who might steal'). Such excuses are routinely met in work experience placements. Education has a complex task here – to raise the awareness of employers about what 'disabled' pupils *can* do (as opposed to *can't* do), by mentoring relationships for example which might in time lead to work experience. Disability is a socially imposed label for people who could contribute given sympathetic provision (Ashcroft, Bigger and Coates 1996). Teachers also need to build up pupils' confidence and develop abilities and skills of use in adult life and in employment, teaching them to be independent rather than dependent. An emphasis on values creates an agenda to help young people to become employable. Pupils need skills and they need to *feel* employable. There are today academic and vocational qualifications appropriate to their needs at each level. 'Able'[1] pupils have different needs – perhaps to be challenged; perhaps to remedy underachievement; certainly to be empowered, enabled and encouraged. Underachievers need to be identified and supported. Teacher expectation is crucially important since this affects self-image: bright dyslexic students, for example, may grow up feeling stupid and incompetent because their ability has been judged on writing skills. Sympathetic understanding and support can make all the difference.

Spiritual aspects

There are religious 'vocations' which might be described as 'spiritual': priests, missionaries, monks. But 'spiritual' and 'religious' are not interchangeable today. My spirituality does not depend on me accepting religious dogma. It is however interesting how this word 'vocation', meaning 'calling' (by God, presumably), has given us the word 'vocational'. 'Vocation' implies an inner voice, a metaphor representing inner conviction. We talk of people with a burning drive to be a teacher, doctor, vet, musician or writer. 'Vocations' (as opposed to careers) have traditionally been 'rewarded' by lower salaries, relying on job satisfaction to help to retain employees (not always successfully). Young people are encouraged to search for the career they would find deeply satisfying, and employers are encouraged to make work more satisfying: the spirituality of vocations provides a helpful metaphor.

The spiritual is about how meaningfully I view myself and my work. The 'who am I?' question explores my sense of identity and self-worth and promotes self-understanding. Personal realisation covers intellectual, emotional, physical and social domains including concepts such as commitment, motivation, value, worth, esteem and relationship. Progress will involve personal growth, developing an holistic perspective, noting and creating inter-connections, in which new meanings are perceived and new insights challenge the fabric of thinking. To the religious, this might be channelled through belief in God; to the secularist, it invites reflection on world views and life-stances. Both are spiritual in different ways; but dogmatic beliefs, whether religious or ideological, can also restrict insight and prevent personal growth.

Job satisfaction raises wider issues of personal fulfilment and self-esteem. Those starting in vocations might grow to hate the job, whilst others grow to find fulfilment. Personal identity, esteem and self-realisation are issues of spiritual health. A job can express inner needs and feelings, give opportunities for self expression and build up a sense of self-worth. This is not the same as being self-centred and egotistical, which stems from a desire for power and personal advantage. Many jobs do not give a high level of pleasure and employees have to reach a personal compromise. An unhappy workforce is far less productive than a content workforce suitably self-directed, so achieving satisfaction and motivation needs be high on management's priorities. Education needs to help students to cultivate a positive ethos to working with others with the sensitivity to be constructive in their own endeavours to bring about positive change.

Self-realisation through work assists the process of self-improvement in which we seek to free ourselves to work in more focused and effective ways. This might involve self-respect. Underestimating our own potential might create a barrier which holds us back: we need to believe in ourselves. (Inappropriate self-confidence might equally hold us back in other ways if it makes it harder for us to learn.) If work can become dynamically empowering, motivation ceases to be a problem. Self-worth leads to recognising worth in others. The concept of worth implies a belief that something or someone *matters*. Directed towards ourselves, this leads to self-respect and self-esteem, a recognition that we personally matter and that our contribution also matters. This needs also to lead to a recognition that the contribution of others also matters.

Respect implies an openness to other people's ideas and beliefs, a willingness to listen, to see things from someone else's point of view. It is the opposite of the closed mind, the egocentric compulsion for everyone to see things our way. Respect implies humility as regards our own situation, a view that assumes that there is much more to be known than is appreciated already. We see our current views as partial and temporary, subject to future development with new information and insights. In relation to work, this touches on important aspects of teamwork and cooperation, the willingness to work things out together, to accept other people's ideas and to welcome critical assessment of our own suggestions. Employers look for team players who can bond an institution, even if they sometimes mistake these for conventional people who don't rock the boat but equally don't have brilliant ideas. A company is as good as the way in which it harnesses its teams and allows them to be creative. A business which is a learning and developing community should welcome constructive critique even if it is uncomfortable. The opposite is the company run by a dominant autocrat who needs power but is not sensitive to the needs of others, whether customers or employees. Such a company will not be empowered by the collective energies of its employees, because it does not value them.

Self-realisation brings the self into the work equation: work is viewed as a vital form of human self-expression, full of dignity, leading to personal commitment to a job worth doing, and a personal growth which is at the same time intellectual, emotional, social and ethical.

Moral aspects

Work has its fair share of ethical dilemmas because decisions and choices have constantly to be made. The values which inform these choices impact upon the ethics both of the industry and of individual employees. Education needs to teach young people to:

- analyse ethical issues in particular circumstances and from different standpoints;

- explore general moral principles and society's expectations;

- apply concepts such as justice, honesty, trust and truthfulness;

- examine the effects and possible consequences of negative concepts such as prejudice, discrimination, exploitation, deceit and malice.

Ethical analysis does not have a fore-ordained right answer. Each situation is unique. In setting out the situation, what happened is set against general ethical principles, against ethical standards and guidelines set for the industry, and against legal requirements. Standards are continually evolving in the light of new cases as new industries test the boundaries and limits. Recently, ethical guidelines have been discussed concerning, for example:

- cloning;

- biotechnology and especially gene manipulation;

- food technologies including genetically altered crops and irradiation treatment for preservation;

- the treatment of food animals;

- tobacco advertising.

New processes demand new general principles and the reapplication of existing ones.

The prime objective of most work is to *make a profit* (the exceptions are voluntary and not-for-profit organisations). Some ways of making a profit are legally restrained as criminal; or socially stigmatised such as intrusive freelance photography. Issues such as exploitation, victimisation, deception, endangering life, or public decency can be discussed. Concepts such as these provide our first level of ethical analysis. Exploitation which is regarded as morally acceptable (and therefore happens routinely) may become the target of ethical controversy which may in time change the moral climate. Smoking is a case in point: selling tobacco is legal but ethically disputed. Advertising tobacco was morally and legally accepted but is rapidly becoming viewed as unacceptable. Child labour worldwide has become an ethical flashpoint; the emotional argument about life chances and education being more desirable than child labour has to be weighed against questions of whether a family can survive without the income children produce.

These raise at a deeper level ethical concerns about the global distribution of profits from work, where workers get paid little and multinational companies make huge profits. Environmental issues highlight pollution and its effects on people, animals and habitats. Here, animal habitats may be set against human needs (for work, income and products) to produce a complex ethical debate. Work is not about making maximum profit at any cost.

When work is viewed as a service, the language of customer satisfaction is often used as an indicator of success. Analysing employment opportunities in terms of *benefits to others* can give pupils a way of thinking about work. Who benefits? Can benefits be maximised? How can customers best be satisfied? Pupils will be creative in deriving their own category headings. A more complex level of analysis comes when comparing the relative values of producing luxuries when many have insufficient basic necessities. The economic system produces winners and losers, rich and poor both in national and international terms. A concept that will be helpful in these debates is that of *social justice* which addresses the global creation, use and distribution of wealth.

There are ethical issues in work processes which involve

- employee relations, and

- employee empowerment.

A contented, motivated workforce gives effective underpinning to management and outcomes but it is notoriously difficult to achieve. Fair practices are enshrined in equal opportunities procedures but most are rhetoric. Employee relations become destabilised by personal ambitions, empire building, and back-stabbing. Person specifications say they want consultative team members but interviewers may value the opinionated, assertive and dominant, who may in practice be ego-centric autocrats who pervert management practices to their own ends. Teamwork contains skills which can be developed in schools, not least through active projects:

- valuing consultation;

- seeking consensus but knowing its limitations;

- being aware of the value of outstanding individual contributions and flair;

- understanding that leadership may facilitate decision-making;

- understanding that hierarchy can be ultimately restricting.

In real work situations, open critique of the effective functioning of hierarchy might be perilous but it is vital for the health of an organisation. This may be contained in the concept of accountability. Working practices consisting of properly constituted teams can lead to empowerment if the results of their work are valued: teams which are used to being overruled will not retain motivation for long.

Areas for exploration in education

1. Define and give examples of useful work.

2. What is meant by exploitation? Where should we draw the line to identify unacceptable practice?

3. How should staff relate to each other? How should managers manage?

4. What working practices help to motivate staff?

5. How can fair play at work be assured – in selection, appraisal, promotion and general treatment?

6. How equal are opportunities?

7. What are our global responsibilities?

   • To what extent is wealth fairly distributed?

   • To what extent does trade favour rich countries or multinationals?

   • How acceptable is the arms trade?

   • Should we invest only in companies and areas with a good ethical record?

8. How might we define, in personal and company terms:

   • Quality?

   • Efficiency?

   • Effectiveness?

Figure 5.1

Social aspects

Social perspectives to careers and vocational education cover an understanding of the role of work in society and in adult life. Pupils understand the range of occupations throughout society and their contribution to national and international well-being. They understand the importance of companies making a profit to provide funds for continued employment, known as 'wealth creation'. And they understand the relationship between employed and employers, with potential for both conflict and empowerment. We do them a service if we help them to navigate through the tensions at work and find a degree of fulfilment.

Positive and negative issues might be raised.

Positive

- work providing an income and sustaining life;

- providing meaning, purpose, status and independence;

- providing companionship.

Negative

- boring, demotivating jobs;

- long hours threatening family life;

- demeaning authority structures.

Discussion of work raises interestingly contrasting notions, such as that preference be given according to *merit*, and that procedures are *fair* in the broadest sense. Pupils can explore how '*merit*' can be interpreted – through qualifications in the traditional way but also by other factors such as attitude, social skills, aptitude, confidence, ability to tackle problems, and willingness to take responsibility. Focusing on these might broaden their preparation for work. Too narrow a view of merit might disadvantage those struggling against material disadvantage, and seem unfair. The phrase 'affirmative action' is used in the USA to promote greater black involvement in the economy: it is controversial and not infrequently tested in law. In Britain, discrimination is outlawed by equal opportunity legislation, which does not differentiate between positive and negative discrimination. Affirmative action takes the form of targeting under-represented minorities in ways which do not discriminate against others, and monitoring recruitment decisions. Yet if merit is redefined in a broader way, more young people from disadvantaged backgrounds might find appropriate opportunities 'on merit'. Selection which relies only on qualifications covering a narrow area of interest (e.g. A levels, or a degree) might unfairly advantage those operating in their first language from affluent homes, who haven't had to work their way through college. So 'merit' and 'fairness' are appropriate partners.

Our individual sense of identity has a social dimension. By having a job or career we regard ourselves as *something*; by being unemployed we do not. Careers are linked with ambition and aspiration – getting the right job is part of becoming the person we wish to be. Our definition of 'the right job' will modify in time: it may involve personal enjoyment and a feeling that the job is worthwhile; it may also involve personal status, that it is a 'fitting' job. Pupils can explore why people work, and what they think of work, to get a flavour of people's motivation. Such a critique of attitudes to work might bring long term benefit – the understanding that everyone, however apparently lowly, needs to benefit from the personal satisfaction of employment that gives them meaning and fulfilment. Relationships with colleagues should not be affected by their 'high status' (i.e. their rate of pay) but everyone should be valued for the contribution they make. Indeed, the higher the pay the greater should be the accountability. In economic terms, young people are learning to be critically aware of the needs of the whole company and the effectiveness of the various contributions to it. Ineffective performance might threaten the survival of all jobs; ineffectiveness at the top causes maximum vulnerability.

Social skills can be developed in schools and colleges throughout the whole curriculum. These might include developing the ability to:

- work in teams;
- behave sympathetically and with respect;
- communicate clearly in a range of contexts;
- give presentations confidently;
- explain circumstances to others;
- teach, instruct, supervise and train;
- inspire confidence in others;
- apologise where appropriate;
- negotiate;
- offer critique sensitively;
- foster the well-being of the group.

Such a list could be derived from a pupil brainstorming activity. Assessment can be based on a mix of teacher judgement, peer review and personal self-assessment, such as is found in individual action planning.

An important aspect of social life is the family, and this raises issues of fundamental importance. Work provides income to support family life and yet sets up impeding tensions – long hours, trips away from home and so on. The sharp edge of this dilemma lies in the difficulties many women face to combine a career with raising a family. There are issues here of pupil-care facilities, the insecurity of part-time working, job sharing, coping with sick children, coping with antisocial work schedules and not least the lack of awareness of some senior managers. There are wider issues of the sharing of responsibilities for home making and pupil-care between partners, which can lead to lively debate among young people.

Cultural aspects

Culture is an ambiguous term, but gains some strength from the ambiguity. For the person in the street, culture means the arts (theatre, art galleries, dance and music) and heritage industries (museums, castles and stately homes) – and there are vocational implications in these. But culture is also an anthropological term for the whole attitude, belief system and world view. Thus we speak of monocultural and multicultural perspectives (from one point of view or from many points of view). The 'culture' of 'multicultural' involves beliefs, the arts (dance, story, song), and the characteristic ways in which this set of people view their world.

Culture as a reference to the arts brings into focus the place of the artistic and creative in the world of work. Painting, sculpture, dance, drama, music and creative writing are rarely 'just a job' – they draw power from the heart of the performer and demand ability, dedication and skill. They put the very being 'on the line': performers reveal their deepest selves through their art and make themselves vulnerable. This is not usual in other jobs, where an ordered routine helps efficiency: in the arts, performances need to be vibrant and full of life, not routine. Yet work in the arts is rarely highly paid. The manager might be paid more than the performer. It is seen as individualistic and idiosyncratic. True, it is possible to become rich – the TV and film actor, the pop star, the top artist. Yet the fashionable artist is not the norm; riches are more easily gained from packaging performance commercially than by following the creative flow. Where arts products command high prices, it is often not the performer who benefits but the entrepreneur.

But is there a clear line between commercialism and art? Or put another way, can the work we do be creative, artistic and an expression of our deepest selves? An issue here is that the artistic creation has to pass through the filter of the business consultant who declares 'whether it will sell'. Publishers have their agents and commissioning editors who try to filter out the non-commercial. These people set trends. Books viewed as trend-setting spawn imitations which prevent the next brilliant book being published. Tolkein has been much imitated. Fixed ideas consign great art to the drawer and hype the mediocre. R. M. Pirsig's seminal, best-selling (and unimitated) *Zen and the Art of Motor Cycle Maintenance*, a disturbing account of philosophy and personal awareness, was rejected by 121 publishers because it didn't fit into any mould. This reveals the necessity for talented agents as well as gifted artists, who can sponsor, package and promote art. These can facilitate creativity and add to its quality. Literary editors have a hand both in what is written and how it is presented: 'That's a terrible ending, try it again!' 'Can't you make this character more real?' and so on. So artistic creativity can be both an individual pursuit and a communal activity. Culture needs the promoters and critics as well as the stars, both very influential in the artistic community, and hopefully responsible. There is a strong quality and values dimension to this.

The media is relatively recent as an agent of culture, creating instant stars of film and television. All forms of the arts appear for the benefit of a mass audience. This raises a range of issues about commercialism and quality as the bizarre dominates. Yet there is room for artistic quality to emerge from the writing and performance or films, dramas, soaps and sit coms. A broad global view of culture (what we might call 'multiculture') can also enrich productions. Teachers can encourage pupils to analyse current productions critically and help to shape future taste.

Those that go into media careers will take this critical understanding with them and shape programming accordingly.

Culture is wider than the arts: it covers belief systems and world views. Multicultural perspectives have careers implications. The travel industry needs people who deeply understand the cultures into which they are sending visitors. Companies need people who can negotiate easily in different cultural backgrounds. The caring professions need both accurate information (and preferably experience) and sympathetic understanding of other cultures, their attitudes, expectations, modesty codes and food preferences. Stereotypes about ethnic groups persist and need challenging. Each ethnic group will have its own settlement history and current socio-economic factors may be a consequence of this – poor housing, high unemployment and so on.

Intercultural aspects of careers and vocational education

Challenge stereotypes

Inter-cultural understanding

Religion, festivals, food observances, ethical expectations

Sympathy, empathy and respect

Linguistic skills

Socio-economic needs

Figure 5.2

References

Ashcroft, K., Bigger, S., Coates, D. (1996) *Researching into Equal Opportunities*. London: Kogan Page.

Hyland, T. (1997) 'Reconsidering competence', *Journal of Philosophy of Education* **31**(3), 491–503.

Lewis, T. (1997) 'Towards a liberal vocational education', *Journal of Philosophy of Education* **31**(3), 477–89.

NCC (1990a) *Curriculum Guidance 4: Education for Economic and Industrial Understanding*. York: National Curriculum Council.

NCC (1990b) *Curriculum Guidance 5: Careers Education*. York: National Curriculum Council.

Parkinson, M. (1997a) *How to Master Personality Questionnaires: The Essential Guide*. London: Kogan Page.

Parkinson, M. (1997b) *How to Master Psychometric Tests*. London: Kogan Page.

Tomlinson, S. (1997) *Education 14–19: Critical Perspectives.* London: Athlone Press.

White, J. (1997) 'Education, work and well-being', *Journal of Philosophy of Education* **31**(2), 233–47.

Winch, C. (1998) 'Two rival conceptions of vocational education: Adam Smith and Friedrich List', *Oxford Review of Education* **24**(3), 365–78.

Further reading

J K Galbraith (1996) *The Good Society: The Humane Agenda.* London: Sinclair Stevenson.

A discussion of the social, economic and political issues contributing to the development of a global society.

Handy, C. (1994) *The Empty Raincoat: Making Sense of the Future.* London: Hutchinson.

A series of short studies on the future of business and the economy from a values perspective.

Plender, J. (1997) *A Stake in the Future: The Stakeholding Solution.* London: Nicholas Brealey.

An exploration by an economist of inclusive ways of organising companies, viewing the firm and its network (customers, shareholders, employees and suppliers) as a community within which relationships and mutual support are important.

Note

[1] 'Able' is used for convenience with the understanding that such labels are problematic even when backed by IQ scores.

Part Two

The National Curriculum

Chapter 6

Science

Jennie McFadden

Values can be embedded in the way science is taught. In fulfilling the requirements of 'Experimental and Investigative Science', frequent opportunities are created for the development of social and moral values and potentially for spiritual and cultural education. These values can be clearly identified in the requirements listed in the introductions to the Programmes of Study for each Key Stage of *Science in the National Curriculum, England and Wales* (DFE/WO 1995, especially pages 2, 7, 14, 24–25). The requirements which particularly encourage values education include:

'Science in Everyday Life' (Key Stages 1 and 2) and 'Application of Science' (Key Stages 3 and 4)

'The Nature of Scientific Ideas' (Key Stages 3 and 4)

'Communication' (all Key Stages)

'Health and Safety' (all Key Stages).

In 'Science in Everyday Life' (primary) and 'Application of Science' (secondary), pupils should be given the opportunity to develop an increasing scientific awareness of how to protect and care for living things and the environment. Science is linked to personal health at Key Stages 1 and 2, while at Key Stage 3 and beyond, pupils learn how applications of science can affect the quality of their lives. 'Life Processes and Living Things' (Sc2) entails looking at drugs as medicines (Key Stage 1) and drug abuse from Key Stage 2 onwards. The requirements also state that pupils should be given the opportunity to consider applications of science and to 'evaluate the benefits and drawbacks of scientific and technological developments for individuals, communities and environments' and should 'consider competing priorities and the decisions that have to be made about energy requirements, taking into account relevant social, economic and environmental factors'. Ultimately, the requirements stress, 'the power and limitations of science in addressing industrial, social and environmental issues and some of the ethical dilemmas involved' must be addressed (DFE/WO 1995, p. 24).

'Health and Safety' requirements emphasise that pupils should be given opportunities to control hazards and risks to themselves and to others, giving scope for social, moral and spiritual values. 'The Nature of Scientific Ideas' requires giving pupils the opportunity to 'relate social and historical contexts to scientific ideas by studying how at least one scientific idea has changed over the course of time' (DFE/WO 1995, p. 14). At Key Stage 4 and beyond, pupils 'should consider ways in which scientific ideas may be affected by the social and historical contexts in which they develop, and how these contexts may affect whether or not the ideas are accepted' (DFE/WO 1995, p. 24). These requirements should stimulate a study both of multicultural science and of social values. Non-Statutory Guidance is also available (DES/WO 1989).

The influential Association for Science Education (ASE) has prepared detailed policy statements on many aspects of science education (e.g. 'Values and Science Education' on the ASE website). There is a clear emphasis on learners experiencing a relevant science curriculum that places an understanding of the applications of science in a social, cultural and ethical context, and gives the learner an appreciation that the conduct of science is not value-free (ASE 1998).

Values

Science is concerned with both the fundamental spiritual questions on the origins of the universe and of life itself. Moreover, many vital social and moral issues confronting contemporary society are scientifically based.

- Environmental problems such as pollution and overuse of resources. Is it 'safe' to develop nuclear energy? Are we fast using up resources? Should we plan for distant future generations? Is the planet overpopulated? Should the debts of developing countries be written off by richer nations in the planet's interest?

- Dilemmas raised by the revolution in molecular biology and genetic engineering. Should genetic screening be introduced? Should 'defective' foetuses be aborted? Can society afford to insure and support the genetically disabled? Will a new genetic underclass be created?

- The nature and conduct of modern warfare – use of biological, chemical and nuclear weapons.

Despite this potential, science is often perceived as clinical, impersonal and dehumanised: yet we are surrounded by scientific and technological achievements, which are not developed and used in a moral vacuum. Choices have to be made as to what science is supported. At primary school, children generally show great enthusiasm for science, but this seems to wane in later years. Many reasons for this have been discussed and in particular, the accusation that science is perceived as the domain of white, middle class Western males (see for example, Reiss 1993a, 1993b). Perhaps, however, it is also due to the way pupils come to view science as impersonal and irrelevant. Maybe it is no coincidence that biology is the more popular science, as it appears to be the one with the more overtly human, moral and social content. Such values equally exist in the physical sciences and need to be addressed more explicitly.

Today there is an increased need for people to be scientifically informed. With the meteoric development of genetic engineering, vital decisions will need to be taken. These choices will reflect the values of society but will need to be scientifically informed. Yet it is ironic that at a time when society needs its population to be more scientifically aware, pupils are turning away from science. Commonly, society's response to scientific advances such as cloning (Dolly the sheep) is an emotive, uninformed gut reaction. In the 1998 Oxford Amnesty Lectures, the contrary cases were argued that scientific research should be regulated by public conceptions of morality yet such constraints could potentially deprive society of valuable developments. Who decides? Wakeford (1998, p. 47) states that 'the most striking aspect of the new biotechnologies is how little opportunity ordinary citizens have had to debate and direct them'. Perhaps the ordinary citizen is not scientifically literate enough to make an informed decision.

Spiritual aspects

The concept of promoting spiritual education within the science curriculum may seem incongruous to those who understand 'spiritual' in a religious sense. The Association for Science Education has produced an extremely rich range of materials in the Science and Technology in Society (SATIS) Project for 14–16 years (ASE 1991) and 16–19 Years (ASE 1990). The SATIS 16–19 Unit 77 (ASE 1990) on 'Science and religion – friends or foes?' encourages pupils to 'consider the relationships between science and religion with a view to exploring how far they are conflicting or compatible ways of looking at the world'. It uses evolution and cosmology as exemplars. SCAA (1996, p. 13) asserts that science teachers 'have a role in promoting an objective, balanced and unsentimental approach to spiritual and moral issues'. The following shows how this might be done.

(a) Promotion of inner growth

'Experimental and Investigative Science' (Sc1) can promote inner growth. In order to carry out successful investigations, a pupil will need to develop commitment and honest observation in recording results. In emphasising the need for personal safety and responsibility for the safety of others, a sense of self-worth, self-esteem and the value of individuals should be promoted. Investigations should also help to promote a sense of wonder and curiosity, and to stimulate the inclination to question.

Some science activities that encourage self-worth, trustworthiness, commitment, personal reflection and meaning and purpose of life are listed below. The following also promote development of social, moral and cultural values:

Care for living things and the environment

- Looking after a class pet or plant. This may be especially rewarding for children with special educational needs.

- Raising funds to sponsor an endangered species or a zoo animal. Should zoos exist?

What is life?
At Key Stage 1 pupils are taught the differences between living and non-living things.

- In primary schools, revel in the sheer wonder of the variety of life forms. Collect and display pictures of diverse and bizarre life forms, visit zoos, parks and museums, use CD-ROMs and videos, e.g. David Attenborough's *Life on Earth* series.

- Progress into a discussion of the value of life and later discuss life used as a commodity – for example, embryo research, or animal treatment. Is human life different from other life? Is it right to use animals in research to save human life? Does human life have intrinsic value or purpose?

(b) Expression of creativity and imagination
Science can be highly creative as all the great scientific discoveries and inventions testify. In designing an investigation, pupils of all ages have the opportunity to think creatively and to discover things for themselves. They can also be encouraged to present their work in creative and imaginative ways thereby enhancing self-expression. Not all investigations need to be written up in the formal practical report format. Indeed there is a statutory obligation to make science accessible to all. For a pupil with learning difficulties or for whom English is not their first language, other forms of reporting investigations may be more appropriate. For variety try:

- A verbal presentation to the class or at an assembly. Sometimes this could even take the form of a drama.

- Writing up some investigations, especially environmental work, in the form of letters to a newspaper, as courtroom drama, games, debates, discussions.

- Poster displays can also encourage artistic expression of scientific issues.

- Group reports require active cooperation and development of social skills.

- Placing results on the school website and establishing Internet links with other schools at home or abroad.

- Making videos can provide a highly enjoyable and creative way of reporting an investigation.

Creative methods can provide a stimulating and constructive use of time, satisfying several agendas.

(c) *A sense of wonder, awe and curiosity*

Great scope exists in science for arousing these feelings. Some general themes to focus on might include:

- *Size* – for sheer scale, science is unbeatable! In biology, organisms range from viruses only visible under an electron microscope to the vast blue whale, not to mention the perennially popular dinosaurs. In physical sciences, dimensions are even greater – from the subatomic dimensions of particle physics to the cosmic grandeur of astrophysics (black holes and expanding galaxies).

- *Diversity* – consider the sheer immensity of it, both biological and in the material world. Discuss the importance of the loss of biodiversity. Meaning and purpose to life can be conveyed in the constant classification and ordering of the natural world.

- *Complexity* – consider how things work and interrelationships. Life – growth and reproduction. Physical – Earth in space, or changes which occur when a cake is baked.

- *Time* – consider both the cosmic scale and biological time spans involved in evolution. Use a roll of computer paper/kitchen roll to represent time – say one sheet = 10,000 years of life on Earth. David Attenborough's calendar year analogy is helpful for older pupils.

- *Extremes* – in biology, organisms can live in incredible extremes of temperature, pH, moisture and oxygen levels (Davies 1998). They survive in hydrothermal vents, in deep caves in Romania and Mexico, and in the blackest depths of the oceans.

- *Distance* – astronomical distances to the sun and beyond. The number of drinks cans consumed in the UK in 1988 (8 billion) would stretch from here to the moon (Silver and Vallely 1990). Consider how mobile phones and the Internet ease communication. This must surely engender a sense of wonder, although it soon becomes taken for granted. It is necessary to jolt pupils out of complacency and challenge them as often as possible.

(d) *Expression of innermost thoughts, feelings and beliefs*

Science can address ideas of personal meaning. Students are developing personal beliefs about life and about themselves in particular, and science can help them build an important foundation. For example, Mullinar (1997) has produced a helpful pack entitled, *Genes and You – Teaching About Genetics from a Human Perspective* for the 14–16 age group, although it can be adapted for different ability levels and ages. Role plays and other exercises help young people to acquire the social, moral and spiritual understanding 'necessary to deal with the challenges arising out of advances in modern genetics research' (Mullinar 1997, p. 1). Students reflect upon the value of their own lives and those of other people and creatures. They will meet many alternative views, in literature and religion, but need to be developing personal views out of their own experiences.

Moral aspects

Many moral issues arise within the Science Curriculum. 'Morality', declares the SCAA (1996, p. 13), 'is not the exclusive preserve of non-scientists'. In particular, the rapid development of molecular biology has raised many ethical dilemmas, many still unresolved. You could encourage discussions of the following:

• Genetic screening – if no cure exists for a genetic condition, why screen? What effect will this knowledge have on individuals and their families? Who has the right to this knowledge? What effect will this have on employment and insurance?

• DNA fingerprinting – is it infallible? Should a national database be created to aid the fight against crime?

• Cloning – to what extent should genetic defects be 'corrected'? 'Designer babies' – where should we draw the line?

• Release of genetically engineered organisms into the wild – is this 'safe'?

• Is genetically engineered food 'safe'?

• Human population growth – should the birthrate of developing societies be curbed? How? Why? They consume less of the earth's resources than the energy hungry developed societies.

• Pollution – whose responsibility? Local, national and global perspectives.

• Radiation/nuclear technology – health and safety. Should Britain import so much toxic waste?

• Health issues – reproductive responsibility (teenage pregnancies are on the increase). Divorce rates and substance abuse are at an all time high.

• *In Vitro* Fertilisation (IVF) – is reproduction a human *right?* If treatment is costly who should pay? Could Health Service funds be better spent?

Discussion at appropriate ages and ability levels can provide the opportunity for developing moral understanding and values. Examination of such issues in depth belongs to the secondary age range, but a beginning can be made with younger children: animal welfare, health and safety, pollution and use of diminishing resources are particularly relevant. Different approaches to teaching such controversial areas are examined in Reiss (1993b).

The SATIS materials provide a wide range of resources. Some particularly relevant units from SATIS 16–19 (ASE, 1990) include:

• *Kidney transplants*, Unit 7, considers ethical issues in transplant surgery – brain death and organ transplantation.

• *Problems with embryos*, Unit 8, addresses scientific technological and moral problems related to experiments with embryos.

- *Foetal tissue transplants*, Unit 33, allows students to explore ethical issues involved in a new and controversial experimental treatment for Parkinson's disease.

- *Cystic fibrosis*, Unit 87, discusses ethical issues raised by genetic screening and *in vitro* fertilisation.

- *Life support*, Unit 88, addresses issues and dilemmas involved in high technology medicine.

Another key area where moral values may be developed in Science is 'Care for Living Things and the Environment'. Activities might include:

- Visiting a local wildlife reserve.

- Creating a wildlife corner at school.

- Starting a project to preserve/improve the local environment – planting trees, creating a pond, litter collection (note, observe health and safety requirements).

- An energy audit for self, families, class, school. Developing a sense of personal responsibility and commitment to environmental issues. Some schools have saved a lot of money through developing energy efficiency schemes.

- Carrying out a litter/waste production audit. Commitment to the Wastewatch slogan – 'Reduce, Re-use, Recycle'.

- Holding a poster display or presentation for school, parents or local community to show what has been achieved to promote environmental issues.

Many activities may be appropriately adapted for use at several ages and for different ability levels if a spiral model of learning is adopted.

Social aspects

Increasingly, scientific and technological issues dominate national debate, whether it is the hole in the ozone layer, cloning or the energy crisis. Science education has a responsibility to society to produce a more scientifically literate population that will be able to assess the benefits and risks of scientific and technological advances rationally and to make informed decisions on issues that could fundamentally change our lives. Molecular biology will continue to have an enormous impact on humanity. Yet SCAA (1996, p. 13) states that 'recent curriculum changes have marginalised social and ethical issues in science. For many students, such issues are not addressed in science lessons'. The following suggestions show how science can recover its social agenda.

(a) Practical work in science
When science is taught in a practical problem-solving manner, pupils should gain a wealth of social skills from their investigations. By the very nature of a shared practical experience, pupils are being given the opportunity to develop social skills and moral values. A successful joint investigation will involve groups of pupils in:

- working together cooperatively in planning and in predicting the outcome;

- carrying out the practical manipulations carefully, with due regard to safety;

- analysing and discussing the interpretation of the outcome.

Through practical work, pupils learn to listen to others and to respect their opinions; to reflect upon their own experiences and to evaluate various approaches; to consider advice from the teacher; to be responsible for their actions and to work safely with others. Practical investigations help to fulfil OFSTED (1995) advice that teachers 'should be:

- providing opportunities for pupils to reflect on experience

- teaching the principles separating right from wrong

- encouraging pupils to relate positively to others, to take responsibility and to participate in the community.'

Effective differentiation can be achieved in science practical work by varying the degree of open-endedness of the problem being investigated. For example, in studying plant growth, able pupils could investigate factors affecting plant growth whilst others might investigate, with more direction, whether plants need moisture to grow. In between these extremes a whole range of investigations can be devised. Pupils could also be challenged to think about moral issues. Would you do an experiment like this with a small mammal or an insect? Is it acceptable to kill plants in these types of experiments? Can science contribute to society's ethical codes?

Purnell (1993) maintains that as science is practical, logical and uses everybody's experience, equality of opportunity for pupils with special educational needs can be effectively provided in science. It is necessary to provide appropriate differentiation of tasks that will depend on the nature of the special needs and available resources. Pupils with reading/writing difficulties may thrive in practical science where there is more emphasis on hands-on experience. As Purnell (p. 165) notes, 'children involved in worthwhile practical exercises will improve their knowledge, gain skills and, particularly importantly, gain in self-confidence and self-esteem'. Purnell provides guidance on teaching science to children with special needs, as well as references to specific guidelines and resources.

(b) Citizenship
The broadsheet *Citizenship and Science* (SCIcentre, no date) clearly discusses how science in the primary classroom can provide a firm foundation for producing good citizens. We are challenged to consider 'what styles of teaching and learning can be adopted in science lessons in order to reinforce the principles of good citizenship'. At Key Stage 1 it is suggested that children might 'create a set of rules for science activities that ensures everyone is safe and that everybody gets involved practically'. By discussing issues such as, are rules necessary? who make the rules? how are they enforced? pupils learn about citizenship and the law through science.

(c) Economic and industrial understanding

From the springboard of biotechnology, the enormous economic and industrial impact of developments in molecular biology can be explored. The Medical Research Council provides valuable resources in these areas. Many local industries foster educational visits by schools (e.g. water companies, power stations, sewage works, car works), where pupils can develop an understanding of the practical applications of science and technology in industry and business.

It is essential to promote awareness of the economic and industrial aspects of scientific discovery, as developing science and technology is vital to the economy. Many units in SATIS 16–19 explore the economic and social considerations affecting decisions about:

- environmental issues – the siting of a new reservoir; quarrying sand and gravel; aluminium in tap water; the prospects for wind energy; catalytic converters; the greenhouse effect; the construction of a tidal barrage;

- industrial applications – the benefits and disadvantages of a petrochemical plant; the use of liquid crystals; the use of chemicals to promote milk yields; the production of polyurethane; ethanol – the fuel of the future?

(d) Behaviour and social relationships

Throughout the Science Curriculum there is a requirement of concern for living things and for the health and safety of you and others. All pupils are required to learn about the human life cycle and of the harmful effects of tobacco, alcohol and other drugs. These areas lead to the issues of human social relationships, which obviously require a sensitive approach. While discussion should not be seen as judgemental, the value of positive human relationships should be advanced. Issues that could be discussed in varying depths at different ages and ability levels might include:

- *peer pressure* – to smoke, drink, take drugs and have sex. The effects of these substances and activities on health are part of the Science National Curriculum.

- *sense of self-esteem* – eating disorders, obesity, and fitness. Healthy diet is also part of the programme of study.

Generally pupils of all ages, particularly teenagers, appreciate the opportunity to discuss social expectations and values. It can be a way of helping to define identity, of exploring how they fit into a group and of establishing whether they are followers or independent thinkers. Such discussions may also foster spiritual development in that they provide a vehicle for the expression of innermost feelings. If discussions are handled sensitively, pupils learn to:

- communicate with each other and the teacher;

- develop respect and esteem for their peers;

- practise social skills and behaviour within the social structure of the school.

Cultural aspects

The literature on multicultural and antiracist science education is extensive (Dennick,1993, pp. 149–51). It is acknowledged that many cultures have contributed to the development of scientific knowledge, yet a white, Western, male perspective (Reiss 1993b) has traditionally dominated science teaching. This alienates other pupils and has resulted in the teaching of an impoverished curriculum to the few who progress to A level science (Reiss 1993a). The 'Science for Life' exhibition at the Wellcome Centre for Medical Science in London (moving to Manchester in 1999) has good interactive displays which challenge pupils' images of scientists. Moreover, Reiss claims that (1993a, p. 68), the 'story of Science in the National Curriculum over the years 1988–1992 has been one of a move away from multicultural and antiracist science playing a pivotal role in official publications' (Reiss 1993a, p. 74). This trend continued in the 1995 Science National Curriculum. Values are confined to the Programmes of Study rather than the level descriptions of the Attainment Targets. While there is still a statutory obligation to promote multicultural science education, 'evidence shows that teachers and pupils under-emphasise the parts of any curriculum which they think are not to be assessed' (NCC 1991, p. 118, cited after Reiss 1993a, p. 70). Reiss asserts that many pupils are more likely to learn about the international and human nature of science in other lessons than in their science classes, but maintains that there is still much scope for science education that is appropriate for a pluralist society.

Reiss (1993b) has assembled an extensive array of examples of scientific thinking by non-Western, non-male scientists and in doing so, claims that Woolnough has 'done a great service' in exploding the myth of science being the exclusive preserve of the white, Anglo-Saxon male (Reiss 1993b, p. 9). Examples to help teachers who wish to promote science education for a pluralist society cover all of the four Attainment Targets for Science and both younger and older pupils. Further examples and possible teaching strategies of antiracist science are outlined in another work by Reiss (1993a, Chapter 5), where measuring time is discussed at length. In addition, some 52 examples of Chinese scientific thought and inventions made hundreds of years before they were 'discovered' in the West are given. Reiss explores how science teaching can help to achieve the aims of antiracist education. Apart from the 'well discussed topics of food, sickle-cell anaemia and the concept of race itself', Reiss (1993a, p. 73) suggests exploring fully the issues of:

- human population size and densities in various parts of the world; and

- patterns of energy, water and fuel consumption.

Comparisons of these issues in 'first world' and 'third world' countries may challenge pupils' thinking and broaden their perspectives. Other cultural issues might include the use of rainforest plants as medicines, the international nature of scientific research, a consideration of historic and pre-historic scientific understanding and the role of women in science. The aims of good science teaching may only be realised by adopting a more universal and all-inclusive perspective on science rather than the current white male, Western viewpoint. Other groups have also published and implemented science curricula for multicultural and antiracist education and a comprehensive list of references is given in Dennick (1993, pp. 143–46). In particular, Dennick recommends that the book *Third World Science* provides 'excellent resource material since it provides fascinating and relatively simple activities, which are reasonably open-ended and can develop into extended studies and project work'. Pupils are encouraged to explore how problems are solved in different cultures with different resources.

Conclusions

At present the effort to slim down the curriculum seems to have been at the expense of the 'human' side of science, a reduction in ethical, moral and cultural values. Although much opportunity still exists within the science curriculum to promote values, the teacher may have to work harder to create these opportunities. In an effort to keep up with an increasingly examination-led education system, non-assessed areas may be the first to go. However, it is possible that developing a stronger emphasis on values may restore some of the lost interest in science at A level and beyond.

References

ASE (1990) *Science and Technology in Society* 16–19. Hatfield: Association for Science Education.

ASE (1991) *Science and Technology in Society* 14–16. Hatfield: Association for Science Education.

ASE (1998) Association for Science Education website – http://www.rmplc.co.uk/orgs/asehg/index/html

Davies, P. (1998) 'Survivors from Mars', *New Scientist* **159**(2151), 24–29 (12 September).

Dennick, R. (1993) 'Analysing multicultural and antiracist science education', in Whitelegg, E., Thomas, J., Tresman, S. (eds) *Challenges and Opportunities for Science Education*. London: Paul Chapman Publishing/Open University.

DFE/WO (Department for Education/Welsh Office) (1989) *Science in the National Curriculum*. London: HMSO.

DFE/WO (1995) *Science in the National Curriculum for England and Wales*. London: HMSO.

Mullinar, G. (1997) *Genes and You – Teaching About Genetics from a Human Perspective*. London: The Wellcome Trust.

OFSTED (1995) The OFSTED *Handbook: Guidance on the Inspection of Nursery and Primary Schools*. London: HMSO.

Purnell, R. (1993) 'Teaching science to children with special educational needs', in Whitelegg, E., Thomas, J., Tresman, S. (eds) *Challenges and Opportunities for Science Education.* London, Paul Chapman Publishing/Open University, 164–76.

Reiss, M. J., (1993a) 'Science', in King, A. S. and Reiss, M. J. (eds) *The Multicultural Dimension of the National Curriculum.* London: Falmer Press.

Reiss, M. J. (1993b) *Science Education for a Pluralist Society.* Buckingham: Open University Press.

SCAA (1996) *Education for Adult Life: The Spiritual and Moral Development of Young People.* London: School Curriculum Assessment Authority.

SCIcentre (no date) *Citizenship and Science.* Leicester: SCI Centre, University of Leicester, School of Education, 21 University Road, Leicester LE1 7RF.

Silver, D. and Vallely, B. (1990) *The Young Person's Guide to Saving the Planet.* London: Virago Press.

Wakeford, T. (1998) 'Coming a cropper', *New Scientist*, **158**(2129) 46–47 (11 April).

Further reading

ASE (1990) *Science and Technology in Society* 16–19. Hatfield: Association for Science Education.

ASE (1991) *Science and Technology in Society* 14–16. Hatfield: Association for Science Education.

These two resources provide an extensive array of excellent material for 14-19 years on values in science education.

Mullinar, G. (1997) *Genes and You – Teaching About Genetics From a Human Perspective.* London: The Wellcome Trust.

A useful resource pack, which helps pupils acquire the understanding necessary to face the dilemmas raised by modern molecular biology. One school pack available free from The Marketing Officer, Wellcome Trust, 183 Euston Rd, London NW1 2BE.

Reiss, M. J. (1993b) *Science Education for a Pluralist Society.* Buckingham: Open University Press.

A very useful resource giving extensive examples of scientific thinking by non-western and non-male scientists.

Chapter 7

Mathematics

Margaret Jones

Mathematics is a remarkable sprawling riot of imagination, ranging from pure intellectual curiosity to nuts-and-bolts utility; and it is all one thing.

(Stewart 1989, p. vii)

It is easy to believe that mathematics is abstract, not about anything except mathematics, learning a set of rules and applying them to set problems. However, mathematics is not and can never be context and values free. Choosing suitable activities allows us to address these issues but also within the wider dimension to see the relevance of mathematics both as a tool for everyday life and as a creative discipline in its own right. Our teaching brings with it a set of theories about how children learn mathematics and with our theories come the potential for influencing children's beliefs about mathematics itself.

Spiritual aspects

Mathematics is a creative and beautiful discipline. The approach to teaching and learning can also bring to the forefront an individual's spirituality through encouraging self-worth and self-realisation, and providing time for reflection on and commitment to the subject. The teaching of mathematics can be rational and utilitarian, but it has intrinsic beauty and offers powerful insights to individuals working on complex problems which can be described in spiritual terms.

Over the centuries mathematics has had spiritual overtones within Christianity and other world religions. The decoration of Christian churches has pattern. Consider the design of the 'Rose Window' in the Notre Dame Cathedral in Paris. Its beauty arises from its symmetry. There is symmetry in the arched windows in our churches, and geometry behind their construction. Islam taught that living beings should not be depicted, which led to some great mathematical discoveries as geometric constructions decorated mosques and artefacts (Field 1998). Judaism also used number patterns. Crump (1992; p. 110f) reproduces Psalm 119 in the original Hebrew showing the 'extrinsic numerical pattern' of the verse, stating: 'this consists of 22 eight-lined stanzas, so that in every stanza each line begins with the same letter, in the order of the Hebrew alphabet'. Jewish mysticism makes substantial use of numbers. In history, the ancient Babylonians had many gods, sky gods and gods of the ocean. These gods were believed to control their lives and since many were represented by heavenly bodies, the basic notion of astronomy was born as the Babylonians attempted to predict the positions of the heavenly bodies and hence future events in their lives (MacIntosh-Wilson 1995, p. 58). The Babylonians used the 'sexagesimal' system of counting, one based around the number sixty, possibly because of their observations of the stars. Three hundred and sixty-five is close to three hundred and sixty, which is equal to six times sixty. Our present measurement of time comes from the Babylonians, using sixty minutes in an hour and sixty seconds in a minute.

The need to verify whether the Earth was the centre of the Universe around which all other bodies revolved inspired the great discoveries made by Copernicus, Kepler and Galileo and they completely changed the prevailing view in the middle ages that the Earth was the centre of the Universe into a realisation that we were just another planet. The 'Charis Project' contains a unit entitled 'The Designer Universe' in which students are encouraged to reflect on the possibility of the Universe having been designed. In terms of spiritual and moral development it states: 'The unit aims to promote a sense of wonder about the Universe and also to encourage students to reflect on the possibility of the Universe being designed' (Short and Westwell 1997, p. 11). Mathematics is a discipline containing what many would call the 'Ahh! Factor'. There are the underlying structures such as isomorphisms, meaning similar structures. These can be illustrated if we take two very simple examples.

1. How many different three digit numbers can we make using the digits 1, 2 and 3, once only?

   (Answer: 123, 132, 213, 231, 312, and 321.)

2. How many ways can you colour this flag using red, blue and green?

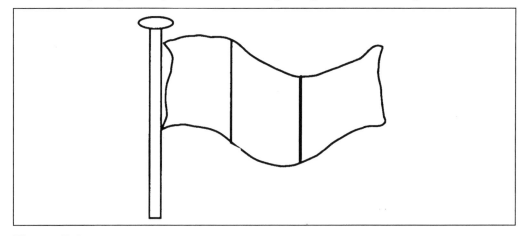

Figure 7.1

This would give us flags which were coloured:
red, blue, green;
red, green, blue;
blue, red, green;
blue, green, red;
green, red, blue;
green, blue, red.

These two simple examples have a similar structure, that if we code red as 1 and blue as 2 and green as 3 we get the same three digit numbers from the flags. It is the realisation of this sameness, the sudden understanding that comes of familiarity that provokes within us the 'Ahh! Factor'. This realisation of the power and beauty of mathematics also comes to us in many other situations. The elegance of a mathematical proof, the fractal and chaos curves and above all the realisation which can come to quite young children that infinity exists, that 'mathematics is shot through with infinity'.

Peter Lacey (1998), considers the humble 100 number square and looks at its extension as he considers inverses as one of the 'big ideas' in mathematics. It is not the idea of inverses that is focused on in this instance but rather the simplicity of the extension of the number square. Infinity is there – suddenly there is an awareness that the square can be extended infinitely in any direction.

-44	-43	-42	-41	-40	-39	-38	-37	-36	-35	-34	-33	-32	-31	-30	-29	-28
-34	-33	-32	-31	-30	-29	-28	-27	-26	-25	-24	-23	-22	-21	-20	-19	-18
-24	-23	-22	-21	-20	-19	-18	-17	-16	-15	-14	-13	-12	-11	-10	-9	-8
-14	-13	-12	-11	-10	-9	-8	-7	-6	-5	-4	-3	-2	-1	0	1	2
-4	-3	-2	-1	0	1	2	3	4	5	6	7	8	9	10	11	12
6	7	8	9	10	11	12	13	14	15	16	17	18	19	20	21	22
16	17	18	19	20	21	22	23	24	25	26	27	28	29	30	31	32
26	27	28	29	30	31	32	33	34	35	36	37	38	39	40	41	42
36	37	38	39	40	41	42	43	44	45	46	47	48	49	50	51	52
46	47	48	49	50	51	52	53	54	55	56	57	58	59	60	61	62
56	57	58	59	60	61	62	63	65	65	66	67	68	69	70	71	72
66	67	68	69	70	71	72	73	74	75	76	77	78	79	80	81	82
76	77	78	79	80	81	82	83	84	85	86	87	88	89	90	91	92
86	87	88	89	90	91	92	93	94	95	96	97	98	99	100	101	102
96	97	98	99	100	101	102	103	104	105	106	107	108	109	110	111	112
106	107	108	109	110	111	112	113	114	115	116	117	118	119	120	121	122
116	117	118	119	120	121	122	123	124	125	126	127	128	129	130	131	132

Figure 7.2 Peter Lacey, 'Educational Research and Advice', *Building Numeracy: Some suggestions for Teaching Basic Arithmetic*. Trowbridge: Robert Powell Publications(1998)

The representation gives a totally different view of the number square which is a spiritual experience in terms of the 'Ahh! Factor' for two separate reasons. First the simplicity of extending in this way; secondly, the realisation that this very simple diagram represents Infinity because its extension is limited only by the size of the paper – but imagination in considering it has no limits. Blatner (1997) similarly finds wonder in Pi.

Values

The values of the teacher are communicated to the child, in mathematics as in other subjects. Ernest (1997, p. 138) identifies five separate ideologies of mathematics education, each with an associated set of moral values. For instance, the '*Old Humanist*' has moral values founded on 'Blind' Justice, Objectivity, Rule-centred Structure, Hierarchy, and a Paternalistic 'Classical View'. The values that are held will affect teaching styles. Perhaps the most difficult task for teachers is to identify personal values and to recognise how these influence teaching style. For effective teaching a broad range of strategies are required. Each ideology has values which relate to a theory of teaching. which include phrases such as authoritarian transmission; drill, no 'frills'; skill instructor; motivate through work-relevance; explain, motivate, pass on structure; facilitate personal exploration; prevent failure; discussion, conflict questioning of content and pedagogy. It is clear in considering this list that each theory has relevance for different aspects of teaching mathematics. The skilled classroom practitioner is able to move between these different modes of teaching according to the needs of the children and the subject matter to be taught. The difficulty comes when the teacher becomes fixed to one set of values and one style of teaching.

The child's development should include self-esteem based on the relationship between teacher and child. This relationship should be exemplified by the celebration of the pupil's effort, whatever the level of success. All pupils need to have an expectation of success. One of the most difficult problems for a teacher to overcome is that of negativity. Pupils who become convinced that they are 'no good at maths!' pose a problem that requires tact and sensitivity: through planning appropriate differentiated teaching children can achieve their potential. Without differentiation a proportion of the class will fail or fail to see the point of the work in which they are engaged. Mathematics has the reputation for having closed tasks, with the implication that the teacher has the answer and it is up to the child to find out what the teacher knows. Open-ended tasks can introduce an ethos of problem-solving, giving pupils active involvement in their own learning and a pride of achievement. Examples of closed tasks are 7 + 8; or How many loaves of bread costing 57p can I buy with £10? Examples of associated open tasks are:

- How many different calculations can you make that give an answer of 15?

- In the case of the loaves of bread look for opportunities to develop interesting maths, such as the school fete or sports day, or set up a mini-enterprise project within the school.

If pupils have good self-esteem in mathematics they are well motivated, but this can sometimes bring with it attendant problems if the esteem is not spread throughout the whole class. For example, George is a very good mathematician and always works very hard and produces excellent answers to all open questions. The problem is that the others, who also produce unexpected and ingenious solutions are convinced that George is always right, that he will have the correct answer. They need to realise that whilst George always produces a good solution, they also have something to offer. Their insights often come from a less conventional perspective and therefore they are capable of producing surprises with their solutions. The teacher's role is to value these contributions and to raise pupil self-esteem. There will always be differences between pupils, but it is these differences which contribute to an ebb and flow of dialogue and the dynamics of interactive teaching and learning. 'Unless the child practises the role of being a mathematician, historian or geographer, learns the issues that excite people, the problems that interest them and the tools that help them to resolve and solve these, then the child may only apply empty tricks or procedures and will not inherit the discipline itself' (Wood 1988, p. 84).

The Implementation of the National Numeracy Strategy Final Report (Numeracy Task Force 1998) suggests teachers engage in whole-class teaching. There are opportunities, within the suggested lesson structure (p. 18) for all children to share their understandings and through discussing and sharing their work arriving at a fuller understanding of the concept or skill which is the focus of the lesson. These opportunities occur within the plenary for each lesson. There is scope for differentiation within the main teaching activity. The report deals with differentiation and emphasises that it should be possible to work across a mixed ability range without resorting to setting. In using the Report's 'Framework for Numeracy' teachers will need to be aware of an inherent paradox. The framework fills in the detail lacking from the National Curriculum, and identifies the teaching progression, but it is easy to focus on the detail and forget the big picture. Mathematics is about making links across the discipline, so for instance, the child who has a good understanding of coordinates, including negative numbers, will have no problem transferring that understanding to vectors. The child can be helped to see the similarities and the differences between vectors and coordinates and thus place this new concept within their mathematical schema.

Much of mathematics is about a process of assimilation, working when we meet a new concept or skill, on what is the same and what is different. Another example is that of explaining the number system. A child's first encounter with mathematics is with integers or whole counting numbers. At a later stage other numbers are introduced such as fractions, negative numbers, decimals and irrational numbers. Those who realise that the rules of operating with whole numbers apply to these new numbers quickly assimilate them into their schema, but those who see each new type of number as something different struggle. The teacher's role has to include helping children to see the bigger mathematical picture. Teachers have to view themselves as professionals whose job is to teach and make links for the children in their care. Tony Cotten in his article 'Mathematics Education and a Curriculum for Justice' (1995, p. 31) made this point when the National Curriculum itself was introduced. He lists some 'How can we?' questions which will help teachers to explore the issues of values within their teaching. These are a selection of the questions he poses:

> How can we support the development of mathematics teachers as positive role models?

> How can we find ways of valuing the progress of all learners?

> How can society's view of mathematics be changed from that of arithmetic with a few frills?

> How can children's views of learning and their expectations of mathematics be valued?

> If the real basics are empowerment and creativity how do we balance these with the rights of the disempowered to qualifications which may enable some form of advancement?

The National Curriculum took us down the path of giving children the opportunity to experience what it was to be a mathematician by including Using and Applying. These problem-solving skills are the basis of modern society. Industry needs problem-solvers and creative thinkers. The physical environment also gives value messages. Classrooms should regularly display children's work in mathematics and consist of displays, both interactive and static, which give children the opportunity to explore mathematics and to see it as an integral part of life.

Moral aspects

In mathematics, moral aspects include norms of socially accepted behaviour, honesty, respecting other people, as well as the moral implications of the material we use to teach. Mathematics is a discipline that is true to itself and seeks to explain and define. By itself it is incapable of making judgements, but it can be used to support judgements made by people who themselves can be either moral or amoral.

Perhaps one of the key aspects of mathematics is the value placed by so many on the 'right' answer. This can sometimes lead to conflict in the classroom in terms of accusations of cheating when pupils are working from textbooks where the answers are provided in the back. In response, it might be better to consider with pupils the purpose of answers in mathematics and whether the answers have invested in them the power that so many assume. Of course pupils need to be able to work quickly and accurately but the answers are merely a manifestation of the thinking that has gone on. There are insights to be gained from knowing an answer and thinking how it was obtained from the information contained in the question. Thinking through processes is a powerful way to consolidate mathematical concepts. The answer becomes an aid which helps the thinking behind the solution to be revealed. Children need therefore to understand that there is nothing dishonest or immoral in working towards a given answer.

Within the mathematics classroom the style of teaching can encourage respect by allowing the pupils to engage in discussion. This encourages listening skills as well as a realisation that mathematics has many faces and many solutions even for seemingly simple problems. The open question considered previously, 'How many different calculations can you make that give an answer of 15?' is capable of many solutions. These will be different for children according to their level of development. A young pupil will possibly reply with addition or subtractions, later multiplications and divisions may be added, later some answers may include answers like 'a quarter of an hour is 15 minutes', or 'a sixth of a right angle is 15 degrees'. Some of the infinite nature of answers through patterning may also emerge:

$$14 + 1; 13 + 2; 12 + 3; \quad 1 + 14; 0 + 15; -1 + 16; -2 + 17;$$

The child who realises that there is a link to infinity here, without even being aware of the mathematical terminology may just say there are hundreds or millions of answers because there is a pattern.

Open-ended questions can produce a variety of responses and working on real life problems can encourage a consideration of moral aspects of our society. For instance, the question 'How much rubbish does our school generate?' can lead to issues of recycling and the use of the world's resources. Even simple activities can have moral overtones. The book *Piers is Lost* (RLDU, undated) looks at real life problem-solving activities in the primary classroom and begins with the account of Piers (age 6), a new boy to the school who doesn't know his way around the building. The response of his class in making signs and maps to help him to become familiar with this new environment seems an eminently suitable activity for pupils and one in which their moral and social development is carried forward.

As pupils develop, some more difficult aspects of morality can be considered, such as the way in which statistics can be used to manipulate society, and the way in which statistics can be used to help them realise some of the moral questions that face them as developing adults. The Charis Project (Shortt and Westwell 1997) produces Christian resources which promote spiritual and moral development within the mathematics curriculum, as well as other areas of the curriculum. For instance, considering the statistics produced during the national census leads to some meaningful work on rounding figures and the consideration of percentage errors, as well as the interpretation of tables of data. Mathematics can make us aware of the choices that face us and the value-laden nature of many decisions.

Social aspects

Mathematics is not like any other subject of the curriculum. It can be taught as a set of rules and facts to be rote learnt but the learning of the facts does not make a mathematician. Rather it is the application of the facts to situations which are either purely mathematical or everyday situations which demonstrate the child's knowledge and understanding in mathematics. Therefore the ethos dictated by the teacher's ideology of the classroom is of paramount importance. In practice the school develops a policy for mathematics, ratified by the governors. The policy should guide classroom practice. Where teachers within the school have cooperated in the formulation of the policy and have a shared understanding of its expectations, policy is much more likely to be implemented in a cohesive manner. Problems can sometimes arise where for expediency the policy has been written by an individual. In those cases there may be a mismatch between policy and practice in the classroom. Therefore the setting of policy which dictates the ethos of the school should be a social, cooperative act.

Policy needs to encourage a number of strands relevant to the social development of the child. The child needs to take responsibility for their own learning, in terms of recognising their responsibility to: discuss and communicate in mathematics; seek help with errors and misunderstandings; take the lead, sometimes, in group work; work as a member of a group with full participation but without dominating; be able to work independently and identify when teacher input is needed. All of these and more may be found in the school policies but they are successful in those schools where all the staff subscribe to these aspects of social development.

Activities to encourage the development of these skills are numerous but there are some planning issues that need to be considered for a lesson that develops these skills. If the pupils are to be encouraged to take responsibility they need to know what they are responsible for. Therefore a key aspect of the lesson would be identifying the objectives to be achieved. This immediately gives pupils the independence to decide what they have learnt and what they need to work on. Often an activity needs to be thought through before giving it to the class: its implications; where it is leading; what questions the children might raise; the possibilities for pupils causing real complications that might have been avoided with a clearer explanation. For instance, in one classroom the children were working on linked machines that produced the same output as the input. Initially they worked with a flow chart that would always produce the same output as input through the use of inverses within the flow chart.

$$\rightarrow \text{Add } 3 \rightarrow \text{Multiply by } 2 \rightarrow \text{Subtract } 6 \rightarrow \text{Divide by } 2 \rightarrow$$

They then worked on a sheet containing various linked machines and through trial and improvement tried to find the input number which would give the same output.

$$\rightarrow \text{Add } 6 \rightarrow \text{Divide by } 2 \rightarrow$$

The number which gives the same output as input is 6.

They were then given another worksheet with blanked outlines and asked to produce linked machines for their partners to solve. They immediately ran into problems because they were not able to solve one another's machines. They completed the machines in an *ad hoc* manner and could not solve what had been written down. They had just written any combination of operations for the machines and the combinations frequently did not have integer answers. For instance:

$$\rightarrow \text{Add 5} \qquad \rightarrow \text{Divide by 8} \rightarrow$$

This has a solution. It is $\frac{5}{7}$, but children who have been working with machines with positive integer solutions using a trial and improvement strategy are unlikely to produce a fraction solution unless it is one of the common fractions such as a half or a quarter. In producing the sheet of problems for their partners the children needed to have secretly thought of a number and then created their machines so that the output was that secret number. They would then have presented their partners with a sheet of questions to which they knew the answers but they would also have been engaged in mathematics in creating the questions. The creation, by the children, of the questions becomes a social as well as a mathematical activity. The activity the child is engaged in when they just write down without thinking through the implications for their partners, is the same as that in which the teacher engages when they hand out a sheet of questions without considering or imagining what the outcomes might be in the classroom.

Mathematics is a powerful discipline in that it has the ability to explain and model all aspects of life. It underpins all aspects of social life and is a passport to understanding the world around us. We cannot open a newspaper without encountering some mathematics within its pages, such as, advertisements showing percentage reductions, tables showing currency exchange values. The weather forecast we look at each day is made up of symbols and icons: pupils who do not understand the use of icons and symbols to explain are impoverished. Inherent within mathematics is logic, the tool which helps us both to live and explain our lives. Even the simple act of clothing ourselves each morning is logical. Early years children first experience time through logical sequencing activities. These activities might consist of listening to a story and ordering a sequence of phrases or pictures which represent stages in the story. Later we might introduce them to ambiguous sequences. For instance Aileen Duncan (1996) has an activity for sequencing pictures for a dog which can be ordered in several different ways. The logic comes from the story the child tells to justify a particular sequence. Therefore using this sequence children can be introduced to both logic and justification at an early age and meet with a mathematical problem in which there is more than one answer. It is often difficult to move the adult mindset away from the idea that each mathematical activity has only one correct answer. Children need to meet situations where there are several solutions. This links back to adult industrial use of problem-solving where there is a problem and a number of viable solutions are considered against cost and other criteria such as marketability.

Cultural aspects

It is easy to believe that mathematics is culture free, or even a Western construct, but in fact mathematics has developed throughout history from early counting for trading purposes through each of the great civilisations that have emerged, each adding a dimension to our understanding of mathematics, some more useful than others. For instance, it is as well we did not continue to use the Roman method of recording numbers because our ability to calculate would have been severely limited. The strength of the Arabic system, which is almost universally used, is that it has the number zero which allows us to have a place holder for nothing within the decimal system.

There are many examples within the Arts of mathematics being used. In *Mathematics Teaching* Ulrich Grevsmühl (1989, p. 54) looks at how modern artists use chance and order within their paintings. Mathematics is intrinsic within musical form, where the round, the canon and the fugue can all be expressed or explained using group theory (Budden 1972, p. 443). The Greeks first discovered the Golden Mean when they described beautiful things as being correct or having pleasing proportion. The Golden Mean can be found in the proportions of the Parthenon (Macintosh-Wilson 1995: 273) and also within the design of the Boeing 747 Jumbo jet (p. 274). There are many examples of the Golden Mean in Art, in Architecture and occurring naturally, for example the ratio of the height from naval to floor to the height of a person.

Mathematics in modern culture underpins the very fabric of our lives, from the running of the trading on the Stock Exchange to the introduction of digital television. It permeates and pervades all, and those who are excluded from understanding this are seriously disadvantaged. Despite the feeling that has been prevalent within society that it is acceptable for individuals to be poor at mathematics, mathematics is still realised to be a powerful tool and one which fascinates even when understanding is limited, otherwise how are we able to explain the fact that Simon Singh's book *Fermat's Last Theorem* (1997) is a number one best seller. The proof of this theorem is understood only by a few mathematicians across the world because of its complexity and yet people have rushed to buy the book. They are reading the story of mathematicians' obsession with proof, which lies at the heart of all mathematics.

References

Blatner, D (1997) *The Joy of Pi.* Harmondsworth: Penguin.

Budden, F. J. (1972) *The Fascination of Groups.* London: Cambridge University Press.

Cotton. T. (1995) 'Mathematics education and a curriculum for justice', *Mathematics Teaching* **150**.

Crump, T. (1992) *The Anthropology of Numbers.* Wiltshire: Cambridge University Press.

Duncan, A. (1996) *What Primary Teachers Should Know About Maths*, 2nd edn. Bath: Hodder & Stoughton.

Ernest, P. (1991) *The Philosophy of Mathematics Education*. Basingstoke: Falmer Press.

Field, R. (1998) *Geometric Patterns from Islamic Art and Architecture*. Diss, Norfolk, UK: Tarquia Publications.

Grevsmühl, U. (1989) 'Mathematics and Modern Art: Chance and Order', *Mathematics Teaching* **127**.

Lacey, P (1998) *Building Numeracy: Some Suggestions for Teaching Basic Arithmetic*. Trowbridge: Robert Powell Publications.

Macintosh-Wilson, A. (1995) *The Infinite in the Finite*. Oxford: Oxford University Press.

Numeracy Task Force (1998) *The Implementation of the National Numeracy Strategy*. Suffolk: DfEE.

RLDU (undated) *Piers is Lost*. Bristol: Resources for Learning Development Unit.

Shortt, J. and Westwell, J. (eds) (1997) *Charis Mathematics Units 10–19*. Nottingham: The Stapleford Centre.

Singh, S. (1997) *Fermat's Last Theorem*. London: Fourth Estate Limited.

Stewart, I. (1989) *Game, Set and Math: Enigmas and Conundrums*. Harmondsworth: Penguin.

Wood, D. (1988) *How Children Think & Learn*. Oxford: Basil Blackwell.

Further reading

Duncan, A. (1996) *What Primary Teachers Should Know About Maths*, 2nd edn. Bath: Hodder & Stoughton.

Lacey, P. (1998) *Building Numeracy: Some Suggestions for Teaching Basic Arithmetic*. Trowbridge: Robert Powell Publications.

Shortt, J. and Westwell, J. (eds) (1997) *Charis Mathematics Units 10–19*. Nottingham: The Stapleford Centre.

These three books give examples of mathematics activities.

Chapter 8

English

Ann Disney and Tim Pound

English in the primary school

Effective English teaching has always included elements of spiritual, moral, social and cultural education. Curriculum guidelines acknowledge the interrelated nature of the three components of speaking and listening; reading and writing and the need to teach these components in their own right and across the curriculum.

Speaking and listening

Spiritual, moral, social and cultural education emerges through a balanced and reflective attitude to planning for talk in any classroom; this acknowledges the importance of oral language in cognitive development, to see language as a tool for thought (Donaldson 1978).[1] The National Oracy Project identified the importance of the teacher's role in organising the classroom and providing opportunities for children to engage in different types of talk, to different audiences and for different purposes. The teacher is modelling the classroom as a microcosm of society and thus planning for spiritual and cultural education.

Methods of planning for talk which consider the importance of the structure of the group can build self-confidence through the support of peers, developing social skills and promoting moral debate and cultural understanding. Baddely (1992) outlines the jigsaw technique which involves the organisation of children into groups described as 'home groups' and 'expert groups'. Children work in both groups and share the knowledge and expertise developed as experts with peers in the home group. Each child plays a vital role in developing the understanding of all the members of the group, operating as a fully-valued member of the culture of the classroom. Written outcomes are not essential and the jigsaw technique can be used with children of all ages and abilities and across all subjects. Browne (1996) outlines further suggestions in structuring groups.

Exposure to the ideas of other people develops a child's sense of herself as a person with distinct spiritual, moral, social and cultural identities; teachers need, in Jerome Bruner's well-known phrase, to 'scaffold' the development of these value systems. Organising a democratic classroom, where the opinions and values of children are given equal importance alongside that of the teacher, can be supported through the negotiated establishment of classroom rules. With the teacher as scribe and chairperson, the class can discuss issues which affect everyone; rules for the class should then be written down, formally agreed, displayed and infringements discussed. This activity develops moral and social values through cooperative relationships.

Whole-class talk can also be structured through circle time activities. Talk can be managed democratically by using a 'prop' which is passed around the circle, the rule being that only the person holding the prop can talk. The prop can vary with the age of the children but fluffy toys, microphones, 'magic' stones or speaking stones have all been used to good effect. The teacher's position at the same physical level as the children is important in establishing partnership rather than superiority. Children learn to value talk by establishing relationships and listening carefully to other people.

Most children are aware that both they and their parents use very different words and sentence construction when talking to the teacher or to a peer. Children learn to experiment with different types, styles and structures (or registers) of talk by finding themselves in situations where talk can be observed and used in a supportive environment. Very young children acquire language skills through sharing experiences with parents and carers. This can be developed in school through the use of the role-play corner. A visit to the local Health Centre can lead to the establishment of a Health Centre in the classroom. Planning this role-play corner gives all children the opportunity to share observations and expertise. The finished role-play corner will give everyone the opportunity to explore the formal nature of talk through 'being the doctor' and the informal nature of talk through 'being the parent or child'.

Drama provides a different experience of talk. The teacher (or a child) adopts the role of a character from a familiar book; the motivation of the character assumed can be examined through questioning. Goldilocks can explain why she went into the Three Bears Cottage or Melanie Prosser (from Aidan Chambers' *The Present Takers*) can explain her behaviour. Opportunity to reflect on and explore the meaning of a text facilitates development of a personal moral code.

Children can learn the importance of their own cultural identities by exploring and valuing accent and dialect. Children who have attended several schools in different locations can develop discussion of variety in language by sharing names for everyday objects (e.g. PE shoes). Children can write to classes in other geographical areas to share and celebrate similarities and differences. Everyone can celebrate cultural diversity by learning ways to say 'Good Morning' in different languages. Public acknowledgement of such rich cultural differences promotes positive attitudes to diversity and has implications for a child's self-confidence and self-worth.

Writing

Children need to develop and demonstrate an awareness of the needs of the audience together with an awareness of the purpose for the writing. Very young children can explore this through opportunities to write through play. Appointment books, prescription pads, note pads, and health records can be provided so that the writing opportunities in the role-play Health Centre have real purpose and a real audience. The teacher might choose to write to the children as a fictitious character, for example, a developer who wants to demolish the Health Centre and build a shopping centre. A meaningful two-way correspondence can be established and the children develop a sound knowledge of the purpose of their writing and a good understanding of the societal conventions of the letter-writing form. Children from different schools in different areas or countries might be encouraged to write to each other. Through this children can acquire a good understanding of the cultural diversity between two mainly English speaking groups.

Exploring different types of text helps children to develop a range of social competence through writing. Skills in choosing words which help to shape the opinions of the reader can be explored. The study of an existing text and the identification of the adjectives (for example) used to describe the character can help children to use this technique in reverse when working on the draft of a piece of writing. Children need to be taught to identify the grammatical features of a particular text type. A helpful outline for planning the teaching of writing to encompass the skills of textual structure and drafting is provided by Rees (1996). The importance of a writer's lexical choice in the shaping of the reader's opinion can be extended to the comparative study of non-fiction texts. Children can study texts from different newspapers on the same subjects and compare different presentation of facts and description of individuals. Newspaper reports which demonstrate an understanding of opposing points of view can then be written. Examples of working with non-fiction texts are provided by Wray and Lewis (1997).

Examining the choice of words used to describe a person or situation can give children a very real understanding of the use of language in constructing cultural identity. Children can begin to see that the reader's concept of character is constructed by the writer's choice of words: one writer's freedom fighter can be another writer's guerrilla. Reflective readers will want to determine the writer's position and to detect bias. *The True Story of the Three Little Pigs by A. Wolf,* written by Jon Scieska and Lane Smith, provides an excellent example of persuasive writing. Through examination of the text, children can rewrite familiar tales from different points of view. Reflective readers will also consider the reliability of the main character's representation of himself.

Writing is often a solitary process but collaborative writing situations provide children with the opportunity to share individual expertise. Children with good handwriting skills can benefit from the input of peers with good compositional skills. Collaboration develops writers with greater awareness of their own skills, and the skills of others, thus developing social skills and spiritual awareness through self-worth.

Reading

In reading fiction we teach children to develop their ability to read across a broad range of narrative structures and genre; to read the lines and to read between and beyond the lines. In reading non-fiction texts children need to experience a different range of structures and styles of reading; to identify bias and prejudice and to accept that 'fact' can have degrees of accuracy. We also need to encompass different demands involved in reading the media.

The teacher's thorough understanding of the extent of literature available for children is fundamental to the effective teaching of reading. This should encompass a consideration of the text in what the Cox Report (Cox 1989) identifies as its narrative, symbolic and stylistic levels. The narrative level will identify the sequence and storyline of a text and will usually relate to 'text level' of the National Literacy Strategy (DfEE 1998). The symbolic level relates to the meaning and circumstances beyond the literal level of the text and may relate to text and sentence level. The stylistic level will identify the crafting of the book and may relate to word, sentence or text level. The teacher's own understanding of the text enables planning at word, text, and sentence level as outlined in the National Literacy Strategy.

A reader's response to any text needs to be developed through talk. Chambers (1993) outlines the process of 'Booktalk' through which the class can come to a deeper understanding of the text at all levels. This involves reflective reading of the text and preparation and of open-ended questions by the teacher. The agenda for discussion is identified by the children through their discussion of 'likes, dislikes, puzzles and patterns' but the teacher's questions will shape the discussion. Booktalk can be used with children of all ages in whole class and in small groups. Children's responses to the texts demonstrates abilities in sharing ideas and beliefs; developing social skills in managing their own contributions to the discussion; and sharing a wider knowledge through their personal cultural experience.

Books should be read and studied in this way because the chosen book is one of quality which will facilitate the child's further development as a reader and may have something to communicate to her at a particular time in her life. Teachers have no control over individual responses and should not seek that control, but we do have a duty and a responsibility to present material of range and quality. The teacher's knowledge of books provides encounters with a range of literature of the highest quality and thus develops all aspects of spiritual, moral, cultural and social education through interactions between children and texts.

Literature can help children to work through problems at a subliminal level. In considering the development of spirituality we may read books where relationships are explored. Children may delight in *Charlotte's Web* by E. B. White where cycles of life are explored and death is situated as a natural part of that cycle. The anthropomorphic nature of the story provides a supportive background for class discussion where children can bring their knowledge of the world to an understanding of the text. A challenging range of human experiences is explored in Katherine Paterson's *Bridge to Terabithia*. John Burningham's picture book *Granpa* presents challenges in terms of the narrative structure of the text and in the treatment of the human experiences of a growing child and an ageing grandfather. Books help children to identify purpose in life which may (but does not necessarily) have a religious expression. Children developing spiritually need to find a range of mediums through which personal beliefs and values can be explored. Poetry will provide an opportunity for this. Jackie Kay's (1994) poem 'Names' gives children the opportunity to explore both friendship and the destructive power of words.

Moral education must present children with a range of possibilities, not an absolute standard of morality. Older children can explore their own construct of morality through a novel like Robert Cormier's *The Chocolate War*. This novel presents a community where certain behavioural choices have been made by adults and children and the main character must survive within that community. Books which explore issues encountered by most children can lead to moral development. Aidan Chamber's *The Present Takers* can provide the opportunities to discuss bullying. Picture books which present the point of view of a character can lead to exploration through drama of the symbolic level of the text. Maurice Sendak's *Where the Wild Things Are* might lead the teacher to adopt the role of Max's mother and thereby help the children to gain insight into Max's motivation from a personal point of view; through this the symbolic level of the text can be explored.

Texts should reflect a range of possible narrative structures so that children may experience a text such as Hazel Townson's *The Deathwood Letters*, where the narrative is told entirely through letters. This text, at a symbolic level, has much to say about family structures and the part they play in the life of the protagonists. In *The Story of Bobble Who Wanted to be Rich* by Joke Van Leeuwen the narrative structure uses several different mediums; the family portrayed is unconventional in its lifestyle and warm and loving in its behaviour. Through consideration of a range of types of text and situations demonstrated the reader can come, through experience and discussion, to an understanding of where and how he or she might play a full part in society. A range of possible social and cultural models is experienced and the notion that there are ranges of possible lifestyles and family structures current in society can be explored.

Traditional tales help children to develop a broad picture of the culture of which they are part and the ways in which their culture is influenced by other cultures. Neil Philip's book *The Cinderella Story* includes tales from all over the world which share features and structure of the Cinderella story but differences in terms of geography and culture. In a world where the Walt Disney adaptation is becoming the most widely known version children need to be alive to cultural diversity. Storytelling can further help children to develop their own versions of a familiar tale. Poetry encourages celebration of cultural diversity: children enjoy reading and learning nursery rhymes from the English tradition; *The Kiskadee Queen* by Faustin Charles and *No Hickory, No Dickory, No Dock* by John Agard and Grace Nichols add a parallel strand from the Caribbean tradition. Poets like Charles Causley whose work often uses traditional forms like those of the ballad and limerick can be read and enjoyed alongside poets like Grace Nichols or Benjamin Zephaniah who, in their poetry, experiment with the patterns of spoken language.

The possibilities for planning spiritual, moral, social and cultural education within the English curriculum are diverse and exciting. As teachers we need to begin from a firm understanding of the learning process: thorough subject knowledge, an overwhelming love of books and boundless enthusiasm.

References

Baddely, G. (1992) *Learning Together Through Talk*. London: Hodder & Stoughton.
Browne, A. (1996) *Language and Literacy 3 to 8*. London: Paul Chapman Publishing.
Chambers, A. (1993) *Tell Me: Children, Reading and Talk*. Stroud: Thimble Press.
Cox, C. B. (1989) *English for Ages 5 to 16*. London: Department of Education and Science.
DfE (1995) *English in the National Curriculum*. London: HMSO.
DfEE (1998) *The National Literacy Strategy*. London: DfEE.
Donaldson, M. (1978) *Children's Minds*. Glasgow: Fontana.
Rees, F. (1996) *Planning the Writing Curriculum at Key Stage 2*. Slough: NFER.
Wray, D. and Lewis, M. (1997) *Extending Literacy*. London: Routledge.

Children's books cited.

Agard, J. and Nichols, G. (1991) *No Hickory, No Dickory, No Dock*. London: Viking.
Burningham , J. (1984) *Granpa*. London: Cape.
Causley, C. (1996) *Collected Poems for Children*. London: Macmillan.
Chambers, A. (1993) *The Present Takers*. London: Mammoth.
Charles, F. (1991) *The Kiskadee Queen*. London: Blackie.
Cormier, R. (1974) *The Chocolate War*. New York: Pantheon Books.
Kay, J. (1994) *Three Has Gone*. London: Blackie/Penguin.
Paterson, K. (1977) *Bridge to Terabithia*. London: Penguin.
Philip, N. (1989) *The Cinderella Story*. London: Penguin.
Scieska, J. and Smith, L. (1989) *The True Story of the Three Little Pigs by A. Wolf*. London: Viking.
Sendak, M. (1967) *Where the Wild Things Are*. London: The Bodley Head.

Townson, H. (1990) *The Deathwood Letters*. London: Red Fox.
Van Leeuwen, J. (1987) *The Story of Bobble Who Wanted to be Rich*. Stroud: Turton and Chambers.
White, E. B. (1952) *Charlotte's Web*. London: Penguin.

English in the secondary school

If this concluding part of the chapter goes somewhat against the grain of the previous section by examining rather more extensively the polemics rather than the practice of its curricular focus, it does so because English at secondary level is generally acknowledged to make a greater contribution to the growth of spiritual, moral, social and cultural awareness in our students than any other subject apart from RE. The fact that the kind of literature which we teach invariably engages with what might be loosely termed the 'human condition' effectively means that the raw materials for nurturing such a development are readily to hand, embedded in a range of creative responses to a variety of individual emotions, aspirations and desires, all of which are explored in the context of a diversity of social, historical and cultural contexts.

Our predilection for singling out these implicit thematic threads as points of discussion has been largely shaped through our assimilation of a critical tradition which has emphasised the importance of an experiential or 'personal response' to literary study at the expense of more theoretical approaches. Indeed, despite the undoubted impact of recent critical theory on ways of interpreting texts at university level, the study of English within the school curriculum – most obviously at Key Stage 4 and A level – remains very much in the thrall of a critical practice the origins of which can be traced back, through the critic F. R. Leavis and the Cambridge School, to the work of Matthew Arnold.

With Leavis in particular, literary studies assumed a moral, even a religious significance. Clearly indebted to the work of I. A. Richards (1929), Leavis became associated with a critical methodology based on the 'close reading' of literary texts that revolutionised the study of literature and inspired a generation of teachers in schools and universities. While largely accredited with reconfigurating the 'great tradition' of English literature, Leavis undoubtedly benefited from the pre-war activities of the English Association (established 1906) in promoting literary study in schools and universities; and from the post-war impact of the publication of the Newbolt Report (1921), both of which succeeded in fashioning an equation between a sense of 'Englishness' and the literary heritage which helped to shape it. As one of its early members remarked, the function of the English Association was not simply to stimulate an interest in the subject, but 'to make the next and younger generation understand exactly what this country stands for' (English Association, 1916, pp. 8–9).

It was not until the late 1960s that the assault on this empirical tradition of English criticism first began. Initially in the form of structuralism – more recently categorised under the generic term literary theory – it severely dented the assumptions of the English critical establishment within the universities, while leaving the teaching of English in schools comparatively unscathed. However, a number of tensions began to manifest themselves at the upper end of the secondary curriculum, particularly in both the form and content of A level syllabuses, where more progressive approaches to syllabus construction and examining were beginning to erode the traditional consensus about what constituted the core of the English literary curriculum.

During the 1970s, a number of self-styled 'alternative' A level syllabuses appeared and by the 1980s, several of these had been adopted as mainstream examinations. The fact that up to 50 per cent of students' marks could now be derived from their response to texts selected by their teachers, ensured that works which, in terms of their cultural origin, fell outside the traditional Anglo-centric canon, could also become a focus of study. The reasons for this development lay simultaneously in the belief that black or post-colonial literature possessed a distinctive voice worth appreciating in its own right; and also, in the desire to make literary study post-16 relevant to the increasingly multicultural complexion of society. This, together with the emergence of the GCSE, engendered something of a sea-change in the ethos and culture of English teaching in the mid-1980s.

To those on the political right, however, such developments were symptomatic of a more general decline in educational, cultural and moral standards, and at very least it seemed that the subject of English could no longer be relied upon to transmit the values of a traditional Anglo-centric culture. Small wonder, then, that when questioned about the government's plans for a new national curriculum, the Secretary of State responsible for its introduction, Kenneth Baker, frankly admitted that one of the purposes behind such a curriculum was not simply that of raising levels of educational achievement, but also that of imposing a sense of cultural homogeneity on to an ethnically diverse nation. As Baker himself put it: 'I see the national curriculum as a way of increasing our social coherence. There is so much distraction, variety and uncertainty in the modern world that in our country today our children are in danger of losing any sense at all of a common culture and a common heritage' (cited in Sarup 1991, p. 107). What the fiercely-contested debate over the construction of English within the National Curriculum amply demonstrated was thus not simply a matter of how one taught Standard English or which texts should be studied across the Key Stages – it was, once again, the issue of national identity, and the tacit desire to rekindle a deference towards the cultural authority of an established, ethno-centric tradition.

While few would deny that the 1988 Education Reform Act's prescription for all maintained schools to promote the spiritual, moral, cultural, mental and physical development of pupils was prompted by concerns other than the perceived erosion of a common, cultural identity, subsequent events would seem to suggest that the function of the school curriculum in nurturing these aspects of individual growth may still be prone to ideological influence or control. For example, as the

OFSTED discussion document *Spiritual, Moral, Social and Cultural Development* (1994) makes clear, provision must now be made within each subject area to facilitate such development in pupils. No doubt as teachers of English working broadly within the critical tradition outlined above, we may already feel that most of the literature we teach leads naturally to the discussion of a range of moral, social, cultural and even spiritual issues. The question that remains, however, is to what extent the cultivation of that touchstone of academic ability and potential – an 'informed, personal response', still given pride of place in examination syllabuses – becomes incompatible with the need to develop the spiritual, moral, social and cultural awareness of our students. As far as the Qualifications and Curriculum Authority (QCA) is concerned – if the views of Nicholas Tate accurately represent its policy – the individual voice is acceptable, *providing* it conforms to an agreed notion of what constitutes these aspects of our lives.

For example, in his opening address to a conference on the spiritual and moral aspects of the curriculum organised by the then School Curriculum and Assessment Authority (SCAA) early in 1996, Tate (1996a) urged his fellow delegates to work towards the creation of an educational climate in which 'young people grow up with a sense that there are objectives and enduring values, that some things are certain, that there is some kind of lodestar within all this flux...to ensure that we do not lose the best of what previous societies had to offer – and above all, their moral wisdom'. In a further SCAA conference held within weeks of the first, Tate (1996b) expanded on his metaphorical allusion to a moral or cultural 'lodestar', claiming that a 'sense of rootlessness and confusion' in modern life could be curtailed by our 'preserving and· transmitting...the best of what we have inherited from the past'. It is perhaps hardly surprising that the teaching of English language and literature was perceived as a crucial means of inculcating a respect for such an inheritance, firstly, as Tate suggests, through its ability to place 'western cultural traditions at the heart of our curriculum'; and secondly, by its capacity to sustain 'the idea of a national language as a force for cohesion within national life'.

But what should our approach to such contentious issues be as we continue to teach our subject in the classroom? Can we – and indeed should we – attempt to steer a course between the monocultural approach favoured by Tate (and presumably the QCA) while simultaneously avoiding the kind of cultural relativism which he discredits? Or is this merely an unacceptable compromise? And finally, in our discussion and examination of the moral, spiritual, social and cultural aspects of the literary texts which we encounter, how can we ensure, as an OFSTED paper (1994, p. 10) puts it, that our students 'acquire value-systems which are their own (rather than simply transmitted by others and accepted uncritically)'?

Whatever approach we adopt, it seems that we must at very least remain critically sensitive not only to the multiple interpretations of the texts we teach, but also to the variations, both in terms of culture and ethnicity, of our students. One could argue, of course, that the key to their moral, spiritual and social development in particular still remains inextricably embedded in the growth and maturity of their 'personal response' – to issues such as love and personal relationships, conflict and suffering, life and death which they vicariously experience through their reading. Many of these issues can be explored in a monocultural context at Key Stage 3, for example, through our teaching of texts which have entered the canon of adolescent fiction, such as *Lord of the Flies* and *Kes*. A number of more recent texts, however, not only engage directly with a range of contemporary preoccupations, but also embody a multicultural perspective. *The Present Takers*, for instance, raises issues of more immediate relevance such as bullying, peer-group pressure and social difference, while texts such as *Walkabout, The Cay* and *Sumitra's Story* deal explicitly with aspects of racism, cultural traditions and the interdependence of blacks and whites.

As far as the teaching of Shakespeare at Key Stage 3 is concerned, the gradual replacement of the current set texts – *Romeo and Juliet, A Midsummer Night's Dream* and *Julius Caesar* – by *Henry V, Twelfth Night* and *Macbeth*, will ensure that his plays remain central to the task of raising awareness of spiritual, moral, social and cultural concerns, since they raise a range of issues such as violence and the value of human life; war and patriotism; human ideals, ambitions and aspirations; sexuality and marriage. And once we broaden our notion of 'text', even an overtly *monocultural* Shakespeare play can be reinvested with a multicultural dimension, as the recent and successful film adaptation of *Romeo and Juliet* vividly demonstrates.

At Key Stage 4, wider contextual considerations become an important element in both GCSE syllabus construction and in assessment criteria, particularly with the higher grade descriptors. A Midland Examining Group (MEG) 1998 syllabus, for example, delineates one of its aims as that of encouraging students to develop an 'awareness of social, historical and cultural contexts and influences in the study of literature' (1998, p. 4); while the marking criteria for awarding a grade A for a drama script demands that candidates show 'how knowledge of social, cultural and historical influences affects appreciation' (1998, p. 22).

This emphasis on the social and cultural aspects of the candidate's response does not, of course, preclude a critical examination of spiritual and moral issues, but it very much depends on the nature of the text being studied. For example, some texts traditionally studied at the level of GCSE such as *Macbeth* cannot be fully understood without an appreciation of basic moral concepts such as right and wrong, good and evil or the spiritual implications of an unbridled lust for earthly power (see *Charis English*, 1996).

As far as post-16 English is concerned, the explosion of the monocultural canon during the 1980s referred to above has left us with a rich vein of post-colonial writing to exploit. As a 1999 Associated Examining Board A level syllabus makes evident 'thought and discussion about current and philosophical issues, evaluation of experience, and the exploration and practice of different kinds of writing' (AEB 1999, p. 9) form the bedrock of success in such an examination. The danger is, though, that our understanding and appreciation of literature from other cultures can be all too easily assimilated within a broadly liberal humanistic tradition. As the following Northern Examination and Assessment Board specimen questions (NEAB 1996, p. 11) for texts by Kazuo Ishiguro, Timothy Mo and James Berry make evident, such an approach can effectively obscure – or indeed deny – this kind of writing its multicultural heritage:

> 'Despite the authors' sensitive insights into oriental attitudes and ways, what impresses us most is their fundamental understanding of humanity.' What are your reactions to this view of the book? (on *An Artist of the Floating World* and *Sour Sweet*);

and

> How does *Fantasy of an African Boy* reflect James Berry's interest in the human condition? Discuss some of his other poems that, in your view, have a similar purpose.

Not only are both questions linked by their explicit focus on humane values, but each provides a striking illustration of the ways in which the cultural contexts of multi-ethnic literature can be so readily transcended through an instinctive reliance on the moral touchstones of an Anglo-centric critical orthodoxy.

Perhaps nowhere is this orthodoxy more entrenched than in the teaching of Shakespeare. For example, plays commonly set at A level such as *Othello, Twelfth Night, The Winter's Tale* and *The Tempest* can be approached solely from the perspective of the transcendental values which they embody – values such as 'love' in all its manifestations (including jealousy); and as far as the latter two plays are concerned, reconciliation and forgiveness. But apart from the spiritual and moral aspects of the plays, given the new critical impetus provided by literary theory, any reading of, say *The Tempest* which avoids matters of dispossession and cultural exploitation – or which fails to raise the issue of 'class' in *Twelfth Night* – would surely be incomplete. The fact remains that we owe it to our students to be receptive to as wide a range of interpretations as possible. What we bring to our study of the text really does make a difference.

References

AEB (Associated Examining Board) (1999) *English Literature Syllabus.*
Charis English (1996) *Macbeth.* St. Albans: Association of Christian Teachers.
English Association (1916) *Bulletin No. 29,* July.
Midland Examining Group (1998) *English Literature.*
NEAB (Northern Examinations and Assessment Board) (1996) *Specimen Material for English Literature: GCE Syllabuses for 1996.*
Newbolt Report (1921) *The Teaching of English in England.* London: HMSO.
OFSTED (1994) *Spiritual, Moral, Social and Cultural Development.* London: OFSTED

Richards, I. A. (1929) *Practical Criticism.* London: Kegan Paul.

Sarup, M. (1991) *Education and the Ideologies of Racism.* Stoke-on-Trent: Trentham.

Tate, N. (1996a) *Education for Adult Life: Spiritual and Moral Aspects of the Curriculum* (unpublished transcript of SCAA conference speech).

Tate, N. (1996b) *Curriculum, Culture and Society* (unpublished transcript of SCAA conference speech).

Note

[1] References and details of children's books are given on pp. 91–2.

Chapter 9

Modern Languages

David Smith and Shirley Dobson

A French lesson is underway. The class, a mixed ability Year 8 group, are working through worksheets. One student raises a hand. The surprising question is: 'Sir, how can the Bible be true, what with the way we get taught history?' As the questioner seems serious, the teacher tries to show respect for the question while suggesting that it might be more appropriate to another occasion. The response is another totally unexpected question: 'Sir, are you afraid of dying?'

Here is a student who has not yet learned to stay within the neat divisions of the school timetable, a student who brings her whole self, her existential concerns and difficult questions, into the modern language classroom. Does this make her an oddity to be ironed out, or is she very normal? Do her concerns about meaning have any relevance in the modern language classroom or are they a distraction from the real business at hand? Could they have any connection with learning French, or should she be told to keep them to herself until a more appropriate time? And what might all of this have to do with spiritual, moral, social and cultural development, which is sought by OFSTED across the entire curriculum, including modern languages?

In the recent flurry of discussion concerning cross-curricular spiritual and moral development, modern language teaching has gone almost unmentioned. The often laborious acquisition of new language skills in the modern language classroom seems to be regarded as an unlikely context for encountering the spiritual. While cultural development is part of the stock in trade of modern language teachers, and social development has become an equally natural part of the communicative classroom, the near silence both among commentators on spiritual and moral development and within the modern language teaching world seems to suggest that a consideration of these dimensions comes far less naturally. An increasing number of teachers are dissatisfied with the superficiality of much language learning at Key Stage 4, but many are still wary of 'SMSC' – as one teacher put it, 'I'm not paid to do this, I'm paid to teach German!'

This perception should be somewhat surprising. The idea of relating modern language teaching to broader educational goals is hardly new – Kelly, writing in 1969, surveys religious, moral, social and cultural aims as recurrent emphases throughout the history of language teaching (1969, pp. 369–79). Modern language teaching in recent times has focused increasingly on personal interaction, on communication across language barriers. Does such communication have no moral or spiritual dimensions? Modern language textbooks offer learners selected images of native speakers and of their societies and cultures. Should the beliefs and values which shape and are expressed by those individuals and societies be of no account? Is our own culture somehow the privileged possessor of the spiritual and moral dimensions of human existence? Can they quietly fall away when we turn our gaze to other cultures? Does a tourist-oriented vision of France, Germany, or any other country tell the whole story, or even the most educationally interesting story? As such questions multiply, it must surely be apparent that to answer any of them in the affirmative is to accept a reduced and impoverished version of what modern language teaching could be.

Spiritual aspects

Spirituality has proved difficult to define. A helpful approach in the present context is to see it as having to do with the different responses which we make to the basic questions of life – questions of security, of meaning, of trust, power and freedom, of love, truth and purpose (Beesley 1993, pp. 22–28, Smith 1997, pp. 24–38). Encountering and reflecting on the beliefs and values of others is an aspect of spiritual development mentioned in many recent documents (e.g. NCC 1993, pp. 2–3).

This is surely an area where modern language learning can both contribute and benefit. It represents an obvious curricular opportunity for extended exposure to the beliefs and values of others in a foreign community and culture – Spanish, French or Italian people also hope, fear, love, suffer, pray, worship, weep as well as travel, eat and shop. Encountering them in this light need not mean leaping for the advanced learner's dictionary – in most European languages 'I pray in the morning' is less linguistically complex than 'I get up in the morning'. If native speakers are encountered as persons with spiritual depth, the scope for learners to develop spiritually in terms of their own attitudes and responses to those who are culturally different will be increased, and there is potential for increased learner interest and identification with the subject. Some learners will find affirmation and personal relevance in seeing some of their own beliefs and values, including religious beliefs, shared by people in other cultural settings. Learning to communicate across cultural boundaries involves both learning to listen to those whose beliefs and values differ and discovering spiritual affinities in spite of cultural differences.

If the spiritual dimension seems somewhat remote from GCSE language learning, a major reason is the pragmatic, transactional emphasis which has pervaded so many course materials. The world of the GCSE language learner has often revolved around a private realm of personal preferences in matters such as food, clothing, pets, television or sport, and a public realm which has to do with the subsistence needs of the tourist abroad, whose interactions consist of buying, navigating, obtaining information and perhaps complaining. Efforts to justify foreign language learning for all, meanwhile, often focus narrowly on the economic benefits of becoming more employable, to the comparative neglect of broader educational considerations. If the syllabus is interpreted as basically the consumer lifestyle writ large, or as little more than a tool for enhancing employment prospects, spiritual development seems a somewhat distant concept.

If it is further assumed that this approach is the only way to cover the vocabulary necessary at this stage and that more meaningful questions require language which is too advanced for GCSE learners, then a serious concern for spiritual development might seem not only distant but impractical and unrealistic. That this assumption is common is suggested by the traditional reservation of more spiritually significant topics for A level, leaving the GCSE learner in a more mundane world of utilitarian transactions.

These obstacles are more perceived than real. The National Curriculum does not define content in any detail, as can be seen from a careful look at the Areas of Experience (AoE). As our examples will show, it is possible to find alternative contexts for teaching GCSE level language in ways which open up new areas of meaning for learners. It is also possible to promote reflection on serious spiritual issues without recourse to complex language and without turning aside from the business of mastering the language itself. In fact, the modern language classroom has a substantial contribution to make to cross-curricular spiritual development, and can in turn raise its own profile among students and colleagues as a site of personally significant learning.

Spirituality will in many cultural contexts be more to the fore than is often the case in our more secularised culture. Teenagers in Burkina Faso, who were interviewed in the process of developing a unit of GCSE work for French (*Charis Français, unité 8*), willingly discussed not only their daily routine and their career aspirations, but also their expectations of life after death and views of heaven. Most were Christians or Muslims. Such material offers opportunities as outlined in the Programme of Study for learners to encounter and identify with the perspectives of those in other countries.

For spiritual development to be an integral part of foreign language learning the materials must be rooted in the culture of the language being learnt. Work with Year 10 students based on the story of the White Rose resistance group offers another example of this. Members of the White Rose were motivated to act against Hitler's regime in part by reading in the Bible that they should act upon the truth and not just hear it (see *Charis Deutsch, Einheiten 1–5*).

Encountering such stories offers multifaceted educational opportunities – encountering people of depth from the target culture, learning about their culture and history while at the same time glimpsing the moral and spiritual dimensions of their lives. The story form helps to keep the language concrete and accessible – learning to talk about myself is complemented by learning to hear the stories of others. One group of Year 10 learners who filled in response forms after working through a unit from *Charis Deutsch* built around the story of the White Rose responded to the question 'what have you learned from this unit?' with responses such as 'I have learnt that all the Germans did not like Hitler' and 'I've learnt that you've got to stand up for what you believe in'.

If the educational benefit of foreign language study includes the experience of learning about and meeting (in the flesh or through course materials) members of other cultures, and if both these others and our learners are spiritual beings with spiritual concerns, then the modern language classroom has its own legitimate interest in exploring spiritual issues.

Moral aspects

There is a long tradition of linking language teaching with moral objectives. Traditionally, the moral virtue was supposed to be linked to the discipline involved in mastering a new language, and to exposure to its literary treasures. Now that language teaching has set its sights more firmly on communication with other speakers, the moral dimension takes on new contours.

Encountering speakers of other languages involves encountering people who make moral decisions, who struggle with right and wrong, who are imperfect, who pursue ideals and do good to others and who get things wrong and need forgiveness. The kinds of dialogues which students are asked to enact can provide opportunities for moral reflection, from the small-scale (you are given too much change in a shop – what do you do?), through the humorous (a class once asked why, in an activity in *Escalier*, they were supposed to be giving directions to a robber to help him avoid the police, instead of turning him in!), to big issues (such as environmental questions). This implies a need for native speakers to be presented in materials as people who are affected by moral issues.

A unit for the Charis French materials was based on questionnaires completed by French teenagers concerning the issue of truth – how often were they untruthful, and to whom? When might it be justified to lie? How would they react if a best friend lied to them? The responses yielded a wide range of sometimes contradictory answers – for many it was acceptable to lie but quite objectionable for a friend to lie to them. The material gathered was linked with proverbs and activities about truth-telling. One opportunity for personal response involved ranking various reasons given by the French students for being honest.

As the language classroom has in recent times become a place where language is no longer studied as an inert entity, but is put to work in a myriad of interactions, there is increased scope for the moral dimension of communication to emerge through developing the ability to listen carefully, patiently, and supportively to others. We rehearse the kinds of communication which we hope will be practised when native speakers are encountered, and work to overcome prejudices which block communication. We hope that if our learners travel abroad, or encounter foreign visitors at home, they will be good communicators not only in terms of skills, but in terms of attitudes and behaviour.

This can lead to questioning some of our practices. For instance, where fictional role-playing activities or drills are not clearly and overtly distinguished from communication of personal information, students can pick up the idea that it really doesn't matter exactly what they say as long as it is in the target language – some even verbalise this as 'it's OK to lie in French, isn't it, sir?' Clearly we must attend to the ethics of communication rehearsed in the classroom and the learners' perceptions of what is going on, which may not match the teacher's rationale (Smith 1997b).

To take other examples, is it relevant that students are routinely taught to apologise in the target language ('Sorry I'm late') but are not as commonly given the linguistic resources to offer forgiveness? Or that time is set aside to practise complaining ('My food is cold') with less attention given to learning how to thank or express appreciation, how to encourage rather than discourage? Too hard for Key Stages 3/4? No, being constructive is no more linguistically complicated than being negative.

It should be clear by now that there is great scope for reflecting upon the moral dimensions of our teaching. As we consider and help students to consider how we should pattern our lives in a world awash with opportunities for cross-cultural communication, we find ourselves back in the vicinity of the spiritual, of questions concerning meaning, how we should live, and what spirit our lives manifest.

Social aspects

Like moral development, social development can take place through the content of the learning and through classroom interactions. The modern language curriculum includes many themes relevant to social development. Students learn to express themselves in a new medium about their families, friends, immediate social surroundings, school life, job aspirations, leisure pursuits, and so on. They learn the social norms of interaction in various settings in the target culture, and practise speaking in socially appropriate ways, using appropriate forms of address or writing in appropriate styles. In the short narratives and video sequences which they encounter in course materials, they have a chance to observe the social (and sometimes the antisocial) behaviour of others.

At the same time the communicative classroom is a context where the social dimensions of learning are accentuated. Students are asked to express themselves to the class, in small groups, and in pairs. They learn to cooperate in communicative tasks with one other student or with several, solving problems together by sharing information, and the need to *participate* is emphasised to students. In fact, all of this seems to be in some way basic to learning a language, something which it is remarkably difficult to do on one's own – so much so that where people do learn languages alone, those who are most successful seem to be those who imagine conversation partners with whom they can interact (Rowsell and Libben 1994, pp. 668–87).

Moral and social aspects are interconnected. Participation in the modern language classroom often involves some degree of personal exposure – letting funny and possibly incorrect sounds come out of one's mouth, divulging personal information in response to questions. If a classroom ethos is allowed to develop in which students take advantage of these moments of vulnerability in negative ways, rather than supporting each other in the learning task, then the inescapable social dimension of learning a foreign language communicatively can become a *barrier* to learning rather than part of one's progress.

Cultural aspects

The idea that modern language teaching has to do with cultural development scarcely needs justification – learning from an encounter with another culture has always been one of its central educational concerns. With OFSTED reporting that some schools need a better balance between pupils' own cultures and learning about other cultures, modern language learning surely has a particularly important role to play (OFSTED 1998, p. 41). This does not, of course, mean that cultural development happens automatically in modern language lessons, and teachers may too often have assumed that it will take care of itself as language skills are practised. It does, however, mean that the term is familiar and its relevance fairly obvious.

It will be clear already that the importance of the cultural dimension in modern languages qualifies our approach to the other three areas under discussion. The texts, topics and activities used to promote spiritual, moral and social development must reflect the fact that the particular context for such development which we have in view here is that of encountering and learning about another language and culture. This is what makes our approach different from Religious Education or Personal and Social Education. There are good reasons to deal with religious belief and practice, but we will do so not in general but as part of learning about native speakers, many of whom themselves believe and live in the light of those beliefs. When we encounter moral issues, it will be in the light of their relevance to the lives of the speakers of the target language and to the ways in which we communicate with them.

Work in German can, for instance, launch off from the word *Licht*, exploring light as a symbol of purity in a way which is firmly rooted in German culture. Candles as symbolic sources of light can be related to the advent wreath and to candle-lit protests in relation to the fall of the Berlin wall and the large-scale demonstrations in Germany against racism (for examples, see *Charis Deutsch, Einheiten 6-10*, p. 27–48).

To encounter another culture is to encounter the spiritual, the moral and the social at every turn. A different culture embodies the responses of another community or range of communities to basic spiritual and moral questions, the working out of these responses in the social life of another group of human beings. There are opportunities here for students to learn that such questions are important beyond the confines of their own culture and that the target culture has the same depth and earnestness as their own, to the point where the different responses found in that culture can challenge their own ways of thinking.

The spiritual, moral, social and cultural dimensions of learning illuminate each other. It is with this in mind that we turn to examples of approaches which can integrate the four areas.

Themes

One approach involves starting from language which already occurs in the syllabus but exploring some of its wider networks of meaning. Take the word 'bread' – in most existing materials this is dealt with predominantly as an item for consumption, in the context of either family meals or shopping transactions. Is this the only or the most educationally interesting way to configure the language being learned? Jacques Ellul reflects that

> Even the simplest word – *bread*, for instance – involves all sorts of connotations. When the word *bread* is pronounced, I cannot help but think of the millions of people who have none...The communion service comes to me: the breaking of bread at the Last Supper...I pass quickly to the moral lessons I learned as a child: that it is a crime to throw away a piece of bread, since it is a sacred substance. And from there, of course, I arrive at the enormous, incredible amount of wastefulness in our society...Memories come back to me: the warm, crusty bread of my childhood. The promised bread of life that will satisfy all hunger. And not living by bread alone...Not all of these memories are conjured up every time I hear the word, and they do not all come at once, but it is a rarity when none of them follows the oft-repeated request: 'pass the bread.' (1985, pp. 17–18)[1]

This does not suggest that every vocabulary item should be subjected to large-scale word-association – it might, however, provide a reminder that consumer contexts are not the only possible contexts within which the same words can be encountered as meaningful. Ask a Muslim or a Christian what significance bread has for them and we are into a new multicultural and spiritual dimension. This in turn can broaden the context within which learners can think about the meanings which bread has for them.

Poetry, parables, dreams

While poetry is often linguistically difficult, it can also have the advantage of expressing abstract issues not by means of abstract discussion, but through striking concrete images, repetitions and thought-provoking phrases. These benefits can also characterise proverbs, parables, dreams and short stories. Two examples illustrate how deeper issues can become concrete through imagery, and how learners can be helped to respond in a personally significant way.

Sophie Scholl, a key member of the White Rose resistance movement in Nazi Germany, had a dream the night before her execution. In her dream she was walking up a steep mountain path to a church, carrying a baby in a christening gown. Suddenly a crevasse opened in front of her and she plunged in, but was able to put the baby safely on the other side. She drew from the dream hope that the cause for which they had fought was not over with their deaths. Resistance, disaster, hope, death, life beyond death – all in a text expressed in language concrete and vivid enough to be accessible to most GCSE students (*Charis Deutsch, Einheiten 1–5*, p. 12).

In the same period of German history, Dietrich Bonhoeffer wrote his well-known letters and papers in prison, including a number of poems. In one of them, 'Wer bin ich?', he agonises over the gap between others' perceptions of him as brave and firm and his own inner experience of weariness and isolation in prison, before leaving the question of his 'real' identity to God. The problem with using this poem in a unit of German work was that it was too difficult as it stood for most learners. It was adapted as follows. First, learners were familiarised with a range of vocabulary for describing character and feelings. They were then asked to circle the words which others have used to describe them, put a square round words which they would choose to describe themselves, and put a triangle round words representing qualities which they aspire to. These three sets of words were then used to compose a poem, using the basic structure of Bonhoeffer's poem, in which learners could express their own and others' perceptions of who they are (*Charis Deutsch, Einheiten 1–5*, pp. 55–76). Learners were enabled to engage with Bonhoeffer's ideas at the level of single words.

Biography and History

Moral development involves helping students to make wise choices, to distinguish between right and wrong, and directing them to patterns of behaviour which consider others before ourselves. One way of provoking reflection is to show them examples which may inspire them. Biography is a way of presenting choices made by others and the motivations behind them in a way which carries a ring of authenticity. The moral choices made by people are grounded in their spirituality, their beliefs and values, the meaning that they see for their own lives and the lives of others.

Historical topics also provide opportunities for students to make comparisons between their own values and those lived out in other times and places. A unit of work in *Charis Français* focuses on the founding of Montreal as a Utopian Catholic colony in the seventeenth century. Students are asked to imagine themselves similarly founding a new community and to decide whom they should take with them in terms of skills and professions, what buildings they would build first, and what rules they would establish for their community (thus practising some familiar areas of GCSE vocabulary). They can then compare their choices with those made by the original settlers in Montreal.

Art

Art is clearly part of culture, and also offers a way into the social and spiritual values of the artist. Students can practise a wide range of questions by asking them in relation to a painting: How many people do they see? What are they wearing? Who seems to be the most important person? Why? What is she/he thinking? What are the surroundings like? When applied to a painting such as Gaugin's *Adoration of the Shepherds*, such questioning can provide a helpful context for work on religious festivals, leading into reading the stories associated with the pictures (in this case the Nativity). The same questions can be asked of secular and religious Christmas cards. Written activities could include a letter to the artist asking further questions. This use of questions can introduce learners to a cultural heritage and to its spiritual dimension.

Teaching methods

We need to consider more than content. Covering vocabulary related to spiritual or moral issues does not in and of itself promote spiritual or moral development – a token romp through the names of the main religious festivals in an otherwise tourist-oriented course does little to promote exploration of the ways in which spirituality informs everyday life. There may be little gain in adding spiritually significant material to course content if the ways in which students interact with that content neither bring out its significance nor encourage students to relate that significance to their own lives. More concretely, if a text which raises personally significant issues is dealt with by means of questions which test comprehension of individual factual details, then can spiritual or moral development be assumed to have taken place? Does the drilling of 'Ich bin anglikanisch' to prepare for personal questions in the oral exam show that spiritual development is being catered for? Surely the answer is 'no'.

Whatever else spiritual development might require, opportunity for open-ended personal response is essential. Spiritually meaningful responses cannot be guaranteed – it is always open to a student to complete an activity in an unreflective, mechanical manner. Learning activities can, however, either close out opportunities for spiritually meaningful responses or create spaces for them to occur. The latter kind will not be made up of tasks which all have fixed right–wrong answers. Activities oriented toward spiritual and moral development will seek to engage learners in reflection on the subject matter, to enable them to *explore* its meaning, and to help them to *express* a personal response whatever their level of linguistic ability.

In an activity in *Charis Français* students place words such as bread, family, education, money and love in order of importance based on discussion in pairs using the comparative (more/less important than). In linguistic terms this is a grammar exercise; in terms of meaning it is a discussion of basic values. The two kinds of learning are not rivals – they can go hand in hand.

Conclusion

It might be tempting to the already stressed modern language teacher to see 'SMSC' as an alien imposition, a burden imposed by OFSTED and a distraction from the immediate business of teaching language skills. We suggest that such a response, however understandable, would be sadly mistaken. The requirement can be regarded as an opportunity to move beyond the somewhat limited horizons of GCSE language courses and to engage learners with themes which have greater personal and educative significance. It is an opportunity to re-establish modern language learning as contributing to the heart of the school's task, rather than as the acquisition of skills which are of interest mainly to the enthusiast. It is an opportunity to move beyond the tendency in public rhetoric to justify language learning mainly in terms of economic competition and to re-explore its broader educational value. It is a springboard to help our students to re-examine spiritual, moral, social and cultural questions in a broader context than that provided by their own immediate experience. What is more, with a little imagination and appropriate resources, spiritual, moral, social and cultural dimensions can be addressed in ways which enhance rather than detract from the regular day-to-day tasks of language teaching and learning.

References

Beesley, M. (1993) 'Spiritual education in schools', *Pastoral Care in Education* **11**(3), 22–28.

Charis Deutsch, Einheiten 1–5 (1996) St. Albans: Association of Christian Teachers.

Charis Deutsch, Einheiten 6–10 (1998) Nottingham: The Stapleford Centre.

Charis Français unités 6–10 (1998) Nottingham: The Stapleford Centre.

Ellul, J. (1985) *The Humiliation of the Word.* Grand Rapids: Eerdmans.

Kelly, L. G. (1969) *25 Centuries of Language Teaching 500 BC–1969.* Rowley, Mass.: Newbury House.

NCC (National Curriculum Council) (1993) *Spiritual and Moral Development: A Discussion Paper.* York: National Curriculum Council.

OFSTED (1998) *The Annual Report of Her Majesty's Chief Inspector of Schools: Standards and Quality in Education 1996/97.* London: HMSO.

Rowsell, L. V. and Libben, G. (1994) 'The sound of one hand clapping: how to succeed in independent language learning', *Canadian Modern Language Review* **50**(4), 668–87.

Smith, D. (1997b) 'Communication and integrity: moral development and modern languages', *Language Learning Journal* **15**, 31–35.

Smith, D. (1997a) 'Facing the challenge of educational change', in Shortt, J. and Cooling, T. (eds) *Agenda for Educational Change.* Leicester: Apollos, 24–38.

Further reading

Charis Deutsch. Nottingham: The Stapleford Centre, 1996–8.
Two volumes of teaching resources which address 'SMSC' in German at Key Stage 4.

Charis Français. Nottingham: The Stapleford Centre, 1996–8.
Two volumes of teaching resources which address 'SMSC' in French at Key Stage 4.

Smith, D. (1999) *Making Sense of Spiritual Development*. Nottingham: The Stapleford Centre.
A practical introduction to and survey of spiritual development across the curriculum, including examples from modern languages.

Note:
[1] From Jacques Ellul, *The Humiliation of the Word*, © 1985 Wm. B Erdmans Publishing Company (US).

Chapter 10

Geography
Avril Maddrell and Stuart May

Geographical studies deal with the real world, looking at both the physical and human environments. As well as giving pupils the opportunity to explore the natural world, to consider how people live, and how these interact with each other, they help pupils to develop a 'sense of place'. By considering what makes where *they* live special to *them*, they are helped to understand how other people identify with their own places. This in turn is a springboard to understanding and respecting differences between places and societies.

Through these opportunities, pupils can develop:

- their own spiritual understanding (through identifying places, both natural and human, of 'special' value to them and developing respect and understanding of the natural world);

- moral and ethical awareness, including issues of equality (of people, gender, race, culture and opportunity);

- social understanding and development (through working together, interacting with others and studying other places, societies and cultures);

- respect and empathy for other peoples, cultures and societies through understanding of their own and other cultures, their similarities (common elements) as well as their differences/contrasts, and some of the reasons for these.

Social, moral, cultural and spiritual issues have been increasingly integrated into academic geography in the last 20 years, through the emergence of new research themes often combined with new theoretical approaches to geographical relationships and phenomena. Notably, this includes the burgeoning research on environmental issues, which geographers with an understanding of both physical processes and social relations feel they are well placed to interrogate. Other examples include social geography informed by radical politics with a strong moral agenda – for example:

- David Harvey's (1973) *Social Justice and the City* in both industrialised and industrialising/developing countries;

- humanist approaches including spiritual and cultural influences on sense of place, which have been developed within the growing field of cultural geography (including popular culture, landscape studies, and consumption);

- feminist concerns about gender and sexuality and post-modernist debates centring on recognition of difference between groups have also had a clear influence on the subject matter, methodologies and analysis of contemporary geographical issues – for example the Institute of British Geographers Women and Geography Study Group (1997).

However, these concerns and approaches have not necessarily filtered down in their variety and complexity to school curriculum geography. The following examples aim to illustrate both some well-known and less common topics and approaches to geography which integrate 'SMSC' themes.

Geographical studies seek to develop pupils' knowledge and understanding of *places, patterns and processes*, and *environmental issues*, together with the skills necessary to gather and interpret information and to communicate this understanding to others.

The process of *enquiry*, by posing relevant questions about *what* places are like, *why* they are like that, *how* they might change and the possible consequences of this for the people who live there, helps pupils to understand the processes of change and the way in which decisions are made. By making them consider their own attitudes as well as other people's, they are developing their own sense of 'right' and 'wrong', of 'natural' justice, as well as recognising the fact that other people may have differing points of view – and respecting these. Pupils can understand that decisions are made on the basis of some of these points of view but that some voices may be excluded from the process. This can be further developed through role-play, which enables pupils to develop an empathy for others and to develop positive attitudes and values towards other people. The enquiry process involves pupils in considerations of the complexity of the 'real world' – real issues and choices, involving real people, in real situations in real places.

Fieldwork, one of the core strands of geography, involves interaction with the outside world in a different, complementary way – fieldwork and enquiry can be combined, as enquiry can often require fieldwork of one sort or another to obtain information from primary sources. Working in the field brings the pupil into contact with the 'natural' and 'built' environment and helps to develop understanding of ideas of stewardship, responsibility and care for the environment. Planning and carrying out fieldwork or an enquiry enables pupils to develop the ability to work with others, the skills of negotiation and to respect points of view other than their own.

The study of places underlies geographical studies. In the study of human geography they are brought into contact with other people, places and cultures. These studies enable stereotypes to be challenged and promote an understanding of how people all over the world have common needs and have to meet similar challenges. By studying how these common elements produce different solutions in different situations helps to promote an understanding of, and empathy for, other cultures.

Human geography promotes an understanding of how societies work on a variety of scales, from local to global (e.g. village/local community – area – region – national; global economy; trade links). It will also promote the understanding of issues such as the empowerment – and exclusion – of people. Who makes decisions? Are all people involved in decision-making? How much are specific groups involved in the decisions which affect their everyday lives?

In studying their own 'place', in all its aspects – physical, human and environmental – pupils are led to develop a 'Sense of Place'; a sense of identity with their own place, an understanding of what makes this place unique in their own lives. Through this, they increase their understanding of the importance of other people's and societies' 'Sense of Place'.

In studying *patterns and processes*, pupils begin to understand concepts of how and why things change and to recognise similarities in contrasting situations. In their studies of the natural world (physical geography) they develop their understanding of small- and large-scale processes operating over timescales varying from short to unimaginably long. In this contact with the natural environment there is the opportunity to develop the spiritual side of ourselves – the magnitude of natural forces, whether in the form of an earthquake (huge power in a short time span) or of mountain building and erosion (imperceptible movement over a huge timescale), the beauty of a waterfall, the magnificence of a high cliff or large cataract. It is in the context of such natural phenomena that a sense of 'awe and wonder' is developed.

Studies of human geography develop an understanding of the pressures, challenges and trends which shape the development of places. It brings pupils into contact with issues involving differing points of view and how people react to various issues; it looks at conflict and consensus and their role in decision-making and management, as well as questions of who makes decisions (see above). In considering the process of change, it also brings up issues of cause and effect, of how decisions made now will affect the future for good or ill, and so develops the concept of responsibility, of selfishness and of right and wrong. Through these considerations, questions of how we use, treat and manage the human and natural environment are raised.

Environmental issues form an integral part of geographical study. Through these studies, which lie at the interface of physical and human geography, pupils consider not only the quality and value of environments but also questions of improvement and management of environments. They also look at the issues surrounding the use of natural resources for the good of the community and the potential conflicts arising from differing uses of land, in both the human and natural environment. All of this work provides the opportunity to develop many aspects of 'SMSC' through consideration of human needs and responsibilities, by developing the concept of 'trusteeship' by understanding how conflicts of interest can arise; how decisions are made; and the need for people's involvement in decision-making. Such work develops the concept of citizenship and can lead on to considerations of, for instance, UN Local Agenda 21, which, with its emphasis on the power of the individual and the small community, on *local* action to make a difference on a much larger scale, is one embodiment of the saying 'Think globally, act locally'.

Differentiation

It is essential that there is a clear *entitlement* to the study, that we ensure 'access for all'. This includes an entitlement to fieldwork for the physically disabled (e.g. wheelchair access, provision for visually impaired pupils, provision for hearing impairment), opportunities for those with severe learning difficulties to experience the real world beyond the classroom, and for pupils whose behaviour might be thought to exclude them from outdoor activities (such pupils often respond well to the outside environment). It also imposes an obligation to ensure that pupils are sufficiently and appropriately challenged in their work, to ensure progression and stimulation.

Access can be differentiated through careful selection and use of resources, so that less able pupils may be asked to respond to a task by looking for evidence from, for instance, a photograph or piece of text; the use of multiple sources (whether all different, e.g. pictorial, graphical, textual, map; or more than one of the same type) demands a level of synthesis on the part of the pupil and so is more challenging. In a similar way, tasks may be made more or less challenging by either concentrating on one aspect or issue, or by demanding a more penetrative response on the part of the pupil, perhaps giving more detail or a more developed reasoning. Thus, in studying another country or locality, some pupils might be asked to identify what groups are affected by a given change, or how one group is affected; others could be guided to consider how and why the various groups are affected, and perhaps whether this might be part of a more general pattern or trend, or have parallels elsewhere.

To achieve this, various types of support can be given. At one level, for example, some simple headings will help a pupil to structure the answer, directing attention to specific evidence in the source material; at another level, headings might be used to ensure that the pupil is challenged to consider all aspects, looking for a variety of information which is available in the supplied resources, though not necessarily in all of them nor explicitly stated, and to use this information to draw conclusions and make inferences. In this way, pupils can be challenged to consider the issues and implications behind the knowledge they have acquired.

By actively involving pupils in work which is matched to their ability and attainment, they are able to develop their geographical understanding and, through this, to enhance their personal development in the various strands of 'SMSC'; if the concepts we try to teach are too advanced, then, although we may get a mechanistic response in terms of geographical knowledge, there will be no extension of understanding in either geography or themselves. As geographical learning develops so increasing *breadth* and *depth* of study enables the pupil to develop a deeper awareness and understanding of the importance not only of 'place' but of a sense of belonging which is achieved by being involved as a part of society.

Spiritual aspects

At the primary stage, there are a number of opportunities for spiritual development. The first opportunity relates directly to religions – through visits to local places of worship, through visits from local people relating to religious establishments. Geographical aspects of such studies will include the mapping of places of worship – where are they in relation to the people who use them? Why have they been built here? What impact have they had on the local community, both direct and indirect? Where do people come from to attend these places? How far do they travel?

The second opportunity relates to the environment, to 'getting in touch with nature'; this includes contact on a local and personal scale, as well as, for instance, visits to World Heritage sites. This is more fully developed in the 'Environmental Geography' section of Figure 10.1 'Environmental Education'.

Thirdly, arising partly from the 'Environmental Geography' strand, is the personal development of spirituality through the experience of 'awe and wonder' in the natural world, on a variety of scales. Such experiences may be small and personal, perhaps a favourite corner of the local park or a quiet place overlooking the local stream; they may be on a much grander scale, perhaps on first seeing an alpine valley. These experiences can contribute to a sense of well-being, which helps us to establish a positive self-image, and/or an awareness of individual place in a larger landscape, ecosystem or world.

Geography of religious practices

This topic appeared on the agenda of Humanist geography and has become a feature of historical and cultural geography, including landscape studies. Historical studies include the spread of a particular religion or denomination, e.g. the spread of Islam and/or Christianity in East Africa in relation to population, settlement and economic activity; the location of Druid sites in the British Isles (including those still standing and/or still in use).

The Sacred Land Project (the religious and environmental millennium project of the World Wide Fund for Nature (WWF) UK and ARC (Alliance for Religions and Conservation)), launched in 1997, is based on the belief that 'land and our physical surroundings have emotional and spiritual significance'. The project includes environmental groups, schools, government, local authorities, churches, temples and mosques and offers ideas for class and fieldwork activities, as well as the opportunity to place individual studies within the nation-wide project. Key Stage 3 pupils could explore their ideas of 'sacred places' and their knowledge and understanding of local religious sites and what these represent. Key Stage 4 pupils could examine the spiritual aspect of cultural landscapes as an especially fertile ground for the understanding of difference, e.g. where religious groups are mixed as in areas of London or Cardiff. Maps can be used to locate synagogues, mosques, churches and temples and the spatial pattern of these related to broader socio-economic and historical patterns, including migration and employment, continuity and change. A field trip or use of video, slides or CD-ROM could be used to explore how pupils' sense of place is affected by religious buildings in their broader context, including aesthetics, affinity, sense of threat, inclusion and exclusion.

Environmental Education

This cross-curricular theme has many strong links to geography in school, in particular with 'environmental geography'. Environmental Education has been defined as (NCC 1991, p. 7):

Education

– about the environment (knowledge)

– for the environment (values, attitudes, positive action)

– in or through the environment (a resource).

Another useful definition in the present context is that
environmental education is about education in the *head* (knowledge)
hands (practical work)
heart (emotional)

(Chambers 1996)

Environmental Geography

This theme runs throughout the school geography curriculum. It begins in the Early Years with an awareness of the immediate world of the child, and looking after this environment, and develops towards an understanding of the many environmental issues facing the world today and our responsibility and ability to affect the environment and to manage change. Through environmental education and the study of environmental geography, the pupil is brought into touch with the world and develops the concept of stewardship.

Suitable projects might be:

Early Years:

My favourite places, e.g. quiet places, exciting places.

Why do I like them?

When do I like them?

KS1:

Places I like and dislike.

Why I feel this way about this place – what I like about it (and some bad points?); what I dislike about it (and some good points?).

How this place is changing, and why. Why we look after places; how we can look after the place; how we can improve this place; who looks after this place?

Figure 10.1

KS2:

A broader perspective is developed at this stage. The pupil can look at various types of environment (urban, rural, wild) and at 'pockets' of one within another, e.g. parks within the built environment, buildings in the landscape. In these studies, they will look at:

– those which are 'worth' preserving (conservation);

– those which 'could be looked after' (management);

– those 'in need of improvement/repair' (restoration).

The last of these, in particular, will bring up issues of how and why environments have become damaged (e.g. extractive industry; pollution – of all types; decline – industrial, inner city; overuse – tourist 'honey-pots', over-grazing; insensitive development).

KS 3-4:

Pupils can integrate knowledge of environment (e.g. types of ecosystem) with knowledge of location (e.g. industrialised country) in order to make contextualised evaluations of the value attributed to particular environments and the management issues associated with those places (e.g. competing interests and sustainable development). Such studies can draw on a wide range of pupil skills (e.g. empathy, data and map analysis) and resources (CD-ROMs, newspapers, local interest groups, videos, role plays). Pupils could explore the following issues:

Differing values and competing uses of game reserves, National Parks, UN World Heritage Sites, Areas of Outstanding Natural Beauty (AONB) or Sites of Special Scientific Interest (SSSI) (e.g. Norfolk Broads game, Land use in Kenya role play).

Differing impact of environmental change and/or hazards, and effects of alternative environmental management policies (e.g. The Relative Drought Game, Floods in Bangladesh role play (Maddrell, 1993)).

Figure 10.1 continued

Moral aspects

In studying people and places, whether aspects of our own area or elsewhere, pupils will meet many instances of inequality, unfairness and injustice, as well as their opposites. In considering these issues, they will develop their own sense of right and wrong, their own sense of justice and, through understanding and empathy can be encouraged to develop a respect for people, truth and property. This can only be done by ensuring an understanding of the societies which they study and a recognition of the issues of inclusion and exclusion which arise within that society. Knowledge and description is not enough, there must be discussion and understanding as well. Thus, gender and socio-economic issues may arise through consideration of the effects of the closure of local shops or services, or in the growth of superstore shopping with its increasing automation and decreasing personal/social contact. Local shops have always been centres of social interaction – who loses out when they disappear? Who loses out when increasing car ownership, for instance, reduces or removes public transport facilities – or increases fares? Equally, similar issues will arise when pupils study other places.

By studying food supply and provision (Wrigley and Lowe 1996), pupils can develop an understanding of the concept of 'Fair Trade', and will be able to compare this with the reality of experience of production for many workers (e.g. coffee growing, the banana trade, child/cheap labour and cheap consumer goods such as tee-shirts). Social justice – addressing issues of social and economic inequality on local, national and international scales – is particularly well developed within geography in the area of development studies.

Pupils will also develop their sense of justice, respect for people and place and concern for others through studying environmental issues, by developing an understanding of how people's actions affect others, how environments can be damaged by our own (perhaps unthinking) actions and through a growing understanding of the meaning of sustainable management/development and the concept of stewardship – of looking after our world for future generations. This may be through discussion of our immediate 'needs' (e.g. energy) against the requirements of conservation and sustainability, and the moral issues underlying this – for example the immediate effect on the environment (both direct and indirect), the immediate 'good', considered against the long-term effect of the use of one resource, or of a number of resources, at an increasing rate. For example, all of the above could be considered through the study of oil: its uses, including cars and plastics; of transport, recyclability, biodegradability, the effect of exploration and extraction on local and indigenous people – both positive and negative. Issues of land use, conservation, tradition and inclusion/exclusion can also be developed through the study of National Parks, Nature and Game reserves.

Through all of the preceding examples pupils will be developing their sensitivity and respect for other's viewpoints; this will be aided by their working alongside their peers and by studying various geographical issues, at local, national and global scales, and recognising how different people will have differing, equally valid, points of view for a variety of reasons. In these studies, the use of games and role-play can play an important part.

Social aspects

During their geographical studies, both inside and outside the classroom, pupils will have many opportunities to develop their ability to handle relationships, to exercise responsibility and initiative and to show their increasing ability to work both independently and with others. In particular, through organising enquiry and fieldwork, they will have opportunities to interact with their peers and with adults, including members of the public.

Pupils' understanding of society starts in the home at a very early age. Pre-school and school geographical experiences help pupils to broaden their awareness from the immediate family and friends to the local community and to an awareness of belonging to an ever-widening hierarchy of communities up to national level, and beyond through international treaties and trading networks. Shopping studies, for instance, will enable pupils to look at the links both within and between communities, from a local to a global scale, as well as considering the contribution of shops to the immediate community and, as trade outlets, to other communities.

By studying places and communities of varying sizes around the world, pupils will be led to a deepening understanding of how communities function and of the role, rights, responsibilities and contribution of the individual members. They should thus acquire the skills, attitudes and understanding necessary for them to take full part in the community as adults, as well as developing an awareness of socio-economic, gender and ethnicity issues.

Environmental issues contribute to the development of understanding of the potential conflict of the needs, desires and aspirations of members of a society, of the range of possible viewpoints, of how conflict may be resolved and how decisions are made. By studying such issues in a range of places worldwide, pupils will gain an understanding of how (and why) similar changes, hazards or pressures for change often have widely different impacts in different parts of the world.

A theme running through all of the above is the concept of 'Place'. Pupils will develop an awareness and concept of a 'Sense of Place' – a feeling of identity and of belonging, an understanding of what makes one place different from another, of what makes 'my place' special to me – and 'your place' special to you.

Cultural aspects

Cultural aspects include both 'high' and 'popular' culture and can include everything from football to opera houses and art galleries to shopping. Pupils will discover that different cultural forms are often reflections of gender, class and ethnicity divides, although they can also represent a bringing together of those groups.

One of the most important contributions of geography in the Primary age range is in the pupil's growing awareness of the wider world. Through the study of a variety of localities – their own and contrasting ones around the world – pupils will develop an awareness of other cultures and the patterns and processes of cultural development, a growing understanding of what it means to live in a 'multicultural society'. An example of this on a local scale would be fieldwork in their own shopping area, using all their senses – touch, sight, hearing, smell and taste – to look at the cultural diversity of the High Street. Such understanding on a local scale will help them to understand and respect other cultures and societies with which they come into contact, whether through study or by personal contact. (See Figure 10.2 for survey and project activities related to 'Shopping').

Shopping

Shopping surveys have tended to be empirical studies of numbers and types of shops. Academic retailing geography has recently undergone something of a revolution (see Wrigley and Lowe 1996), expanding its remit to consider issues relating to consumption as well as retailing patterns and practices. 'Shopping' as a theme may be developed at all levels of the curriculum.

Early Years:

Walk to the local shop.

Talk to the shopkeeper about what is sold, who uses the shop.

Where do deliveries come from, who brings them?

Are any services provided locally (e.g. sub Post Office)?

KS1:

Who uses our local shops?

What is available?

Study the range of goods, the range of shops and local services.

When and why do we shop locally?

Where do we do our main shopping?

Where does food come from?

In studying a contrasting locality, compare and contrast shops in the locality and the goods and services provided.

KS2:

Where do people shop?

Look at local shops, town centre shops, out-of-town shops.

Gather firsthand information on where people come from to shop here, and how far they travel.

Why do they travel this distance?

Is there a difference in the responses obtained in the three types of centre?

Figure 10.2

Consider the implications of the findings for

(a) shopkeepers (trading hours, Sunday trading, tele-shopping),

(b) various groups of people – e.g. age, access, mobility, cultural differences.

Look at the effect of cultural issues in the development of shops – specialist shops, and growing cultural diversity in the 'High Street'. Cultural diversity can be developed into a study of where food comes from, how it reaches us and how the price we pay is split between various groups. How much do the growers (e.g. of coffee, bananas) get? Develop the concept of 'Fair Trade'. Environmental links can also be developed here, looking at transport (of both goods to the shops, and of people when shopping); packaging and recycling. It is also possible to develop an understanding of gender and class issues in changing shopping habits – the number of women who shop, and the social contact which this gives. What happens to people without cars if the local shops close down? How good is the local bus service?

KS 3/4:
Recent research on the huge growth of charity shops in the 1980s and 1990s raise:

– environmental concerns and recycling of second hand goods;

– attitudes to charity and the role of non-governmental organisations (NGOs);

– economic divisions in society (the 'haves' and the 'have-nots');

– changing employment patterns and voluntary work.

PROJECT
(a) Exploring customer motivation – why we buy the things we do as individuals (brand names, own identity, hobbies, peer pressure, 'buying British/Welsh/Scottish').
(b) Mapping the supply chain: the geography of students' food/ clothes/ gameboys/ music: local, national and global production processes – issues including international division of labour.
(c) Child labour issues and how it relates to products bought in Britain. For information and activity packs contact the Bureau of Public Information, International Labour Office, 4, route des Morillons, CH–1211 Geneva 22, Switzerland http://www.unicc.org/ilo). CD-ROM newspaper search – Manchester United merchandise and allegations of the use of child labour.
(d) Fair trade role play – arguments for and against fair trade products – followed by debriefing and own response to issues.

Figure 10.2 continued

Key Stage 3 pupils could study the spatial distribution of those people associated with particular cultural activities, e.g. mapping the nationwide support base for football teams such as Glasgow Rangers or Manchester United. Information on the geographical distribution of visitors to a local art gallery, library, music shop, sports centre and cinema could be collected, mapped and analysed and compared. The question of access is a crucial element that links cultural expressions to moral and social issues.

Key Stage 4 pupils could debate whether the United Kingdom's cultural resources are too centralised in London, Cardiff, Edinburgh and Belfast. Recent discussions about the location and nature of the Millennium Dome and debates about the merits of touring opera companies versus those permanently located in London offer specific case study material on which to base discussion (pupils with access to CD-ROM or Internet news coverage could do a search of articles related to their topic).

References and further reading

Action Aid (1997) 'Sacha Mama, Eco-tourism in the Amazonian Rainforest' (KS3 Study Pack, Ecuador). Action Aid, Chataway House, Leah Road, Chard, Somerset TA20 1FA.

Atkins, J. (1995) *Aani and the Tree Huggers.* New York: Lee & Low Books Inc.

Chambers, W. (1996) 'Environmental quality and change', *Primary Geographer* **27**, October 1996. Sheffield: The Geographical Association.

Harvey, D. (1973) *Social Justice and the City.* Oxford: Blackwell.

Maddrell, A. (1993) *Geography in Action.* London: Hodder and Stoughton.

May, S., Richardson, P., Waugh, D. (1998) *Forward In Geography* (KS2 textbook series). Walton-On-Thames: Thomas Nelson.

NCC (1990) *Curriculum Guidance 7: Environmental Education.* York: National Curriculum Council.

The Sacred Land Project. ICOREC 9a, Didsbury Park, Manchester M20 5LH. 0161 434 0828.

Women and Geography Study Group of the Institute of British Geographers (1997) *Feminist Geographies. Explorations in Diversity and Difference.* London: Longman.

Wrigley, N. and Lowe, M. (eds) (1996) *Retailing, Consumption and Capital: Towards the New Retail Geography.* London: Longman.

Chapter 11

History
Ann Jordan and Paul Taylor

History has always been a medium for delivering essential skills at all stages of education. It is a subject which seeks to place children in a context of time and place, and thereby allow them to see what has gone before. Therefore the environment and society in which they now function can be given a clearer focus. It was the ancient philosopher Cicero who believed that to know nothing of what happened before you were born was to remain forever a child. Given that a key purpose of a child's education and full-time schooling is to prepare them for life as an adult, and, presuming that this is more than a mere collection of assorted abilities to do different things, then history can be seen as a platform from which to understand aspects of spiritual, moral, social and cultural values, not only of the past but also of the present. As teachers of history we are not seeking, as such, to turn pupils into historians but rather to encourage the ability to select and interpret data from a range of historical sources and a variety of perspectives. Ultimately, adults choose and reflect on what is of value to themselves, their community and the world in which they live. This chapter considers how history may be used as a means to develop and foster that wider sense of values on which any society ultimately places its standards.

Policy

The framework for History that is taught to children between the ages of 5 to 14, when the subject is compulsory, has been laid down in a series of Education Acts and corresponding statutory orders for England and Wales (DfE 1995). From the ages of 14 to 18 a number of GCSE and GCE syllabuses across the country further determine the course of study for those children who continue with the subject. Obviously, the Department for Education and Employment (DfEE) and Office for Standards in Education (OFSTED) perform a supervisory role over what takes place, while history itself has been alluded to in a number of documents produced by the National Curriculum Council (NCC), School Curriculum and Assessment Authority (SCAA) and OFSTED during the course of the 1990s on a number of matters concerned with issues relevant to this book.

Despite recent and possible future changes in the National Curriculum there is no question of removing from schools their option to deliver history as part of a 'broad and balanced curriculum'. Under the 1995 National Curriculum History Orders for each Key Stage there was a presumption about the development of Key Elements, and as these were based around the essence of what the subject is about, then any change in the nomenclature could not fundamentally disguise or remove the essence of the subject which these contained. Given that these Key Elements were to do with chronology, organisation and communication, knowledge and understanding, interpretation and enquiry, it can reasonably be stated that the final three in this list can have direct links to the delivery of spiritual, moral, social and cultural education. Indeed, at Key Stages 2 and 3, and implied at Key Stage 1, there was an expectation that political, economic, social, cultural and religious perspectives would be delivered through the Programmes of Study. These were designed to broaden understanding of the history studied and expand the context in which pupils would study and reflect on content of the past.

Values

The basis of History is enquiry and through this the question of why certain events and actions took place. It widens appreciation of different thoughts, perceptions and experiences of people in the past and the values they placed on issues of significance to them. By gaining a sense of perspective, and arriving at a thoughtful and considered view of what has occurred, present-day attitudes and developments can be put into a more meaningful context. It does not have to be the role of an historian to inculcate or enforce a particular set of values to the detriment and denigration of all other viewpoints and opinions. Yet all history involves a process of interpretation which to some extent reveals, and is possibly controlled by, the values of the individual historian.

However, this is not to say that, through a reflective and open-minded approach, certain widely held and worthy aspirations of particular individuals and people over time cannot be noted and thereby implicitly recognised. History cannot, by itself, make someone become antiracist or anti-sexist, but it can show the consequences of following a set of practices or ideas, either as an individual, class, society or government. This may lead to a particular outcome and to this extent therefore can be very explicit in an articulation of values. This enables teachers and pupils to contemplate the results of, for instance, condemning and victimising people based on religion, colour, race, gender or class. Therefore, history does have a role in fostering understanding and tolerance, but also a questioning approach to values so that the present is not discussed in a vacuum and that values can be seen as having emerged through a set of complex processes. This can begin with the youngest pupils and progress through a series of 'steps' which lead to a fuller and deeper contact with the issue of values. This could be explored through the following developmental points:

- looking at how values emerge from observing a series of events in the past;

- taking into consideration the different interpretations of those events and how these can alter initial perceptions of value judgements;

- considering wider contributory factors beyond the events themselves which have a role to play in value constructions;

- analysing a variety of perspectives from a range of historical sources in order to identify and distinguish motivations behind events and the subsequent values placed upon them;

- stressing the need to discuss the validity of information, motivations and personal opinions, in the widest possible sense, in order to explore the essence of what a value judgement is.

These points will have relevance to the sections which follow.

Spiritual aspects

Progression is an important theme in history and most children develop a wider understanding and appreciation of a range of issues, concerns and attitudes over time. Therefore, history can move from observing, to discussing and then analysing more complex spiritual matters which in themselves involve deep-seated and often abstract concepts.

A number of schools touch upon religion through their history content. At Key Stage 1 often famous people are studied who have a religious connection, such as Dr Barnardo, Elizabeth Fry and William Booth. At Key Stage 2 and 3 there is often an examination of religious issues: in the Tudor period Henry VIII's break with Rome, and schooling in Victorian times. Issues such as relations between the monarchy and the church during the Medieval era, along with questions of religious change and tension during the sixteenth and seventeenth centuries and the origins of religions and denominations provide opportunities to discuss the wider religious context.

History can foster a wider spiritual understanding beyond just a religious/church dimension. In order for the pupils to explore who they are and how they fit into the world at large, they need to explore a range of spiritual perspectives from the past. Sensitive questions need to be answered which enable pupils to develop understanding about the variety of contexts in which people have developed their spiritual awareness. By looking at the form of communities over time, whether it be for instance, the Anglo-Saxons in England, the society of Mesopotamia, or the native peoples of America, the nature of the relationships within these societies and their differing belief and value systems may well enable pupils to see and understand that there was more to people's lives than merely the concrete and materialistic. It can obviously be difficult for many children to understand belief systems which seem to be so alien to themselves and the selection of sources needs to at least raise some questions which might be explored further. The use of empathy can be a method for exploring the meaning, purpose, motivations and feelings of people in the past. It can be employed as a means of raising issues of identity in topics which involve consideration of, for instance, war, poverty, famine, disease and suffering.

Moral aspects

History shows us that over different time periods and cultures the interpretation by governments, organisations and individuals of what is 'morally correct' have differed widely. By developing knowledge and understanding pupils can see, even if they do not accept, why, at certain points in the past, communities and societies acted in the way they did. Interpreting these events is one thing, making judgements quite another.

At Key Stage 1, exploring seemingly simple issues of right and wrong can be problematic. For instance, in a study of Guy Fawkes, a basic question such as 'should he have been executed, given that he did not actually kill anyone?' invites discussion on capital punishment and what it is to be used for, if at all. Obviously, some pupils will be able to have a deeper grasp of the complexities of this question than others. Similarly, any discussion on the sinking of the Titanic might superficially lead to a view that the owners were morally wrong not to have sufficient lifeboats for everyone, but on the other hand they seemed to genuinely believe it was unsinkable. Therefore, these raise issues of justification at a fundamental level.

By Key Stage 2 the questioning can become more complicated. For instance, Ancient Greece is regarded as a great civilisation, yet it kept slaves and did not offer equal rights to women. Pupils may well approach this topic without seeing the links between the various aspects of that society which led to this situation. Therefore, they do at least have some moral dilemmas raised by teaching the topic, and will begin to address some of these, possibly through drama, even if they do not have a full and rounded picture of the society as a whole. The more able children may seek to question how such a society that produced great philosophers and thinkers, with seemingly clear insights and sensibilities, managed to hold such beliefs. Equal rights could therefore be an ongoing discussion across each of the strands of this project which constantly involves the pupils in a search for new evidence against which to make and refine their moral judgements. Similarly, as with a study of conscientious objection to conscription into the armed forces within Britain during the Second World War, the morality of whether, and on what terms, this was, and should have been, allowed, can raise interesting questions with children about the nature of conscience, and the role and expectations of a citizen within society.

At Key Stage 3, and in a number of GCSE syllabuses, pupils are asked to consider deep questions of the rights and wrongs of wartime actions. For instance, how does a person judge the morality of the deaths of hundreds of thousands of civilians at Hiroshima and Nagaski in Japan through dropping two atomic bombs, against the lives of hundreds of thousands of British and American soldiers whose deaths were possibly avoided by the Japanese surrender? This raises questions of the idea of a 'just war' and the value and sanctity of human life. This can be approached in a number of ways to take account of differentiation:

- Some pupils might see the issue as being one of a straightforward case of 'us versus them' and that they were an enemy who got what they deserved. This may be through an initial emotional response which at least raises a talking point on which to discuss the nature of life and its value.

- At another level pupils may see the issue as a pragmatic one in which the decision was not an easy one to take but necessary in the circumstances. This allows a discussion of to what extent pragmatic decisions, however reasoned, should potentially override moral perspectives.

- A further refinement would be for pupils to follow on from the pragmatic argument, but argue that there was a certain morality in what occurred given the circumstances of the time. This allows reflection on the issue of balance and whether this comes into a moral discussion.

- At a more sophisticated level, pupils could consider whether the decision was necessary, become aware of the moral repugnance involved in dropping the bombs, but also in the loss of life that would have come through invasion, and thereby seeing both sides of the argument clearly. This allows a debate over whether there are 'two moralities' or indeed no morality at all.

The danger with morality is that judgements are sometimes made on insufficient knowledge, undue subjectivity and a present-day view which may not correspond with the realities or perceptions of people in a different time or place. Asking pupils to develop a personal view on the ethical issues raised by a number of subjects, including history (OFSTED 1994), may not always end up with the result you might want or expect if pupils decide to take a negative, pragmatic or narrow view of the issue. Even so, it could be argued that history can play a role in developing tolerance (NCC 1993) to the extent that it can make pupils aware of the practicalities and motivations which informed people's decisions in the past. Given that moral questions are often abstract, and that the level of ability, understanding and maturity in pupils varies widely, there is particular need for care when it comes to the differentiation of tasks for pupils to undertake, thereby avoiding the dangers of oversimplification.

Some people believe in moral absolutes, while others contend that relativism needs to be a factor at play. Although few today would deny that slavery and imperialism are inherently wrong, both have in the past been regarded as inherently sound. This is not to say that they were, but to judge those in the past by present criteria can be to alter the historical truth. In the future, if society largely decided that abortion is immoral and makes it illegal, would that mean that a study of Britain in the 1990s would be a study of an immoral society? In other words, diversity in society and the acceptance of a pluralistic ethos can be a challenge to some people's moral orthodoxies. History can illuminate moral dilemmas without seeking to give moral answers. That is not to say that a historian as an individual is morally neutral. Though the process of selecting, sifting, sorting and interpreting data into a thesis may still allow bias to be present, this need not in itself dictate the teaching and learning context with pupils and students.

Social aspects

The social context of the past underpins much of the delivery of the subject right across the Key Stages. By its very essence this involves studying past societies and being able to describe and identify reasons for and results of certain historical situations and changes. Social history concentrates around the everyday lives, roles and relationships of peoples at different levels of society, and this may include issues of status, class, hierarchy and power. It is important that pupils at an early age are provided with opportunities to develop understanding of various aspects of social life such as homes, houses and family. For instance, the immediate environment of school and home at Key Stage 1 can develop into looking at the wider local history of the community at Key Stage 2 and on to the study and development of national parliaments, the European Union and the United Nations at Key Stage 3 and GCSE.

It is also from within a social context that wider cross-curricular elements such as environmental education, economic and industrial understanding, and citizenship can be explored. In the case of environmental education the construction of new roads can lead to debate and argument about the effect on places of historic importance such as buildings, monuments and battlefields, and how you judge issues of valuing the heritage of the past when placed against the perceived need of the present. The effect of the workplace and industry in general on the nature of communities and their evolution or decline, whether it be the rise of those towns and cities based on the car industry in the 1930s, or the fall of the coal mining villages during the 1980s, are valid areas of enquiry for an evaluation of the nature of society.

With regard to citizenship, history can show how this concept has altered significantly over time, and allow an examination of what this might have meant to say a peasant in feudal England, a Chartist in Victorian times, or a teenager in the Britain of the 1960s. Given that the role of the citizen is such a topical and relevant issue, particularly given the whole question of the idea of European citizenship, the role of history in fostering some awareness of this difficult and potentially ambiguous concept becomes all the more pertinent. Taking the example of a teenager in 1960's Britain, one could approach the topic in the following way with, perhaps, upper Key Stage 2 pupils:

- *Background.* In 1960's Britain you had to be 21 years of age to vote in Parliamentary elections. Yet, increasing numbers of young people were entering the workplace at 15 and therefore contributing to a society in which they did not have a right to vote. Those pupils staying on at school after 15 and possibly going on to further and higher education also had no right to express their opinion in the electoral process.

- *Task.* This could lead to a discussion of the current place of teenagers in society and how this has evolved since 1945. This might involve an examination of rights and responsibilities and the relationship between the two. It also involves looking at the role of the law in defining these.

- *Differentiation.* The pupils could trace a range of themes of relevance and significance to young people over which decisions are made which directly affect them such as the age of drinking in public houses, or the age at which they can learn to drive. Irrespective of the pupils' ability, and given that decisions of this nature are not made on the basis of educational or social aptitude when it comes to legislation, it should be possible to devise tasks which require different levels of analysis but which involve all ability groups. This could be achieved through oral history such as examining people's recollections of the past, or by including a selection of multimedia broadcasts, such as television documentaries of which there are many.

- Therefore, assessment can arise through the level of questioning and understanding expected rather than through different tasks being undertaken. In other words, all pupils could take part and express an opinion, just as all citizens have the right to formulate their views through the electoral system.

Cultural aspects

History opens the door to the cultural inheritance of the past. Indeed it has been stated that teaching history can encourage 'a lifelong curiosity of the past which is also likely to increase individuals' sense of involvement and heritage ... The use of objects, archives and buildings is important if pupils are to gain a feel for, and a sense of, the past and make links with it' (SCAA 1997, pp. 39–40). There are a range of historical venues, theme parks and events which are now available to explore and experience around the country. These can vary enormously in terms of their usefulness for practical teaching purposes. Many of the English Heritage sites are particularly useful and appealing due to their educational focus, for example the home of Queen Victoria at Osborne House on the Isle of Wight, Kenilworth Castle in Warwickshire, and Riveaux Abbey in North Yorkshire. There are many places dedicated to particular aspects of cultural history such as the museum dedicated to packaging and advertising at Gloucester, or the Ashmolean Museum in Oxford.

There is a danger that certain venues offer a stereotypical view of an imagined past in which cultural differences are obscured or ignored. Given careful selection of material history can seek to enhance an understanding of aspects of the past through an examination of the architecture, art and music of the time, thereby broadening a pupil's vision of the interests and experiences of those who lived then. There is a danger of imposing a set of middle-class cultural values as the norm, or the most accepted way, of appreciating cultural questions or diversity. It has, though, rightly been claimed, that the role of schools is to, 'have a responsibility to extend cultural horizons beyond the immediate and the local to, for example, the highest artistic, musical and literary achievements of human beings' (OFSTED 1994, p. 17).

Obviously there are a range of different cultures that can be studied over time and at certain points these have come into collision such as over the Crusades, the spread of European Empires, and the move west of American settlers. Therefore there is a need to broaden the study of culture beyond Britain to look at the diversity of European and non-European societies. This was reflected in the views of the Curriculum, Culture and Society Conference of 1996, where it was stated that pupils, 'should understand the ways in which British culture and traditions have been shaped by the classical and Christian heritages, and also by the pluralism and diversity which have always been a part of British society' (SCAA 1997, p. 4). At Key Stage 1 teachers explore individuals such as Mary Seacole and their cultural influences. At Key Stage 2 pupils often examine topics such as the Ancient Greeks and Egyptians, while at Key Stage 3 and at GCSE the study of European history becomes more of a focus and the impact of events such as the French and Russian Revolutions, with all their cultural overtones and influences, can be examined.

The debate over the Millennium Dome and what both it and its contents are supposed to represent and say about the culture of Britain today, was raised over the Great Exhibition of 1851 and the Festival of Britain of 1951. Therefore, if culture is about a sense of identity and what that means, children need to be exposed to a questioning and challenging discussion, not a dictated, deterministic and rigid cultural edifice in which opinions and arguments have been nullified. Pupils and students should have the opportunity to accept or reject cultural norms and expectations based on what they have seen, heard or experienced of the past. In essence, a lively debate over cultural meaning, interpretation and difference through history is an enlightening and enhancing process which in itself can give enrichment to an understanding of culture as part of the wider value of a liberal arts-based education.

Conclusion

There is much overlap between the categories. In history there can be a danger of seeing spiritual and moral as always one category for debate, with social and cultural as another. In fact each strand can be seen as complementary. History can enhance the profile of these issues and give meaning and context to the discussions. Ultimately the emphasis in any approach the teacher undertakes and the nature of its delivery will depend on their aptitudes, interests and expertise. History can provide a forum for a meaningful discussion to take place and at times an exciting and positive exchange of views can be generated.

History should not be used as a vehicle to enforce a specific set of explicit values, however worthy they are felt to be, or to favour a particular viewpoint. Rather history should enhance a reasoned and humane approach to sensitive issues, almost all of which are the result of a set of historical processes. Therefore, it is not the role of the history teacher alone to set values but rather to work with colleagues, coordinators, parents and support staff to have a clear view of history as an informative channel, from which values of understanding and tolerance, along with a rejection of bigotry, can flourish.

References.

DfE (1995) *History in the National Curriculum.* London: HMSO.

NCC (1993) *Spiritual and Moral Development: A discussion paper.* London: National Curriculum Council.

OFSTED (1994) *Spiritual, Moral, Social and Cultural Development: A discussion paper.* London: HMSO

SCAA (1997) *Curriculum, Culture and Society Conference Report.* London: School Curriculum and Assessment Authority.

Further reading

Hoodless, P. (ed.) (1998) *History and English in the Primary School: Exploiting the Links.* London: Routledge.
The close relationship between these subjects and the way values can be articulated through differing approaches makes this a useful book for contemplating practical approaches to subject teaching.

Edwards, J. and Fogelman, K. (1993) *Developing Citizenship in the Curriculum.* London: David Fulton Publishers.
It is important to link History with citizenship education both to provide a background for modern citizenship, and to provide a tool for interpreting the past.

Watts, R. and Grosvenor, I. (eds) (1995) *Crossing the Key Stages of History: Effective History Teaching 5–16 and Beyond.* London: David Fulton Publishers.
A number of chapters discuss issues related to values and the book gives an overview of the place of history in the curriculum as a whole.

Chapter 12

Music

Peter Stead

Although the National Curriculum orders are specific about the areas of musical skill and understanding to be covered (DES 1991, DfE 1995), there is considerable scope for teachers to follow their own interests and enthusiasms in its delivery. The orders require that the repertoire chosen for performing and listening should extend pupils' musical experience and should be drawn from a wide variety of types and styles of music, although the choice of styles is left to the teacher. Emphasis is placed on teaching music as a practical and creative subject, allowing pupils to learn through direct experience of music by composing and performing. The orders require that pupils learn to explore, select, combine, organise and refine sounds to create musical ideas using notations and IT as a support, but there is no requirement to concentrate specifically on the study of musical theory or traditional staff notation. The National Curriculum offers all pupils, whatever their level of musical or academic ability, the opportunity to be involved in practical and creative music-making in order to develop the aural and coordination skills necessary to express themselves musically, and the knowledge and experience to allow them to develop their appreciation of the richness of the diverse cultural heritages of the world.

As an expressive art which is almost always enjoyed in a social context, the practice of music offers unique opportunities for the development of self-expression, social skills and cultural awareness, and there is an implicit recognition in the National Curriculum of the value of music in developing these skills and understandings. Concentration, perseverance and cooperation are fundamental to the successful performance of music. Involvement in a musical performance requires discipline, commitment and reliability and, as anyone who has attended a successful school performance knows from the delight on the faces of the pupils, performing music brings its own powerful reward.

Music is a useful educational tool with pupils of all abilities. It is valuable in its use as a therapy to aid the physically or mentally handicapped and as an activity to extend the most able pupils. As a fundamental vehicle for human expression, it could hardly be otherwise. In almost all schools, music forms an important part of the extended provision for pupils with particular interests or abilities, and school orchestras, bands, choirs or recorder groups provide enjoyment and fulfilment for participants, and pleasure for audiences. These activities also provide an important means of reinforcing the identity of a school as well as developing the self-esteem of the individual performers. Within curriculum time, activities should be accessible to pupils of all abilities, and each pupil should have the opportunity to perform, compose or respond to music at his or her own level. In a class performance, differentiated parts should be available for pupils of differing abilities. In a composing project or in responding to music, the differentiation will be by outcome.

Spiritual aspects

Music has traditionally formed a large part of most activities which we would associate with the human search for, and exploration of, spirituality. We are familiar with its use in worship, in school assemblies and in other forms of religious expression. Music has been used as a means of heightening sensitivity and spiritual awareness in most cultures and throughout all times in human history. Music is universally used to provide a calm environment for reflection, excitement for praise, and to move us deeply at the significant moments of our lives. It would be an unusual wedding, funeral or state occasion in any culture which did not make some use of music. Music is also used in some parts of the world as a means of transcending the mundane, of going beyond emotional states into trance or altered states of mind. Quite apart from any religious connotations, practical and creative involvement in music provides a means of self-expression at the deepest level. It offers opportunities for the development of self-esteem and self-worth through personal expression and involvement in social activities. The human ability to be creative, to rework the environment in the imagination, is an important means of coming to terms with, and learning to understand, our inner world of feelings and emotions. Macquarrie (1992, p. 40) believes that the more people go out from themselves or go beyond themselves, the more the spiritual dimension of life is deepened, and the more they become truly human. Music, the least tangible of the arts, is an ideal medium for that expression, that 'reaching out'. Whether as listener or performer, involvement in music is, by common consent, a life-enhancing activity, and is a powerful way of enhancing that which makes us meaningful beings. At crucial moments in our lives, whether they are times of crisis or at a football match, it is to song, to music, that people turn to lift their spirits or to move or inspire them. It is clear that through music people find a vital expression of their feelings.

Education concerns itself mostly with learning about the physical world which surrounds us, but we all have an inner world of feeling and emotions which we also need to explore, understand and come to terms with. Creative activity in the arts may be seen as a process of exploring this inner world, and music offers unique opportunities for this exploration. Because music is abstract, and because it can mirror so closely our 'feelingful' world, it carries a unique form of meaning for us. It is this meaning which sheds light upon that which animates us, that which makes us human in the fullest sense of the word. For music to be meaningful to pupils, it has to become part of their own experience by experiencing it directly, practically and creatively. This they may do through the central musical activities of listening, performing and composing. As teachers and educators, we can provide opportunities for pupils to develop those areas of understanding which will enable them to gain the maximum personal benefit from involvement in music. It is a measure of the importance that has been attached to music over the ages that it has always played an important part in education.

Listening lies at the heart of all musical activity, and the development of listening skills is central in the classroom. We live in a society in which we are surrounded by music, and music is accepted as part of the general background noise of life. Through music education we can open pupils' ears, teach them to listen attentively, and show them something of the power and effect that music may have. Through focused listening, pupils may come to an understanding of the power upon their minds and feelings of those patterns of sound which we call music, and learn something of the ways in which music may be used to manipulate their state of mind. It is generally accepted that pupils will come to a better understanding of the power of music if they are allowed to work with the raw materials of music, to express themselves in sound through playing, singing and composing. Engaging in these activities is an important way in which we may reach out and communicate something of our inner feelingful selves to the wider world, and a way in which we can find personal fulfilment.

In music lessons, pupils have opportunities to take part and express themselves at their own level of ability, and to derive personal satisfaction and fulfilment from music, however small their role may be. A pupil may derive the same excitement from a single triangle stroke as another may gain from playing a complicated piece of the traditional piano repertoire. Each is important in its own way, each allows access to the satisfaction and fulfilment of musical performance, and each allows individual access to the excitement of self-expression through sound. Recognising this power of music and working with its effect sheds light on our experiences and insights into our human condition. The Indian musician, Ravi Shankar, puts it this way: 'It is like feeling God...the miracle of the music is in the beautiful rapport that occurs when a deeply spiritual performer performs for a receptive group of listeners' (Shankar 1969, p. 57). As teachers of music, our aims will be to develop insight through the application of creative thought, to enhance self-knowledge and understanding and, ultimately, to reset values through this most potent form of human expression and communication. In the classroom this may come about by giving pupils opportunities to explore and experiment with sounds – the basic materials of music – through performing and composing. Understanding is built by direct experience of, and practical involvement with, the music itself. If, fundamentally, spirituality has to do with becoming a person in the fullest sense, then building an understanding and love of music is a unique education of the spirit.

Moral aspects

In exploring the question of musical values, the composer Hindemith draws on Augustine's notion that moral power is generated from active mental participation in and with music (Plummeridge 1991, p. 18). This leads Hindemith (1952) to conclude that the eternal and lasting values in music are not to be found in the musical works themselves, but rather in that form of mental activity which converts sounds or acoustic effects into meaningful structures. In performing or composing music, whether through learning a traditional instrument or taking part in group or class musical activities, practical and creative involvement in music offers opportunities to develop positive moral qualities. These qualities are intrinsic to all musical activity and may be a reason why learning music has always been considered such a valuable part of education.

Preparing a performance of a piece of music is a process which requires commitment, concentration and dedication on the part of the performer. Its success depends to a large extent on the amount of effort and application invested by the player. In the case of a solo performance this may mean many hours of solitary practice working towards a goal. The effort requires sustained concentration and perseverance to overcome the frustrations and difficulties of mastering technique. The problems are overcome through diligence and hard work and the reward is fulfilment through successful performance. In the early stages of learning an instrument the goals are set by the teacher, but as skill and commitment develops, the goals are increasingly set by the student. Learning to play a musical instrument and to rehearse music effectively requires the development of self-discipline, an ability to set one's own goals and sustained attention to a task.

Taking part in group music making such as singing in a choir or playing in an orchestra offers other opportunities for reinforcing positive values. Playing or singing in any group develops a sense of purpose, a commitment to the endeavour, and a sense of responsibility towards fellow performers. It means attending rehearsals reliably, accepting responsibility for your role by doing whatever preparation is necessary, and finally being able to perform the piece as it is intended. A performance is only as good as the weakest member of the group, and a commitment is required of everyone to perform at their highest level of ability. These are values which we would broadly define as positive, and they are moral and social skills and understanding which are well developed through involvement in music. The role of the individual is vital in group music making because performing music is always a very personal expression, but that personal expression must always be secondary to the needs of the whole performance. In this sense, performing music is a reconciliation of individualism and communalism. It is a clear parallel with an individual's role in society.

In return for an investment of time, dedication and commitment to working towards a goal, music offers a very powerful reward. That reward comes through success in performance, the positive feeling of having taken part in a successful mutual endeavour and the excitement and fulfilment which are gained from expressing oneself in sound. It may be achieved in a solo performance, but it will be further enhanced where the music making is a social or group activity. Because of music's ability to move and inspire us, the rewards of such efforts can be very great indeed. In the classroom the reward may come in a simple way from, for example, a group of pupils maintaining a steady beat on drums, varying the loudness to create moments of excitement. In the concert hall, the reward may come from a successful choral or orchestral performance. Although the end result of a formal concert may be more sophisticated, the careful preparation and rehearsal are the same process wherever they take place.

Whilst nowadays we may argue as to whether or not music has any intrinsic moral values, there can be no doubt that it has been used down the ages as a force to inculcate or impose moral beliefs. Fletcher (1987, p. 18) points to Wesley and Whitfield's use of the hymn as a means of 'rousing the masses of English and Welsh workers to a concern with heaven and hell'. With the advent of education for all during the nineteenth century, music was seen not as a moral force in its own right, but as a vehicle for Christian evangelism. The fact that music can so easily be used to rouse our emotions and to lift our spirits has been used for both good and evil. Music acquires 'moral' qualities on the basis of its association with extra musical factors – words, actions of individuals, association with a story and so on. The music of a rock group whose actions are judged immoral by society would not nowadays be said to be intrinsically immoral. Nevertheless, it would be naive to suggest that music does not have an effect on the behaviour of those who listen to it, even if that effect is only by association. In this sense, music may condition moral behaviour even if it is itself morally neutral. In the early middle ages, European culture nurtured a 'love of art' on the basis that beauty leads to goodness and truth (Fletcher 1987, p. 112). Although it has been fashionable to deride such ideas, contemporary evidence has emerged to show that listening to certain types of music can at least modify behaviour. Music in contemporary society is used to manipulate us to believe certain things, even to buy certain products. We have a responsibility to help our pupils towards an understanding of this power of music to affect our lives.

In a broader context, music may be seen as a moral force because it is the purpose of the artist to reflect something of the values of the time. Because of the abstract nature of music, the links between social morals and the output of contemporary composers are not always obvious, but where they are they strike a powerful chord. Whether it is the music of the blues illuminating the plight of the Negro slaves in America, the grandiose works of Elgar reflecting the moral confidence of the British Empire at its height or the exuberance of the youthful culture of rock and roll in the fifties and sixties, music gives insights into the attitudes and morals of our society. The true value of art or music lies not in its capacity to entertain us or to add that little cultural gloss to our lives, but rather in the way in which *through active involvement with it* we gain insight into what Langer (1957) has called 'the central facts of our sentient existence' (cited in Paynter 1982, p. 135). In this way, music touches and moves us deeply and because of this it has the capacity to shape or change values at the deepest level.

Social aspects

Participation in music offers unique opportunities to develop social skills ranging from basic sharing and turn-taking to the sophisticated social interaction needed to perform a piece as a member of a group. Every group of performers, whether classroom ensemble or full orchestra, needs sophisticated social rules in order to work successfully. In group music-making activities in the classroom, questions prompted by the teacher may be: Can we agree which instruments to choose? Do we need a leader to direct this piece? How are we going to start all at the same time? Can we listen to each other and stay in time or in rhythm in our performance? How do we know when to stop? What happens if someone in our group disagrees with the rest? Can we negotiate to a successful conclusion both socially and musically? In the classroom, whether in singing, performing or composing in a group, cooperation is vital to success. Music generates a common commitment to the success of the venture (Plummeridge 1991, p. 117) and it is the success generated by this common commitment which provides an ideal motivation for cooperation.

In any musical performance, each player or singer must make his or her personal contribution to the performance whilst at the same time taking into account the greater needs of the whole. In this sense, group music-making is a microcosm of an individual's role in society. Any performance of music only 'works' if the whole class is committed to its success, conscious of the need to listen carefully and respect the contribution of other members of the class, and work together to achieve a successful result. In these respects music makes considerable demands on pupils' abilities to concentrate and cooperate.

Listening is the basis of all musical skill, and listening in itself demands sensitivity to the needs of others. All musical activities in the classroom are designed to enhance the skill of discriminating listening in one way or another, and all musical skills require an awareness and appreciation of the contribution of the other members of the performing group or audience. At their most basic, these skills involve an appreciation of the need to perform at the correct time, at the correct volume and at the right speed. Social skills are also literally and metaphorically about listening – listening to the needs of others and responding sympathetically to them. In a music lesson there are opportunities to focus upon these fundamental skills of social interaction and develop the understanding necessary to live and work together in harmony. Although musical games and activities in the classroom are designed primarily to develop auditory discrimination skills, their success depends on social skills as well as musical ones and they provide an ideal medium for their development within an activity which is intrinsically enjoyable and motivating.

Self-esteem is an important part of relating well to other people, and music offers excellent opportunities to build and develop self-esteem. Everyone loves to be applauded, to be the centre of attention and to feel that by their efforts they have brought pleasure into the lives of others. These are powerful tools which teachers use to develop self-esteem in many contexts, but which are particularly easy to use in music lessons and performances.

Recent research evidence confirms the benefit of practical and creative music lessons to the development of social skills. In a two-year Swiss experiment 'Music Makes the School' (Weber *et al.* 1993), the improvement in social abilities in classes taking extended music lessons compared with control classes was particularly clear. The researchers attribute this improvement to the need to listen and cooperate. It was also found that classes receiving extra music lessons were closer, and fewer pupils were rejected or disliked by the others. The results are echoed in a US study (Gardiner *et al.* 1996, p. 381) which shows that classroom attitudes and behaviour ratings improved substantially in classes which had increased levels of music provision by comparison with a control group. Practical music making in the classroom (Mills 1991) provides an ideal medium to show the benefit derived from turn-taking, sharing, cooperating and responding to the needs of others. It provides opportunities for pupils to build self-esteem through controlling their environment, and developing listening skills necessary for good social interaction.

Cultural aspects

The arts form one of the major ways of expressing our cultural identity and defining who we are. They are symbolic modes of thinking and understanding which express the human condition in a unique manner. The arts in general, and music in particular, provide us with insights into the ways in which people think, feel and express themselves. Whilst this would be important in any context, it is especially important in the multicultural society in which we live. Swanwick (1979, 1988) gives a psychological reason why music is such a powerful expression of group culture: 'Musical expressiveness is a form of imitation when we take on and to some extent become like someone or something other than ourselves; it is the point at which music touches "real life", the world outside of itself' (Swanwick 1988, p. 99). Involvement in music is an important means of enculturation, of developing the common ground which enables us to feel a part of our own society. From nursery rhymes to pop music, from hymnody to classical symphony, our music plays an important part in defining us both as individuals and as a society. Singing is an important means of enculturation (Dowling and Harwood

1986). Music also helps us to a better understanding of cultures other than our own and provides us with a point of entry to explore the wonders of a wider world. Music has always developed, progressed and evolved through the interaction of one culture with another. New and exciting forms of self-expression spring from the combination of the sounds of different cultures. Although Fletcher (1987) speaks disparagingly of the 'watering down' of cultures in this way, all musical cultures have evolved through mutual interaction.

Simply requiring pupils to listen to music which they find difficult or unfamiliar is not likely to be the best way to bring about tolerance and understanding. A music which is unfamiliar is likely only to reinforce prejudice, and for many pupils, the classical music of Western culture is likely to sound as difficult to listen to as the music of other more obviously 'foreign' cultures. Education can reduce prejudice and create tolerance and understanding but, in order for music to do so, we need to give pupils aural discrimination skills and the opportunity to rework sounds in their imagination so that they can make the music their own.

The National Curriculum requires that pupils should be introduced to music from contrasting traditions, but if we are to help pupils to come to a genuine understanding of any music, it will have to be through their own direct experience of working with the elements of music, elements which are relatively independent of cultural ownership and which are accessible to all pupils. All musics have common processes at their roots – the common elements of pitch, duration, dynamics, rhythm, timbre, texture and structure. These can be found in music from all cultures. It is also generally felt that musical meaning is sufficiently abstract to travel across cultural boundaries (Swanwick 1988, p. 101). To take a specific example, the idea of 'ostinato' (a repeating pattern of notes or rhythms) may form the basis of a musical topic. Ostinato may be found in all forms of music. It may be explored in calypso, African drumming, Indonesian Gamelan, the music of Bach, 12 bar blues and contemporary popular music. The pupil is encouraged to listen for the musical procedure, but, in doing so, has an opportunity to appreciate the unique expressive character of the music and to hear how, even with music which may sound very unfamiliar, the same procedures are at work. The key to understanding is then to incorporate the idea of ostinato into the pupils' own creative activities. In this way, either by performing music which includes ostinati, or by composing using ostinato as a procedure, the process becomes integrated into the pupil's own creative imagination.

By working with the common elements and encouraging pupils to develop creative imaginations to deal with those elements, we may realistically hope and expect that they will come to a fuller understanding of their own cultural heritage and have some tools with which they may better understand the heritage of others. Our primary aim is to develop skill and understanding in music, but, in doing so, we may realistically expect that we may also promote a point of access, a common ground between cultures which will allow us to enhance tolerance and cultural understanding.

Music education offers many exciting opportunities to work from the familiar to the unfamiliar and build understanding in this way. The patterns of the Indonesian gamelan or sophisticated rhythms of African or Indian drumming work very well on classroom instruments and offer a delightful opportunity to explore not only other worlds of sound, but also some of the wonders of other cultures. Styles and instruments may be, as they always have been, mixed and matched to powerful effect. African and European elements were fused to create the music of the Afro-American slaves which in turn formed the basis of blues, reggae, jazz and rock styles. In schools today you may hear Western classical melodies hammered out on steel drums, or a fusion of African, Celtic and rock styles. This transformation of musical material allows a genuine and unique interaction of different cultures and a breaking down of barriers. The ultimate goal is personal and social transformation; music-making must be used to enhance personal consciousness and experience in community (Blacking 1987, p. 131).

References and further reading

Blacking, J. (1987) *A Commonsense View of all Music*. Cambridge: Cambridge University Press.

DES (1991) *Music for Ages 5–14*. London: HMSO.

DfE (1995) *Music in the National Curriculum*. London: HMSO.

Dowling, W. and Harwood, D. (1986) *Music Cognition*. San Diego, Calif: Academic Press.

Fletcher, P. (1987) *Education and Music*. New York: Oxford University Press.

Floyd, M. (ed.) (1996) *World Musics in Education*. London: Scolar.

Gardiner, M. F., Shaw, G. L., Levine, L. J., Ky, K. N. and Wright, E. L. (1994) *Music and the spatial task performance: a causal relationship*. Paper presented at the meeting of the American Psychological Association, Los Angeles, California.

Hindemith, P. (1952) *A Composer's World*. Boston, Mass.: Harvard University Press.

Langer, S. (1957) *Philosophy in a New Key*, 3rd edn. Boston: Harvard University Press.

Macquarrie, J. (1992) *Paths in Spirituality*, 2nd edn. London: SCM Press.

Mills, J. (1991) *Music in the Primary School*. Cambridge: Cambridge University Press.

Paynter, J. (1982) *Music in the Secondary School Curriculum*. Cambridge: Cambridge University Press.

Plummeridge, C. (1991) *Music Education in Theory and Practice*. London: Falmer Press.

Shankar, R. (1969) *My Music, My Life*. London: Jonathan Cape.

Swanwick, K. (1979) *A Basis for Music Education*. London: NFER Nelson.

Swanwick, K. (1988) *Music, Mind and Education*. London: Routledge

Weber, E. W., Spychiger, M., Patry, J-L. (1993) Unpublished paper presented at the economic summit of the National Association of Music Merchants, Newport Beach, California.

Chapter 13

Art

Jackie Chapman

Art, a compulsory Foundation subject, is an important component of the curriculum recognised as providing a valuable foundation to a balanced and broadly based curriculum. Chris Smith, MP, as Secretary of State at the Department of Culture, Media and Sport, concluded his speech to the National Association of Head Teachers' conference in 1998 by saying 'time spent on the arts is not peripheral – it is absolutely fundamental to all that we are trying to achieve'. The Labour Party, in a document on the arts (1997), quoted John Ruskin in the preface: 'A person who everyday looks upon a beautiful picture...will soon become a transformed person – one born again.' OFSTED comment (1998, p. 3) that 'the most persuasive argument for an education in the arts (Art, Dance, Drama and Music) concerns the benefits of attainment in the arts for its own sake'. The arts are 'intrinsic components of human culture, heritage and creatively' which 'mirror the whole repertoire of human experience.' Furthermore, they 'give people opportunities to explore their feelings, and come into contact with the spiritual.'

All this might suggest that the arts should have substantial curriculum time; after all, half of our brain is dedicated to our creative side. However, the focus on literacy and numeracy is reducing art to a support role, drawing pictures or painting models, giving even fewer opportunities to explore the broader aspects of visual art. Art is no longer compulsory after Key Stage 3; fortunately, more than one third of Year 10 and 11 pupils currently take art or art and design as a GCSE subject (OFSTED 1998, p. 5).

Appreciating and evaluating others' work is intrinsic to the National Curriculum requirements. Working collaboratively in pairs or groups on projects such as murals or large sculptures, for example, is actively encouraged, and pupils review and evaluate their own and others' work frequently. Pupils can explore packaging, advertising, design, and the issues and values of consumerism. Many well known artists have explored this – recently, Andy Warhol, Roy Lichenstein, and Richard Hamilton.

Ken Robinson, Professor of Arts Education, University of Warwick, tells of a visit to a London school: he walked through the foyer past a beautiful bronze sculpture on a plinth and asked who had made this wonderful piece. The head teacher replied 'That was done by one of our less able pupils'. It is essential to consider the different needs of children *in art* – perhaps their motor skills, their degree of creativity, their ability to understand an abstract concept, their willingness to challenge themselves artistically and to plan differentiated tasks accordingly. For example, a pupil who can draw cartoons (and does so at every opportunity!) may need to practice observational drawing using tone (light and shade) or to adapt a 2D drawing to a 3D construction. Pupils who feel they are 'no good' at art (which usually means they think they cannot draw realistically) may need non-threatening art work to help boost confidence, such as painting with sponges, pattern-making, weaving, computer design and so on.

Spiritual aspects

There are close links between art and religion. We frequently describe art as 'sacred', 'religious' or 'spiritual' without always being sure what we mean. Yeomans (1998) defines sacred art as that which involves a degree of sanctity, bound up with tradition, devotion and acts of worship. Religious art occupies a more generic category embodying elements of narrative and didacticism, spiritual meaning and values; while spiritual art covers a much broader spectrum of human feeling not necessarily bound by any religious creed. Exploring further links, Carr (1995) said 'in a very significant sense religion and art speak a common language', since both are more likely to use the 'spiritual language' of symbols, myths, metaphors, parables and analogies. Art forms such as icons, calligraphy, sculpture, stained glass, mosaics, architecture and religious painting, may provide an important vehicle for developing an understanding of religious ideas, beliefs and concepts. At Westminster College, our students are given the following guidance:

> Children should be given time to experience stillness and silence – to reflect upon works of art – both their own and that of others. They should be encouraged to become more aware of themselves as individuals and be helped to express themselves through their work. They should be encouraged to recognise and wonder at the beauty of the natural world and at how artists have celebrated that beauty through their work. They should respond personally to art in creative and developmental ways.

The spiritual includes emotion, personality and personal commitment – all three often tied closely to modes of expression in art. In their discussion of the spiritual dimension of education, HMI suggested that 'dance, drama, music, art and literature witness to the element of mystery in human experience across the centuries and in every culture'. John Patten, in 1992, then Secretary of State for Education and Science, referred to the 'spiritual questions' raised by 'inspiring' passages of music or 'uplifting' works of art. The arts have a key part to play in making a connection between the temporal and the eternal, the finite and the infinite, the material world and the world of the soul.

If we understand art to be concerned with the striving for something beyond ourselves, the urge to create and express oneself, the drawing on inner resources, the exercise of the imagination and the expression of awe and wonder, then all of these belong to the domain of the human spirit. If by 'spiritual' we mean how meaningfully we view ourselves and our work and link this with self-realisation and self-esteem, then art is well suited to serve this purpose. Sadly many have been set back by insensitive art teaching in the past. The belief that 'I am no good at art' is reinforced by poor art teachers unable to give pupils the confidence to realise some artistic capability. Very few of us go on to earn a living by or even fill our leisure time with artistic pursuits; but inside us all is a creative streak, which manifests itself in various ways – the way we choose to decorate our homes, or the way we combine colours in the clothes we wear. We do not have to be practitioners, 'artists', in order to appreciate beauty and talent; neither do we have to be 'experts' in art theory to be able to appreciate these qualities in a piece of art, be it a painting, a sculpture, a piece of jewellery, a photograph or a weaving.

If art is the expression of the human spirit then through it – both in its creation and in its appreciation – we can express ourselves *and* make personal discoveries. A good starting point for children to explore the self and others is portraiture, and even very young children can be asked to create art which conveys something about themselves – their family, their friends, their hobbies and their interests. We can provide pupils with different magazine pictures and ask them make a photo montage which illustrates their lives, their hopes, their fears, their plans for the future. As they mature and master more skills, they can explore the use of icons both in religious and secular settings. Older children may use a similar technique to express their hopes and fears for a wider 'audience' – for society, for the future, and so on.

There is a wide range of works of art which explore human experience and response to life and death, far too many to list more than a few under some arbitrary categories (see Figure 13.1).

Mother and Child, Motherhood

The Cradle, Berthe Morisot, 19th c.
The First Born, Frederick Elwell, 19th/20th c.
The New Born, Georges de La Tour, *c*. 1650
Mother with Two Children, Egon Schiele, 1917, in Vienna
Maternity, Marc Chagall, 1913
Woman and Child on a Beach or *Hope*, Pablo Picasso, 1921

Marriage

The Marriage, William Hogarth, 1734
The Jewish Bride, Rembrandt, 1668
La Noce (*The Marriage*), Henri Rousseau, 1910
Arnolfini and his Bride, Jan van Eyck, 1434

Figure 13.1

Old Age

Grotesque Old Woman after Quentin Massys, 1520
Old Woman Reading, Rembrandt, 1655
Portrait of an Old Man, Filippino Lippi, 1485
The Stages of Life, Caspar David Friedrich, 1835

Death

Burial at Sea, J. M. W. Turner, 1842
The Dead Christ, Andrea Mantegna, 1480
The Death of St Francis, Giotto, c. 1320
The Angel of Death, Carlos Schwabe, 1900
Guernica, Pablo Picasso, 1937

The Emotions

Weeping Woman, Pablo Picasso, 1937
Pity, William Blake, *c.* 1795
Melencolia, Albrecht Durer, 1514
Alone, George Hicks, 1878
The Scream, Edvard Munch, 1893

Heaven and Hell

Garden of Eden, Adam and Eve and All Creation, Roelandt Savery, 1620
The Peaceable Kingdom, William Penn's Treaty with the Indians, Edward Hicks,
c. 1836
The Last Judgement, Hieronymous Bosch, *c.*1470

War and Conflict

The Death of Major Pierson, John Singleton Copley, 1783
The Battle of Aljubarrota in Spain, Jean de Wavrin, mid 15th c.
Battle between Persia and Turan, Anonymous Provincial Mughal Artist, mid 17th c.
The Execution of the Emperor Maximilian, Edouard Manet, 1867
Tube Shelter, Henry Moore, 1941
Whaam!, Roy Lichtenstein, 1963
Battle – the Cossacks, Wassily Kandinsky, 1910
Guernica, Pablo Picasso, 1937
The Fighting Temeraine, Joseph Turner, 1839
The Third of May 1808, Execution of the Revolutionaries, Goya, 1814

Figure 13.1 continued

Spiritual interpretations about the universe and life are depicted by artists from a variety of genres and cultures. Human potential and achievement through the ages has been depicted in monuments and portraits and religious festivals are amply represented in greetings cards and artefacts. It is important for children to investigate how change, development and recreation has been documented visually and to come to an understanding of the importance of tradition to a community through their crafts. Ideas of beauty, appreciation of colour, shape and texture are all represented in religious and spiritual ideas expressed in visual forms such as icons. Art is used as a means of expressing personal feeling, imagination and creative thought. Spiritual awareness of the human body, its beauty and potential can be seen in the sculptures of, for example, Michelangelo, Rodin, or controversially, Anthony Gormley. Writing about the spiritual dimension of primary art education, Halstead (1997, p. 105) cites a project from *The Arts 5–16: Practice and Innovation* (Arts in Schools Project Team) which is rich in potential. A Year 1 class explore touch and he comments: 'there is wonder at the melting of snowflakes and the shape and texture of shells; imagination and creativity are being developed through the various activities; the children are feeling, exploring, discovering, growing and developing their own individuality in the process, linking the sensuously immediate with the spiritually infinite'.

Moral aspects

To quote again from our guidelines for student teachers, children can be made aware of issues of right and wrong and other moral issues visualised in paintings and drawings. They need to develop an appreciation of living things and could, for example, study and make botanical drawings of plant and animal life. Tolerance can be learned through cooperation with others in group activities – large murals, sculptures. The issue of war and peace can be explored through images depicted by war artists such as Nash, Stanley Spencer and, latterly, photographers, such as those who worked in war zones. Particular attention can be paid to those images which in some way reflect attitudes to war and peace and perhaps strive to change those attitudes (examples could be taken from propaganda posters to John Lennon). An awareness of the use and misuse of Earth's resources and human responses can be raised by making recycling posters for example, and of human exploitation and inequality by studying 'social' artists such as William Hogarth, members of the Pre-Raphaelite Brotherhood or Gerald Scarfe. Figure 13.2 provides some suggestions of works of art a teacher might use.

Social aspects

A theme which can be explored by most age groups is that of *change*. One exciting vehicle for this is the making of banners – starting, perhaps with the traditional Trade Union banners (which could be brought up to date or modified) and moving on to making 'Banners for Change' – and particularly, with the more recent historic developments in Northern Ireland, 'Banners for Peace'. Similarly, there is an American tradition of making patchwork quilts which depict whole

---

General

The Rake's Progress, William Hogarth
Campbell's Soup Can 1, Andy Warhol, 1968
Close Cover Before Striking (Pepsi Cola), Andy Warhol, 1962
Modern Life Collage 1956 and *Modern Life Collage 1996*, Richard Hamilton

Charity

Pity, William Blake, *c.* 1795
Weeping Woman, Pablo Picasso, 1937
An Old Black Man, Andrew Wyeth, *c.* 1935
Feeding the Hungry Boys, Cornelis Buys, 1504
The Blind Hurdy-Gurdy Player, David Vinckboons, 1620
Cimon and Pero: Roman Charity, Theodore van Baburen, 1625

War, Conflict and Propaganda

Death of Wolfe at the Capture of Quebec, Benjamin West, 1771
Akbar's Forces Besieging Ranthanbhor Fort in 1568, Anonymous Mughal Artist 1600
Soldiers Armed with Nadcannon Besieging a Castle, Quinte Curse, *c.* 1468
The Cutting out of the French Corvette 'La Chevrette', Philippe de Loutherbourge, 1801
We are Making a New World, Paul Nash, 1918
Murals (various titles) at Sandham Memorial Chapel, Burghclere, Berkshire, Stanley Spencer, 1927–32
Merry-go-Round, Mark Gertler, 1916

Figure 13.2

family histories or describe communities. The school or local community would make an ideal subject for exploration of change.

Children should be given opportunities to work with others and to listen to their ideas. Activities can be undertaken in groups, sharing expertise and skills, in activities which require communication and interaction and those which relate to issues in society – for example, they could make posters or paintings about drug abuse or homelessness. One Key Stage 2 class I observed made model shelters ranging from tents to tree houses out of scrap material. Designs can be shared and technology used to aid them. Designs can be put to practical use – e.g. making tactile pictures for the blind, designing a play area for handicapped children, making safety posters for areas of the school. Historic aspects of social change are well documented by artists. Wealth and poverty, medicine and care, children's welfare and the influence of the past on the development of society today can be seen through the art of the times. Local studies about the environment, homes and housing can be explored using visual images, as well as by designing new facilities for the community. Children should be encouraged to share their achievements through group presentations, assemblies and performances.

Cultural aspects

Some of us may be quite quick to describe other cultures with reference to stereotypical images such as 'exotic costumes' for 'Indian', or 'carved wooden animals' as 'African', but what actually *is* culture? Culture can indicate a particular way of life or a general process of development or a description of 'great' literature, music and art. Indeed, successive governments have maintained that the arts are, and should remain, central to our culture. One definition developed by Williams (1976) is 'a whole way of life, material, intellectual and spiritual'. Our ideas are largely shaped by the culture in which we live and no one develops in a cultural vacuum. We are surrounded by images of our culture and 'absorb' these images whether we are aware of it or not.

A study of the art of different cultures illustrates this. The development of children's drawing in Britain and America has been well documented by researchers such as Rhoda Kellog and Dr Maureen Cox and it is clear that it does so in quite discernible stages (which may or may not coincide with chronological age). A standard 'test' is to ask children to draw a human figure – a popular choice of subject for most children anyway. One of the earliest representations children make of the human figure (Cox 1997, p. 4) is the 'sun' or 'tadpole' figure where, if there are any limbs at all, they are attached directly to the head. These figures appear frequently between the ages of about two to five years. Gradually, the form develops, adding more and more 'correct' details. This pattern of development is extremely common – most children will 'visit' each of the stages for a varying length of time; occasionally a stage or two will be missed out altogether, or revisited at a later time. Western children draw the human figure as one of the first representations of the world they see around them, but we must not assume that this practice is common in all cultures universally. In some African countries, for example, drawing the cattle which represent the family wealth is more important than drawing people; in other areas, 'pin head' people are drawn with little or no facial detail. Australian Aboriginal children (and adults) represent figures by a simple U-shape. However, it is just as likely to find the familiar 'tadpole' figures in their drawings as they will pick up images from cultures around them just as easily. In some traditional cultures, in which adults produce formal designs but no representational art work, the children may likewise create patterns but no representational pictorial forms. For example, a study in Bali (Belo 1955) showed that when drawing the human figure, the children adopted the style of the figures in shadow puppet plays popular in that culture. So, art is embedded in a culture, but 'culture' is far more – a way of life. Belonging to one's own culture may not be learned so much as assimilated. 'The concept of a widespread, informed participation in creative art-making by the mature population is missing in Western societies; and there is thus an unavoidable temptation to annex as examples those societies in which it is present. This is why Western early learning and the art of so-called "primitive" societies are still theoretically linked, even when many of the original premises have been discredited' (Thistlewood 1986, p. 8). Thistlewood went on to describe encouraging 'universal' principles detected in child art and the art of 'primitive' societies.

The concept of art as being a product of the culture in which it is developed is an important one for children to acquire. But it is equally important for children to learn that one is no 'better' or 'worse' than another – comparisons between Western and non-Western are irrelevant. Far more important to realise the *influence* non-Western art has had on our own culture. One only has to explore the sources of designs in fashion/architecture or interior design so see this influence so clearly. But the teacher must beware of tokenism – and even worse, of patronising the art of other cultures by awarding it a degree of exoticness or labelling it 'primitive'. It is important also to establish progression from infant level to Key Stage 4 and beyond in terms of understanding and criteria used to study the art of other cultures. There needs to be a growth in aesthetic sensitivity. A major aim of art education in this context is to help children achieve their full potential for response to art work, both emotionally and intellectually.

One of the broadest changes in culture is the recognition of the coexistence of different cultures – *not* just ethnic or racial, but also gender and class based, or 'mass culture', 'high art' and 'popular culture'. We are becoming increasingly aware of, sensitive to, and tolerant about the difference between individuals within society.

If we truly want to provide an arts education which is related to the society outside it, we must proceed on as broad and differentiated a series of fronts as possible. Making art is at least partly about the constant process of redefinition and discovery. Pupils should be given access to a wide cultural variety of visual stimulus in all areas of the curriculum; they can be given the opportunity to meet, talk and work with artists of different ethnic backgrounds and encouraged to have a global perspective which positively appreciates the diversity and richness of artistic achievements of cultures worldwide and locally, using the cultural diversity which exists within their own school. Islamic geometric patterns, Indian rangoli designs and puppetry can be used to illustrate different techniques and materials. Art can be seen as an expression of culture – for example, Christmas, Divali, Eid or Jewish New Year cards which show religious pictures and artefacts from a variety of cultures.

The Art and Development Education 5–16 Project *Art as Social Action* described how specific artefacts could be used as bases for enquiry and activity. The objects chosen were an Oceanic mask, a Mexican head-dress and Henry Moore's 'Helmet' and examples of questions to elicit responses are listed. At the first stage, a descriptive response is elicited. Questions about the dimensions, weight, colour, texture and materials used included 'What words can be used to describe the objects?', 'What colour, tonal and textural ranges characterise the objects?' 'What levels of technical development are implicit in the objects?' The next stage of comparison follows, and questions about the function of the objects focused the response, for example; 'In what ways are the objects similar and in what ways are they different?', 'In what ways are the sources of imagery similar or different?', 'What effects has the use of different materials had on the form of the objects?' Only when children have made significant discoveries can they begin to analyse, interpret and evaluate the objects. During these stages, the questions included, 'Which colours in the objects are natural and which are applied?', 'Which shapes are repeated in each object?', 'What cultural symbols can be identified in the objects?'; 'What external references are imposed?', 'What cultural beliefs are projected?', 'Why do you think the objects were made?', 'What criteria can be employed to evaluate the objects?'. At some time in the process, practical work can be undertaken. Suggested activities included using similar materials to make a head or mask which evokes some particular feeling, or adopting similar styles of working using the same materials and techniques as in the objects, or using similar materials to work in a different style.

We might talk about the *functions* or motives for making art and in our society each of those functions have their parallel in other cultures. Children draw for reasons which also echo these functions. Paul Duncum (1993) suggested five such functions:

- The first is to *represent* the world around us and to *record* our place in it. We use pictures or other visual images to help us remember places, events, people – civic statues, or portraits of famous people. Pictures help us to make comparisons and to record a sequence of events. Children can be asked to make visual images for the same purpose – a pictorial record of a birthday party, the building of a new classroom, sports day. This method of helping children understand the world around them by recreating it is the process Piaget claimed to be the way children learn.

- The second function is that of *narration*. Drawing is a tool in art that many teachers have shied away from teaching, as they are not 'experts' themselves. Teaching children *about* drawing is as important as helping them to improve their skills. They need to understand the range of drawing styles – from Leonardo da Vinci to *The Beano*. The cartoon strip is a highly suitable style for children to practise narrative drawing. Amongst the resources you might use for this could be the following: *Human Locomotion*, Eadweard Muybridge, 1887, a series of photos; *Shuffle and Skip*, Dave Sowerby, Museum of the Moving Image; *Asterix and Son*, R. Goscinny and A. Edezzo, 1994. The children could then progress on to the idea of a single picture telling a story. For example,[1] in the fifteenth century, Antonio del Pollaiuolo painted *Apollo and Daphne*, depicting Daphne turning into a tree to prevent Apollo, the sun god from catching her. Similarly, in the sixteenth century, Captain Thomas Lee commissioned a portrait of himself without trousers or shoes to be sent to Queen Elizabeth 1 in order to plead for a reward for fighting so bravely for her.

- The third function is *embellishment*; that is, decoration, ornamentation, patterns and style. This can attempt to make acceptable the otherwise unacceptable –

weapons of war and destruction were often highly ornate, decorated with engravings, jewels, and carvings. Many examples can be seen in our museums and art galleries.

- The fourth function is *commitment* or *persuasion* to an idea or action. This might be said to cover everything from propaganda to television advertising.

- The fifth function is that of *personal expression* – a reason for making and teaching art which is often the very first to be identified by students and teachers when asked the question 'Why do we teach art?'

And finally...

We speak of our spirits being lifted by experiencing something beautiful – God's creation in nature, human creation in the arts. A work of art need not be ecclesiastic in content in order to do this – we may be deeply moved by Michelangelo's *Pieta* – in my own experience, moved to tears by its sheer presence – but equally moving or 'spirit raising' could be a painting by Picasso (*Guernica* springs instantly to mind) or by Jackson Pollock – or a sculpture by Andy Goldsworthy or by Barbara Hepworth – as spiritually uplifting as anything if you have the mind to see...

Practical resources

Elaine Baker (1992) *Art of Different Cultures*. Dunstable: Folens Primary Art Key Stage 1.
Activities using South America, China, Tibet, Egypt, Africa, Polynesia, North America and Australasia as sources of reference. Also Elaine Baker, *Art of Different Cultures*, Key Stage 1 Picture pack, Dunstable: Folens.

Robert Clements (1990) *The Art Teachers' Handbook*. Cheltenham: Stanley Thornes.
Two activities exploring self image: *Self as an object* leading to self-portraits; *Myself and Others*, drawing the pupils and their families from photographs, ranging from infancy to old age and exploring pre-photographic portraits.

Loeb, H., Slight, P. and Stanley, N. (1993) *Designs we Live By*. Corsham: NSEAD.
Designs from many cultures

Margaret Morgan *Art 4–11*. Oxford: Blackwell Education.
Describes four projects on weddings, old age, shelter and the church.

Sightlines, produced by Gloucestershire Education Authority Art and Design Inspection and Advisory Service:

- 'face decoration around the world' (multicultural, images of African tribal face decoration, Japanese Kabuki theatre, circus clowns, punks and hippies, theatrical make-up)

- 'the rainforests' (environmental) – textile-based

References

Belo, J. (1955) 'Balinese children's drawings', in Mead, M. and Wolfenstein, M. (eds) *Childhood in Contemporary Cultures*. Chicago: Chicago University Press.

Carr, D. (1995) 'Towards a distinctive conception of spiritual education', *Oxford Review of Education* **21**(1), 83–98.

Cox, M. (1997) *Drawings of People by the Under 5s*. London: Falmer Press.

Duncum, P. (1993) 'Children and the social functions of pictures', *Journal of Art and Design Education* **12**(2).

Halstead, Mark J. (1997) 'An approach to the spiritual dimension of primary arts education' in Holt, D. (ed.) *Primary Arts Education: Contemporary Issues*. London: Falmer Press.

OFSTED (1998) *The Arts Inspected*. London: Heinemann.

Thistlewood, T. (1986) 'Cultural significance of Art', *Journal of Art and Design Education* **5**(1).

Williams, R. (1976) *Keywords: A Vocabulary of Culture and Society*. Glasgow: Fontana.

Yeomans, R. in Starkings, D. (1998) (ed.) *Religion and the Arts in Education*. London: Hodder and Stoughton.

Note
[1] These two examples are used in *A Child's Book of Play in Art* selected by Lucy Micklethwait and published by Dorling Kindersley, London. The former painting can be seen in the National Gallery, the latter in the Tate, London.

Chapter 14

Physical Education

Jennifer Gray

The term Physical Education is vague and the reasons for its inclusion in the National Curriculum are complex. Schools and teachers place differing values on its inclusion. For many primary schools it is still seen as a time to 'let off steam', 'to get some fresh air' or 'to have a rest from academic subjects'. In this chapter I will use the term physical education (PE) to include all areas of physical activity that are included in the National Curriculum for Physical Education. These include games activities, gymnastics, dance, athletics, outdoor and adventurous activity, and swimming. In some schools, dance is placed within the expressive arts and not considered as a part of PE.

One could question whether PE should be a vehicle for the teaching of values or included in the National Curriculum for its intrinsic worth. Should its objectives be to keep fit? or recreational? Should development of values be an objective, an outcome or by-product? From whichever starting point one comes, it is hard to argue other than PE can play a crucial role in the personal and social development of the pupil and teachers must be aware of the crucial role they play in this process. It is not only possible to build personal and social self-worth, it is also possible to destroy it.

Physical activity has been part of education since primitive times. 'The primitive man's education was focused primarily on hunting and fishing. The strength, endurance, and skills requisite to the hunt were just as essential to the war campaign' (Hackensmith 1965, p. 4). Physical Education was, in these early times, not a form of recreation but an essential aspect of human survival. However, Smidt (cited in Hackensmith 1965, p. 5) argued that primitive man participated in games of survival and endurance activities and he states that 'it is often difficult to determine where primitive man's productive activity ended and his play began'. In these primitive times, the creation of life was expressed through religion which found expression in games, song and dance. So in its earliest forms, physical education was preparation for the skills and rigours of life; attitudes, values and religion were linked through the need to survive. In some schools this general philosophy has not changed, although the rigours of life have.

As early as 1861 when the Clarendon Commission reported on the management of Public Schools, the value of organised games was recognised as character building, but the commission gave little credence to gymnastics as it did not produce the 'desired qualities'. In contrast the elementary schools adopted Swedish gymnastics as the bedrock of their programme. 'Games', were seen as *character building*, whereas the elementary schools' system of physical training was seen as *discipline*. At the beginning of the twentieth century, the Public Schools which catered for the nobility and middle classes taught games where the emphasis was on building the *moral fibre* of boys and preparing them to take decisions in war and leadership, whereas the State schools introduced 'drill' to build the physical well being of the mass classes as well as building the ability to follow instructions. Many secondary schools followed the Public School tradition and organised their PE on the Spartan 'do good to you' principle. This attitude has changed but in some schools, remnants still persist. One can remember the cross country runs where the overweight class member suffered the indignity of always coming last, the clumsy pupil with coordination problems, the freezing cold days when it was 'good for you to go out in your shorts and tee shirt' and suffer from mild hypothermia, and the cold showers. PE often did very little to raise the pupil's self-esteem and taught them very little other than to dislike PE.

Spiritual aspects

PE offers an important opportunity for pupils' spirituality to be developed. Spirituality deals with contemplation about ourselves and our place in the cosmos, our responsibilities and the meaning we give to our lives and our experiences. It is the development of our inner self. PE, if only seen as recreation or keeping fit, misses out on these vital elements of physical development. Confidence and competence are linked; physical and emotional development go hand in hand.

If our PE programme tries to develop the pupil's confidence and competence, then pupils should be set (or set themselves) personal achievable targets to help them make personal progress. It is essential for them to develop their individual competence and not dampen their sense of achievement by always belittling them in the light of best performances. Records of attainment especially in measurable events such as swimming and athletics are often displayed on communal notice boards. For the able, these raise self-esteem, but for the pupil at the bottom of the list, they may destroy confidence and intrinsic pleasure in the activity. This is not to say that there will not be failure. Even the top performers sometimes feel they have failed, and they need to learn how to cope with this; but the teacher's role is to foster success, to develop a sense of personal achievement and to help the pupils recognise their own and their colleagues' strengths and weaknesses, and to learn to share in and celebrate others' successes. Not all pupils can be the best. They cannot all be a member of the school team, but they can find a sense of fulfilment by personal achievement. For the pupil who scores their first goal, who demonstrates their gymnastic sequence, who is praised in the dance lesson for an appropriate action, who is presented with their swimming certificate in assembly the feeling of self-satisfaction and self-worth are enhanced. It is through praise and celebration of a pupils' work that their self-confidence and self-esteem can be raised. At all stages of the National Curriculum pupils are encouraged to self and peer assess. For this to be constructive, pupils need to understand that their comments must be positive. They may be asked, for example, to look to see if the task has been achieved and to find one part that they liked. Teachers may need to assist this observation and focus their attention on specific elements. In the later Key Stages, pupils are also encouraged to look for elements which need development and to give feedback in a constructive manner. The pupil who has experienced success and failure in PE and coped with the emotions these raise, may well be able to cope more adequately with these in other aspects of their life.

Spirituality is also concerned with our place within the cosmos. Outdoor and adventurous activities allow the pupil to pit themselves against the elements, to experience the vulnerability of working in a hostile (albeit controlled) environment and gain the experience of venturing to remote, isolated terrain. Anyone who has sat on the top of a mountain cannot help but wonder in the enormity of the environment and realise what a tiny part they play in the scheme of life. For others, their choice might be walking, running, swimming, athletics or gymnastics, but still pushing themselves to their physical limits. In some cultures, spiritual ideas are expressed physically: Indian dance not only tells stories, but also celebrates cosmic energy and processes, such as the dance of Shiva celebrating creation and dissolution.

Moral aspects

Morality and physical education in particular competitive activities are inextricably linked although it has been argued (Bailey cited in Meakin 1981) 'that games cannot initiate people into morality but can only be played morally if morality is brought by players to the game having been learned in a wider context of a non-game kind'. Teachers should examine their own views, but in my view, the concept of morality can be learned and developed through the context of PE and in particular games. For, as Aspin (1986) argues, the rules of all major games are of a moral nature with the chief ones 'having to do with equality, freedom, honesty, respect for other persons and consideration of other people's interest'. If this is accepted, then the concepts of rules and fair play should be built into the curriculum at the earliest possible opportunity. The pupils need to appreciate that rules, whether in physical education, the classroom or life generally are there for a reason and that there are consequences for not adhering to these rules.

The teacher should offer the opportunity for the pupils to create and apply their own rules in appropriate circumstances. Games-making, where the pupils create their own games and consequently their own rules, offers an ideal opportunity for them to discover the importance of rules. The teacher can devise situations in which ideals and rules can be tested. The pupils soon realise that when an incident in the game occurs, they need a specific rule to deal with it. They also realise that the penalty needs to match the severity of the incident and be fair to both sides. Games-making also gives the pupils the opportunity to deal with the more complex skill of interpreting rules. Some rules, such as the play-on rule in football recognises that it is not fair if stopping the game for an infringement disadvantages the victim who might be close to scoring. Pupils might be encouraged to use a similar rule. Teachers may also give the pupils the opportunity to impose the rules themselves; to self referee. This gets them into the habit of recognising when rules have been infringed and to recognise the fairness of playing to the rules. They should also be encouraged to not argue with the referee or umpire and to take decisions in good faith, even when they consider these decisions to be unfair. When facing defeat, they should be encouraged to recognise their own limitations and not blame outside conditions, especially the officials. It is hoped that through participation in games, pupils will not only gain an awareness of fairness but also a respect for others and an ability to respect their point of view. There is a further step of developing informed opinions about rules, as rules themselves evolve in line with changing perceptions. Boxers no longer, unlike gladiators, fight to the death. Reflection and empathy are important stepping stones to moral autonomy. Adults obey rules not because they are rules but because they are right and fair, and they change rules that need changing on the basis of discussion and consensus. PE can thus be a window into the rules of personal and social morality. Discussions on cheating and drug taking are particularly appropriate. Morality in life is a balance between keeping rules and improving standards in ways which tend to lead to rules becoming updated.

It is essential that the pupils move from heteronomy (obeying external rules) to autonomy (keeping rules we set for ourselves), taking responsibility for their own behaviour. At Key Stage 1, decisions are made by the teacher. Meakin (1982) suggests that with young pupils teachers should develop a set of moral habits based on a content of moral rules that can be rationally defended. During this Key Stage, teachers start to develop moral skills which later can be explored in Games and PE. At Key Stage 2, games-making can be introduced to allow pupils to develop their own rules although it is essential that the pupils possess the required skills and 'moral habit' for the task set. At Key Stages 3 and 4, the skills element will be further developed, but the degree of pupil autonomy within the game will increase. The aim is to 'develop a high degree of moral autonomy based on reason' (Meakin 1982, p. 80).

Moral attitudes towards sport can be discussed from an early age. Pupils can be encouraged to look at the attitudes of their sporting idols, to discuss the morality of certain incidents and to discuss the current issues in sporting morality such as the use of drugs to enhance performance; and violence on and off the games field. What level of aggression is acceptable? When in sport does aggression become violence? Are different standards applied to different sports, so some become more violent than others? Other issues might be racism in sport, both by competitors and spectators; and the relative status of men's and women's sport. Is it fair that the sports pages of the national newspapers are dominated by male sporting activities, and that remuneration is therefore higher? Teachers can try to ensure that their programmes and teaching set good examples and encourage discussion.

Through participation in team activities, whether it be as part of a soccer or netball team or a member of a dance group, pupils can learn the importance of reliability, the need to be there and not 'let the team down' This responsibility may be to attend all sessions or to perform to the best of one's ability. It may involve being tolerant of the performance of other team members; accepting that anyone can miss the vital penalty or drop the relay batten. Such responsibility can be fostered at all levels. The pupil does not have to be a member of a school team to feel responsible for their actions. Curriculum PE is an excellent way of introducing and developing team or group work which fosters a sense of personal responsibility.

It is also necessary to include the moral aspects of being a good spectator; to be able to recognise the skill of another player or the brilliance of a goal being scored even if they are not from 'your' team. Any teacher who has officiated at an inter-school game will recognise that very often parents are not ideal spectators. On occasions, verbal abuse and even violence are experienced. It is important for pupils to recognise that officials are not all infallible, they do make mistakes. Pupils need to recognise that officials, spectators and players see the situation from a different position and therefore may have a different opinion on the decision to be taken. Such situations may be discussion points in post match analysis. Pupils should be encouraged to thank officials who have given up their time to allow them to have such a good game. A useful activity for pupils is to draw up a spectators' code of behaviour. Many schools have such codes in place, so an existing code could be a starting point for discussion.

For outdoor and adventurous activities pupils need behavioural guidelines based on respect for the environment. These should involve conservation of the immediate environment – 'to leave nothing but their footsteps and take nothing but their memories', but they should include more far-reaching moral concerns. Pupils should be encouraged to weigh up the consequences of their actions. Might they be putting themselves and others in danger? In an emergency, in order to rescue them, will others have to put their lives at risk? Will their actions cause mental anguish to others? Pupils should be asked to consider what constitutes an acceptable level of danger? Such a level of moral debate throughout the teaching of PE could make an important contribution to a pupil's overall moral thinking.

Social aspects

Most aspects of PE in school are social. The very nature of the activities encourage pupils to be social beings. At the early Key stages, pupils should be encouraged to work with partners, to share opportunities. Gymnastics and dance are times for cooperation and mutual support. During lessons, these activities are not usually competitive. There needs to be times for the pupils to develop their own skill and to perhaps work with a person with whom they have never worked. It might be a time for an able performer to work with a less able pupil. In such activities as games-making, it is the time for sharing ideas and communication that is important. Collaborative group work ideas can be learned and developed. In all areas of PE, problems may be solved in a variety of ways. There is rarely a right answer. Everybody's views can be valued and incorporated into the final 'performance'.

Social education is also concerned with respect for others. Activities which involve cooperation require others' views to be taken seriously. Cooperation games using parachutes or games such as 'skinning the snake', 'islands', 'tank track' are excellent ways of introducing social skills. These usually involve the pupils working in close proximity to each other or having to hold hands. Teachers may well recognise how the instruction 'now pupils, find a partner and hold hands' can lead to disastrous consequences in even the most organised lesson. By using fun activities where the pupils have to have close contact with their peers, these barriers may be broken down.

Through outdoor and adventurous activities, pupils continually develop their ability to work cooperatively and collaboratively. At Key Stage 2 this may involve the pupils participating in an adventure course away from the school site. The advantage of these opportunities is that the centres are staffed by people with specific expertise, who understand the inherent dangers these activities can pose and ensure the necessary safety precautions are in place. Exciting challenges can also be set up in the school environment: orienteering skills can be developed in the classroom, further developed in the playground and then tested in the local environment. Building rafts to cross the school swimming pool offers an opportunity to develop cooperation skills. At Key Stages 3 and 4, pupils can be given the opportunity to work on planning expeditions and through such activities recognise the need to be responsible for themselves and others. Involvement in such organisations as the Duke of Edinburgh's Award Scheme offers an opportunity for the older pupils to develop their leadership skills.

It has been argued by Lynch (1991) that removing pupils with social and behavioural difficulties from their problem environment can give them an opportunity to succeed. Teachers who have taken pupils into a different environment can see a different side of a pupil's personality. Teachers sometimes threaten to exclude disruptive pupils from such activity but unless such pupils offer a threat to the safety of themselves or others, they should if at all possible, be encouraged to participate. It might be that the perceived lack of formal discipline presented by the experience creates opportunities for mutual respect between teacher and pupil to be fostered. Such outdoor education programmes are used successfully by non-government organisations in the rehabilitation of young offenders.

Pupils who are educationally and behaviourally disturbed may also benefit from a programme of outdoor activities. Many of these pupils have little trust in their peers and in adults. They have often been in their view 'let down' by society and have failed to build relationships. Many outdoor activities require trust in one's own ability and also in others. To abseil down a wall or rock face requires trust in the person holding the rope. Once trust has been established it is hoped that it will continue to other activities. McGowan (1991, p. 26) states that 'the outdoor experience can facilitate major psychological and philosophical change so that life outlook and indeed life itself can be influenced'.

If teachers are truly aiming to build social development through their PE programme, then they should include curricular and extra-curricular activities which are attractive to all the pupils. I know of a school which has introduced a roller disco into curriculum time. You may question the validity of such an activity, but consider how much social development could be developed. There is also no doubt that participation in a particular physical activity can lead to lifelong friendships. To share in a common endeavour suggests a common interest. From this mutual start, diversity can be explored and enjoyed.

Cultural aspects

Cultural diversity can be seen in all aspects of sport. At the school level, there are schools which traditionally play football and those which play rugby. Creative dance was initially seen (and in many secondary schools still is) as an activity for girls; netball was only for girls and football and rugby only for boys. The inclusion of dance for all in the curriculum at Key Stages 1 and 2, and equality of opportunity has changed this, but the gender prejudice is still occasionally encountered.

Major sporting events such as the Olympic and Commonwealth Games and World Cups provide an opportunity for pupils to understand the tradition of such gatherings. They can learn to appreciate cultural diversity and similarity: viewing such events provides the opportunity to view traditional ritualism such as the All Blacks' *Ka Mate Haka*. The *Ka Mate Haka* dance has been performed by the New Zealand All Blacks team at the start of all representative games since 1888. Although resembling a war dance, it is performed without weapons and has been described by Armstrong (1964) as a 'composition played by many instruments. Hands, feet, legs, body, voice, tongue and eyes all play their part in blending together to convey in their fullness the challenge, welcome, exultation, defiance or contempt of the words'. From the study of this dance, pupils are able to learn a little of Maori culture and tradition. When basic ball-handling skills have been mastered, pupils may be introduced to games from other counties such as baseball, Australian Rules football and Gaelic football.

At Key Stage 4, the diversity in cultural attitudes (both current and historical), can be discussed. Postwar initiatives by the Eastern Block countries make an excellent starting point. Such initiatives include the now exposed performance-enhancing drug culture which was particularly prevalent in the German Democratic Republic. The testing and selection of potential talent at an early age and the pursuit of excellence at all costs, make stimulating debate. Current cultural diversity should also be examined. Many countries such as France, where in 1978 the Minister of Sport declared that there would be a change in emphasis from participation to winning, have changed their attitude to performance. The reasons for cultural diversity in achievement can also be discussed. Why do certain nations excel in certain activities? Such debate enhances understanding of cultural diversity and leads to greater acceptance of difference.

The inclusion of dances from different cultures and times including traditional dances from the British Isles allows the pupils to experience the formality of Tudor dance and the exuberance of Maypole dance. It is an opportunity to discover how dance has developed and in many examples is influenced by the geography of the area. Teachers should be careful to develop authentic movements and not follow stereotypical clichés. Dance as an expression of other cultures should also be introduced. There are exciting dance performance groups which can be used as a stimulus for a Programme of Work and introduce us to a wealth of cultural diversity. In schools where the pupils have a variety of cultural backgrounds, it may be possible to involve parents and other relatives in the teaching of dance (but we cannot assume that because a person comes from that country they will know anything of its dance forms). The involvement in dance festivals can not only introduce diversity of culture, but also provide an excellent opportunity to enhance home–school links.

PE includes a wide range of different physical activities, and teachers have different views about the broad objectives and priorities. Yet, we have seen that through PE, pupils can develop and enhance their attitudes, values and behaviour in ways which broaden their spiritual, moral, social and cultural understanding.

Appendix: Games which encourage cooperation

Although these activities are cooperative, competition between groups adds to the excitement.

Skin the snake
A group of at least 6 pupils lines up one behind the other and joins into a line by reaching backwards with one hand through their legs and hold one hand of the person immediately behind. Without breaking contact the back person comes under the legs and moves towards the front of the line. Each person in the group follows through until the back person comes to the front of the line.

Bench games
Each group of about 8 pupils line up on a bench. The floor around the bench is 'shark infested water'. The pupils have to rearrange their line according to the

instructions of the teacher. The aim is to rearrange the line without any part of the body falling into the water (i.e. tallest on right, shortest on left). The person with the largest hands on the right. The teacher can choose any criteria.

Hoops
The group join hands to make one large circle. Different coloured hoops are suspended on the arms. Use about 4 hoops. Without breaking the circle, the pupils have to make the hoops travel around the circle.

Tank tracks
6 to 8 pupils with 2 mats. The pupils start standing on one mat, with the other above their heads. By only travelling on the mats, the pupils must travel along the length of the gym.

References

Armstrong, A. (1964) *Maori Games and Haka*. London: Reed Books.

Aspin, D.N. (1986) 'On the nature and purposes of a sporting activity: the connection between sport, life and politics', *Physical Education Review* **9**(1), 5–13.

Hackensmith, C. W. (1965) *History of Physical Education*. London: Harper & Row.

Lynch, P. (1991) *Journal of Adventure Education and Outdoor Leadership* **8**(3), 27–31.

McGowan, M. L. (1991) 'Encounters with transcendence in Adventure Programmes', *Journal of Adventure Education and Outdoor Leadership* **7**(4), 25–28.

Meakin, D. C. (1981) 'Physical Education: an agency of moral education', *Journal of Philosophy of Education* **15**(2), 241–53.

Meakin, D. C. (1982) 'Moral Values and Physical Education', *Physical Education Review* **5**(1), 62–82.

Further reading

Chedzoy, S. (1996) *Physical Education for Teachers and Coordinators at Key Stages 1 and 2*. London: Falmer Press.

Chapter 15

Design and Technology
David Coates and Nick Rose

Values are an intrinsic part of Design and Technology because the nature of the subject deals with people's spiritual, moral, social and cultural needs and differences. 'What is needed for the future? What do people want? By what means could it be achieved and at what cost? How will what has been planned affect people, their environment now and in the future? Values and value judgements always emerge when striving for the best balance or proposing the most inclusive and potentially enhancing range of possibilities.' (Standen 1992, p. 83). These feelings are expressed through the design and manufacture of products that we are able to evaluate from around the world by designers with different agendas, resources and manufacturing capabilities.

Design and technology education is concerned with pupils designing and making quality products, reflecting what happens in the wider world. It provides excellent opportunities for pupils to apply value judgements of an aesthetic, economic, moral, social and technical nature in two contexts: when evaluating their own work; and when examining existing products and their applications, through, investigate, disassemble and evaluate, activities (NCC 1995). Through design and technology pupils can learn about the inter-relationship of the technical, scientific, environmental, aesthetic, economic, social and moral aspects of society in a practical manner. This is exemplified in the Midlands Examining Group GCSE syllabus for Design and Technology: Resistant Materials (1998): 'When pupils are required to identify and evaluate how existing products fulfil the needs of their intended users they will undertake a range of activities including: market surveys, existing product analysis, in relation to moral, social, economic, environmental and cultural factors' (Midlands Examining Group 1998, p. 10).

Technology is seen as essentially a human activity. Since our earliest times we have been using technology to solve problems, to meet our needs and wants. It has developed our capability to grow food, build shelters and travel from place to place at great speed, for example. It would be easy to limit our definition of technology to simple examination of the finished product in terms of technicality and cost effectiveness, but pupils need to explore decisions that influence what we design and make, which come from balancing these with aesthetic, environmental and moral criteria (DfEE 1995b). The restricted idea of technology by itself ignores the human dimension. 'We create things that we value, the things we think beautiful or useful. We devise tools, machines and systems to accomplish the ends we value' (Prime 1993, p. 30). Consideration of values has the power to soften some perceptions of technology. When pupils design and make products to solve problems they express their creativity, inventiveness, imaginations and sense of worth (that is, their spirituality), from which they develop products which meet precise specifications.

Values are central to 'quality' and 'purpose', and to the development of products in response to needs, desires or opportunities. These can be made explicit. What we design and make may have implications for developers and users, and there may be resource issues or side effects. Take the motor car. Is it a quality product? It clearly meets one purpose, to move people at speed, in comfort and safety. The design has been constantly improved over the years, in terms of speed, safety, reliability and economy. Most, however, use petrol which is manufactured from oil, a scarce resource. They produce pollution which has serious environmental and health effects. There is a potentially contradictory idea of the car as a 'quality product' which is 'fit for its purpose'. We weigh one value judgement against another in our decision to drive. The technology is not value free: value judgements are influenced by personal, social and cultural priorities. This balance between conflicting values can shape the community in which we live. An alternative view sees technology as increasingly pervasive with harmful impact at a natural and a social level. For example, medical technologies have reduced the death rates in developing countries, but have contributed to population growth. Progress has been viewed in technological terms, for example the development of labour-saving devices such as the microwave oven. Technology can be shaped by the values and beliefs of a community. There is more research now into less polluting electrical cars in response to environmental and social values which our society now has begun to more highly regard. Values in the technology must match those of its users. When they do not technological obsolescence occurs. An example of this would be the Sinclair C5 whose concept few people wanted.

School design and technology should be transformative and offer a critique of current values. It involves head, hand and heart. The heart comes through feelings and value judgements which should be considered alongside the cognitive (head) and the manipulative (hand) (Ritchie 1995). Value judgements about technological activities are a significant feature of debate in the real world and schools should reflect this. Pupils will be faced with value judgements of many kinds: what is worthwhile? what is feasible? what might the consequence be? There is never any 'right answer' to a design and technology problem. If technology is about fulfilling human needs, we must define and evaluate need. Needs may be life sustaining (e.g. water, food and shelter) or be luxuries. Design and technology in schools focuses on food and textiles through which we can begin to understand these essential human needs and their provision.

Successful teaching respects pupils' contributions, and creates opportunities for them to evaluate their ideas against criteria of their own, of the class and externally set. Pupils need the opportunity to communicate their ideas in a non-threatening environment where everyone's ideas are valued. If they see that their ideas are valued they will be more prepared to listen to others and begin to appreciate other people's points of view, to realise that questions of values are important in the development of technologies. This way values are born.

Spiritual aspects

Design and Technology can be an expression of creativity and imagination that promotes inner growth. There is a sense of wonder at a pupil's own achievements and in studying the work of talented designers and makers. Personal reflection is a fundamental part of evaluation. Pupils are encouraged to express their feelings about products they are designing and making, and to understand the expression of other designers' products and artefacts. The DfEE has described evaluating products and applications as: 'The aim here is to promote careful thinking, respect for others, concern for the Earth's limited resources, and a readiness to wrestle with conflicting values, including ethical dilemmas' (DfEE 1995a, p. 2). As pupils progress they will be challenged to develop their evaluative thinking from the analysis of 'simple features of familiar products' at Level 1 through to 'recognising the different needs of a variety of users, and use appropriate evaluation techniques to find ways forward' at Level 7 (DfEE 1995a, pp. 14–16).

Does the outcome of a pupil's design and technological activity express that pupil's feelings? Pupils that have been given a task to design for others, such as a toy for a three to seven-year-old, should question themselves to see how much their own childhood and interests have affected their designs. Pupils will often start projects with an evaluation of a familiar product: what was your favourite toy when you were a young child? why was it special to you? When pupils enjoy designing and making, it expresses their own identities.

The Primary school teacher might ask pupils to bring in greeting cards. Pupils would examine these and disassemble the component parts into title, graphics and message. The pupils would be asked to comment on:

- why they like or dislike the card?

- who gave it to them?

- what messages does it send?

- who is it for?

- how does the graphic image convey a message?

After this, pupils can design and produce a greetings card for their own celebration using their own lettering, images and message.

Studying textiles in Secondary school, pupils might create mood boards, with images pasted on them that show their views on designers' creations and interpretations, and provide motivation for design ideas. Given a South American theme they might investigate textiles in terms of colour, texture, pattern and materials. They would use material swatches, colour samples, pasted images and possibly use text to describe the feelings provoked by the textiles. The pupils would then undertake a design-and-make task to produce a bag, drawing inspiration from the images and materials that they had collected. This approach could be applied to other topics.

'Wonder' at the beauty of a designer object can motivate pupils when undertaking a new task. Wonder can be seen in the excitement of experiencing a new technology, for example a laptop computer. There is a joy to be had when encountering a well designed product. The aesthetic beauty of Starcks juicer, the Ferrari motor car or the Forth Bridge can be studied to understand designers' outlooks and perceptions. Pupils using electrical circuits in the Primary school or electronics in a Secondary school for the first time are often in awe at their own ability to perform a seemingly magical task using components whose inner workings they do not fully appreciate. They can explore how designers use beautiful forms found in nature and design artefacts that reflect these.

Designing and making artefacts can benefit a pupil's self-worth and insensitive handling can have the opposite effect. A sense of achievement might come at a time of little success in academic subjects. Pupils are able to risk failure and yet still be rewarded by a teacher for innovation, empathy and experimentation. A teacher can differentiate project tasks to give a pupil success. Some pupils will require greater teacher input and others might be encouraged towards self-expression through colour, shape and through their interests. A project that involves a group of pupils with separate responsibilities will enable them to develop sensitivity to other pupils' ideas and respect for the opinions of others. Key Stage 1 pupils might be designing and building a model house from recycled materials. Key Stage 2 pupils could extend this idea by incorporating simple circuits into their model houses. Key Stage 3 or 4 pupils might design 'a car for the future'. Each pupil could be responsible for one aspect of the design, body styling, interior, energy source, materials and components. Throughout these projects pupils would need to be given time to combine ideas, accommodate other pupils' points of view and develop their role within the group. The social skills of working as a team in design and technology could benefit all pupils' work on group tasks. Pupils learn to value others' views in working towards a collective design and to work together in the manufacture of a large product.

Moral aspects

Technology should be set in contexts that are real to the pupils and not abstract. Contexts should develop from those with which pupils are familiar (for example their own home), to the wider world. A technology curriculum which takes seriously the process of reviewing and evaluating should be one in which the values and beliefs in technologies are made objects of study (Barnett 1994). As the National Curriculum Orders stress, 'Evaluation is part of design and technology capability. In addition to considering the effectiveness and impact of a product, pupils will need to think about the appropriateness of the underlying values ... The evaluation can then refer to the intended purpose and consider not only performance and cost effectiveness, but also implications for the people who develop and use them and the problems associated with resource utilisation and side effects' (DfEE 1995a, p. 2).

There are clear moral dilemmas associated with the evaluation of some products of technology. Land-mines clearly do what the designer wishes (fit for purpose) in a very effective manner (quality design), but is it morally right to use them considering the suffering they cause? One of the moral values that we should consider in schools is the worth associated with the sanctity of life. Secondary pupils might consider the consequences of technology, for example nuclear power produces cheap electricity but also hydrogen bombs. In a Primary school you might consider the design and technology of other times, giving children the opportunity to consider people's real needs and the issues of the past as well as the values they considered important in the technological development. The pyramids are considered to be one of the greatest wonders of the world but were built at great personal sacrifice by large numbers of slaves. Pupils could evaluate the pyramids by answering the following questions:

- Were the pyramids considered to be successful/unsuccessful? By whom?

- Why were the pyramids produced in the first place?

- Should the pyramids have been built in the first place?

Consideration of value judgements enables pupils to harness their creative abilities towards goals they have chosen, with growing sensitivity to the needs of others. Pupils should be taught that there are alternative points of view, that the values of other people are not necessarily the same as their own. Their values may be about personal likes and dislikes and it is up to the teacher to help pupils to recognise the basis for preferences and encourage them to be more open-minded. As pupils get older they can deal with more sophisticated questions that involve value judgement concerned with economic, aesthetic, environmental, technical, social and moral issues, for example on the use of recycled products, e.g. fleece jackets made from plastic bottles.

Social aspects

Products made by pupils, as in industry, are designed to overcome problems and to satisfy needs. Design and Technology can help pupils to understand the social influences on their own lives and how systems and products can affect us all. The critical evaluation of existing products might involve pupils asking whether we buy products that reflect our status in society and social values. The use of logos on designer clothing and labels on food products and their advertising are an enormous influence on young people and projects that explore this would question their views. Key Stage 1 and 2 pupils might examine fizzy drinks cans from various manufacturers, exploring preferences from brandnames before blind tasting. Children might then design and make their own 'healthy' drink and design a package for it. Key Stage 3 or 4 pupils might be asked to look at a number of similar garments with logos on and disassemble them for quality and worth. Pupils might be asked to design a garment and logo for a company that was targeting a particular audience. Pupils could explore issues of 'image' and 'peer pressure' alongside the practical activities.

Problem-solving activities could lead to a deeper understanding of human needs. A brainstorming session to 'design a pedestrianised shopping area' could, if well facilitated, lead to an understanding of the needs of shoppers, the disabled, young families, the elderly, the business environment, the emergency services and tourists.

On the design of aids for people with special needs, primary school pupils could investigate their school for ease of access for disabled people. They could carry out an audit of suitability for wheelchair users by using wheelchairs to get around school. Someone who is wheelchair bound might come in and talk to the pupils about the problems they have. After identification of problems the pupils would then undertake a design-and-make task to overcome one of these problems using models and using Graphics to plan routes around the school for disabled people. This should raise social awareness in pupils.

At Secondary school pupils could investigate the problems people with special needs have when pouring hot water from the kettle into a cup. They could examine familiar products to develop their own designs. The teacher may invite a guest speaker into the classroom to convey first hand the problems encountered by the disabled doing every day tasks and ask them back to evaluate the pupils' work. Pupils would then design and make a product from resistant materials that would try to overcome this problem.

Case studies that feature particular designers might be used as a basis for questioning the work of that designer. Designers of armaments, the means of producing nuclear energy, and motor vehicles could be discussed using the opinions of opposing organisations or pressure groups: e.g. arms manufacturers and Amnesty International; or motor vehicle designers and Friends of the Earth.

Modern advances in communications technology have helped human interactions and possibly hindered them. Correspondence by letter was affected by the invention of the telephone yet e-mail has rejuvenated the written word. How might future technologies like video conferencing change these interactions? The initial motivation behind Trevor Bayliss when inventing the clockwork radio was to help communicate sex education to the African people, that would prevent the spread of the Aids virus; now that the product has been developed to power an electric light and a laptop computer how might this be used in other societies around the world? The development of 'low tech' technology using simple resources is an interesting area to explore with pupils.

Changes in manufacturing industry towards mechanisation and robotics has had far-reaching effects on society. For example, to explore this, pupils could visit a local factory or car plant and see robots in action, giving them some understanding of modern technology and the efficient use of the workforce. Pupils could then model a production line in school, for example by making up model Lego cars. They could first make models on their own, joining all parts together. This would be followed by the pupils working in a production line performing only one task. The time for the manufacture of ten cars could be taken in each case. The pupils could be asked to reflect on the benefits of automation in cost terms and how they might feel working as part of a production line, that is, the social implications. They could also consider the implications for mobility on the increased number of cheaper cars.

There are many social influences and pressures on designers and pupils should research their effects and consider them in their own work. Key Stage 3 and 4 pupils involved in Food Technology could devise a questionnaire that investigates the social pressures on dieting, the image of a super model having the ideal figure, the reasons for anorexia, fitness and acceptability of vegetarianism. In 'Resistant Materials' pupils should be aware of why we restrict the use of hardwoods, how deforestation is motivated by local need, and yet there are far-reaching global needs. Mahogany and teak are used to make furniture. This has lead to deforestation in South America. We need the furniture, the South Americans need the money and the environment needs the trees. Pupils will encounter a range of monitoring organisations in their studies: health and safety is prevalent in all areas of Design and Technology and this will help students to take responsibility for their actions and become aware of how they might affect other pupils and those for whom they design; health and hygiene in 'Food Technology'; the design and manufacture of toys for very young children in 'Resistant Materials'; the use of mains electricity in 'Systems and Control'.

On equal opportunity, Design and Technology has been perceived as traditionally a male domain, although this is beginning to change. Women's and girls' skills in a wide range of technologies, including food and textiles, have not been valued. Less effective lessons can often value and build on boys' interests and experiences more than those of girls. Girls' and boys' attitudes to technology are developed from an early age. Therefore Primary schools have an important role to play in ensuring all pupils participate and experience success in design and technology. Girls generally develop skills of cooperation and like working in groups where they support each other through sharing their ideas, skills and expertise. Design-and-make assignments might be set which allow pupils to work in cooperative groups even though they will be producing an individual final product. Girls react positively when they see the personal and social relevance of what is being taught. Including questions such as 'How does technology affect you, your family, your friends?' and activities which investigate, disassemble and evaluate products, can help to stimulate girls' interest in technology. Equal opportunities for different racial groups can also be explored: pupils could undertake a graphics project on stopping racism in football.

Cultural aspects

Europeans have had a tendency to be rather chauvinistic about technology, to look down on anything that does not come from our culture. Pupils need to become aware that technological advance is not the monopoly of a single culture, but developments over the centuries have taken place in many countries and cultures. A study of the technology during the Crusades gives the lie to many of these ideas. The Islamic culture was far in advance of western Europe. They had systems for moving water around using one way valves to stop back flow, complex water clocks, horizontal windmills and gas masks for miners, medicines, astronomical instruments to name but a few developments. An important aspect of technology is therefore the recognition that there is nothing inevitable about technological developments. Different cultures have found alternative solutions to the same problem. Some ancient technologies such as early porcelain glazes cannot be copied, even with modern resources. Conservation of buildings can help preserve the technical skills used by the builders. Controversies over the ozone layer and the greenhouse effect, and the use of embryo tissue present ethical issues for technology. Technology is fully embedded within culture and reflects its values and norms. Some technological developments are created to celebrate a culture, to show to the world the values that the society has. This is a symbolic use of technology to produce prestigious buildings. The Sydney Opera House is designed to reflect the sails of the (invading, in Aboriginal eyes) ships entering the harbour. It represents the beginnings of modern-day Australia and a society with 'western' values. Products of technology can be status objects (e.g. a Rolls Royce) which signifies wealth, power and grandeur.

The inherent values in a product cannot be discerned by simply examining a technological product. It needs to become meaningful. In a primary school the study of festivals, for example Diwali, could lead into the children designing and making sweetmeats and diva lamps for the celebration and therefore understand inner meaning. Pupils might design and make hats suitable for different climates, for example sun-hats. This would follow an evaluation of hats from different cultures designed to protect the wearer from sun, cold or rain. In a secondary school pupils might study Indian or Caribbean food, musical instruments, toys or cooking utensils from other cultures as 'investigate, disassemble and evaluate' activities to explore the technology of other cultures, and any implications this might have for ourselves. Pupils might then design and make an ecologically-friendly food product that could provide one third of the daily nutritional requirements of a teenager (Runnymede Trust 1993).

We must take care when identifying the contexts for design and technology to avoid reinforcing negative images of people in developing countries. Pupils might study houses from different cultures, or 'primitive' societies. The mud huts from some rural areas of Zimbabwe are a good example of technology that is relevant today. Architects study these to find out more about heating and cooling effects, air flow and solar power to use in their building designs (Mulberg 1992). The Mongul yurt, a tent like structure made from felt, is designed to be easily transportable, but also effective in keeping the people warm through very harsh winters. Design and Technology work can help pupils to understand and appreciate the multicultural society in which we live without being patronising. Pupils bring different values and beliefs into the classroom and teachers will need to approach these with sensitivity. This variety of cultural backgrounds broaden the insight pupils can have into the range of solutions to a problem. It can be a very effective way to show that one culture is not better than another in its design and technology achievements.

The cultural aspects of technology are linked to the idea of *appropriate* technology. This recognises and accepts that human needs are complex. This idea of technology suggests that things are not necessarily transferable from one culture to another. *Appropriate* technology is often specifically local, needs orientated, resource efficient and flexible. Western intensive farming techniques were tried in India and found to decrease not increase yields. Direct drilling of food crops interspersed with ground covering fodder crops was found to increase yields because it restricted the growth of weeds and stopped soil erosion during the rainy season. Technologies transferred from one culture to another can often be radically transformed by the society, but can also transform the recipient culture, not always beneficially. Alongside technology, pupils need also to examine potential consequences.

References

Barnett, M. (1994) 'Designing the future? Technology, values and choice', *International Journal of Technology and Design Education* **4**, 51–63.

DfEE (1995a) *Design and Technology. Characteristics of Good Practice in Secondary Schools*. London: HMSO.

DfEE (1995b) *Looking at Values Through Products and Applications*. London: HMSO.

Midland Examining Group (1998) *Design and Technology: Syllabus D, Resistant Materials*. Cambridge: Midlands Examining Group.

Mulberg, C. (1992) 'Beyond the Looking Glass: Technological myths in Education' in C. Budgett-Meakin (ed.) *Make the Future Work. Appropriate Technology: a Teachers' Guide*. Harlow: Longman.

NCC (1995) *Design and Technology in the National Curriculum*. London: HMSO.

Prime, G. M. (1993) 'Values in Technology: approaches to learning', *Design and Technology Teaching* **25**(3), 30–36.

Ritchie, R. (1995) *Primary Design and Technology. A Process for Learning.* London: David Fulton Publishers.

Runnymede Trust (1993) *Equality Assurance in Schools: Quality, Identity, Society.* Stoke-on-Trent: Trentham Books.

Standen R. (1992) 'The design dimension of the curriculum', in Budgett-Meakin C. (ed.) *Make the Future Work. Appropriate Technology: a Teachers' Guide.* Harlow: Longman.

Further reading

Budgett-Meakin, C. (ed.) (1992) *Make the Future Work. Appropriate Technology: a Teachers' Guide.* Harlow: Longman.

This is an important book that puts technology into a world-wide perspective. Contributors provide a range of perspectives in examining values and appropriate technology.

DfEE (1995) *Looking at Values Through Products and Applications.* London: HMSO.

This book provides guidelines for the discussion of various products, to reveal the values embedded in them, e.g. a collection of dolls.

Chapter 16

Information and Communications Technology

Chris Higgins and Philip Meadows

Policy

When discussing the values dimension of teaching and learning, the use of Information and Communications Technology (ICT) across the curriculum is likely to become increasingly important. ICT has assumed greater prominence in the National Curriculum for schools as time has passed. In 1990, in the first version of the National Curriculum, it appeared as Information Technology (IT) and was to be found in the Technology Order along with Design and Technology. This created some confusion about the status and purpose of IT use in schools, by appearing to define it in terms of the technology. The revision of the National Curriculum in 1995 went some way to rectifying the situation by treating IT as a subject in its own right, and emphasising the use of IT as a cross-curricular tool rather than as a technology.

The latest development is indicated by the adoption of the term ICT in the current documentation. This signals the recognition of the importance of the appearance of communications technology use in the classroom. For our purposes, the addition of communications technology to the equation extends the use of IT in the classroom from the rather mechanistic overtones of manipulation and dissemination of information and data, to include the more humanistic realms of dialogue between users implied by the terminology of communications technology. ICT has also assumed a position of being virtually the fourth core subject in the curriculum after English, Mathematics and Science.

Values

Neither information nor technology is value free, and making explicit the value laden nature of the use of ICT is a complex problem, made even more difficult when the domain of enquiry is education. The aim of this chapter is to address two interrelated questions:

- To what extent does ICT help to shape the student's spiritual, moral, social and cultural values?

- How is this function of ICT to be evaluated and directed?

Initially, ICT was viewed principally as an instructional tool in education, but now it is also seen as a means of enhancing teaching and learning. There are a number of theories of learning which can be considered when discussing ICT use in an educational context, each having different aims and objectives for the learning process and hence incorporating different values. Any piece of ICT software written specifically for educational use incorporates, more or less explicitly, the model of learning its designer espouses, and any use of ICT for educational purposes presupposes, even unconsciously, a model of learning which informs the activity and which requires varying modes of use.

Two broad categories of ICT use can be identified in terms of the learning theory models involved. The first category comprises those uses where a behaviourist view of learning is assumed, and the second is where the activities are based on cognitive theories of learning. The behaviourist approach is posited on the beliefs that the learning process can be rigorously analysed and that knowledge can be specified in language and transmitted to a student. This means that the student is considered to be a passive recipient of teaching and that the main object of learning is the mastery of subject matter. The role of the computer here is to present content in sequence, to prescribe tasks and to motivate the student by feedback. A drill and practice program would be an example of this approach, as would some of the early forms of Integrated Learning Systems (ILS). The cognitive theories consider the student as an active participant in the learning process, which is seen as the development and modification of cognitive structures. The emphasis of this approach is on the internal processing of ideas, and is termed 'constructivist' theory as the learner constructs their own understanding. Learning takes place by exploration and discovery, and the student develops problem-solving skills, hypothesis-testing skills and procedural thinking skills. However, the original constructivist ideas take little account of the social context of the learning process. The implication is that individual exploration of the learning environment will result in development of the student's knowledge structures. Later developments in cognitive theory do not treat learning as a solitary activity but attempt to incorporate the effects of the student's peers and the teaching process. These new developments are commonly termed 'socio-cultural' theory. Simulations and microworlds are based on these theories, giving the student an environment to experience and manipulate.

Any ICT activity in the classroom thus carries with it statements of values in terms of the purposes of the activity and the model of learning inherent in it, and so the medium can be used as a means to exemplify these values. The teacher can make them as explicit as they like to their students. ICT activities incorporating the socio-cultural theory of learning can in particular offer possibilities for the development of the social aspects of education, allowing experimentation with roles, social rules, relationships, communication, cooperation and social structures.

We shall now present a 'values model' to provide us with a framework for analysing values in the use of ICT more generally. The model has three elements – educator, computer and student – and recognises that in the interplay between them, each brings its own set of assumptions. We will apply this model to a number of ICT applications, using it to raise questions of value and direct some preliminary explorations. Our overall aim is not to provide a comprehensive list of value statements pertaining to ICT, but to offer a model and a method which can be used more generally to reflect on the values associated with any educator-computer-student scenario.

The model

1. The role of the educator

The educator is no longer seen as the source of information, rather they become the students' guide and mentor, and we can investigate the forms their guidance takes and the effects it has. The educator can plan the incorporation of the ICT into the rest of the curriculum, suggest investigations, engage in discussion, offer constructive criticism and evaluate progress. They can supplement ICT activities when they lack some particular dimension, and make students aware of the implicit values of the software engineers who decided on the forms of ICT the students find themselves using.

2. The role of the computer

Interpreting the values to be found in the technology itself can be productively approached through a set of criteria, which themselves express certain tensions in the nature and use of ICT:

– ICT as a *resource* versus ICT as a *subject of study* in its own right.
 In our discussion we consider ICT as a resource, as it might apply to the teaching of any area in the curriculum.

– ICT as *tutor* versus ICT as *tool*.
 The use of the computer as a tutor extends from simple drill and practice programs to intelligent tutoring systems. Using the computer as a tool includes applications such as databases and word-processing.

– *Explicit* versus *implicit communication of values* with ICT.
 Explicitly, ICT can be used to communicate values as a subject in its own right. Implicitly, the technology itself can be seen to embody a set of values which can inform the student's world view.

– ICT *serving pedagogy* versus ICT *determining pedagogy*.
 Here we consider to what extent the curriculum is being driven by technological developments, rather than educational needs determining the ICT use.

- *Social/public* versus *individual/private modes of learning* with ICT.
  The computer typically engages the student in solipsistic learning experiences which must be integrated in other ways. With the advent of more advanced forms of computer mediated communication, corporate learning experiences are possible.

3. The role of the student

Students are human beings, and we can turn to philosophy to find a number of interrelated perspectives on what it means to be human. Pedagogically speaking, we reflect upon the activity of *learning and knowing as a human being*, and *learning about or from other human beings*.

- The *personalist perspective* places a premium on the student's personal relationship with that being learnt. That which the student aims to know can be either an object or another person, and the nature of the encounter should determine the mode of enquiry. Relations with objects are properly about the analysis and interrogation of the objects. However, people are not objects but other conscious selves, who we get to know in a mutual process, not by objective interrogation. To treat others as objects effectively depersonalises and dehumanises them. Learning to treat others as persons means developing qualities such as sympathy and empathy.

- The *existentialist perspective* assumes that information has the power to shape the being of the learner. In other words, the handling of information is never a purely objective business, but needs to be dealt with subjectively and personally. Learning constantly places demands upon our world view, and often requires us to make important personal choices. Thus, the existentialist perspective elevates the importance of experience, emotional involvement and personal risk.

- The *spiritual perspective* points out that to be fully personal and live a fully authentic existence also involves transcendence. It means exploring ultimate concerns beyond oneself which can help make sense of one's place in the whole scheme of life. Such ultimate concerns, be they religious or secular, ground the importance of qualities such as truth, faith and commitment. Such spirituality is not, however, something appended to the human being but part of what it means to be human. It is expressed in the capacity for aesthetic appreciation and imagination, the exercise of hope and love, and the experience of wonder and mystery.

We shall now concentrate on four specific ICT applications, discussing and evaluating them in the light of our proposed model.

Computer Mediated Communication (CMC)

CMC is a generic term for a number of different technologies, including electronic mail (e-mail), Internet Relay Chat (IRC), bulletin boards and computer conferencing, all of which are interactive text based technologies. These are obviously ideal for developing literacy skills: CMC tends to encourage students to think through and carefully craft their contributions to an on-line community in a way that face-to-face communication does not. While the spontaneity of face-to-face group discussion is to be valued, it must be recognised that not all students are comfortable with the vulnerability of the classroom context. The more leisurely and anonymous nature of interactivity in CMC can be of value in encouraging the participation of even the most reticent student, building confidence for wider forms of interaction.

In our context, however, the potential of CMC lies in the fact that it is not about face-to-face encounter. There is a cartoon of two dogs sitting at a computer terminal, with one dog saying to the other, 'This is great! On here, no one knows we are dogs!' The very anonymity of CMC tends to open up the possibility of interpersonal relationships and on-line communities which may never have occurred in the ordinary way. People who are alienated by their age, sex, socio-cultural background, occupation, or failing physical embodiment, can find in the indiscriminate levelling nature of CMC a personalising and humanising environment. CMC can be excellent for the excluded, especially if exposure to these technologies helps to foster inclusive attitudes which translate into everyday relations. It has to be questioned, however, whether an inclusivity based on anonymity is necessarily wholesome: attitudes engendered by CMC could, morally speaking, actually become depersonalising and dehumanising.

There is a degree of anonymity built into all human relationships since we all wear different masks in different circumstances. The anonymity of CMC means that it is possible for individuals to construct on-line personae which are quite different from the realities of their own age, occupation, and even gender. An exercise in which students adopted invented personae would allow exploration of these issues, offering a way for students to explore their own sense of self and personal identity. However, one must ask whether it matters that presenting such personae could be construed as a deception, and what this communicates about the values of building right relationships in the ordinary way. Existentially speaking, patterns of experience and learning should encourage students to live authentically.

As a pedagogic device, the use of CMC can offer an example of the role of educator as guide. The tutor enters the community of learning as one participant among many, engaging discursively at the same operational level as the students. To be sure, the tutor brings their own expertise (and even plan) into the conversation, but facilitates and guides learning only as a cooperative venture with the students. Tutoring models based on dialogue emphasise the responsibility and active participation of the student in the learning process. Such methods could also have the virtue of enhancing the student's engagement with material at a personal and existential level.

CMC also offers powerful possibilities for strategies such as peer tutoring and the development of learning communities. Technologies such as computer conferencing engage students in dialogue rather than monologue: answers to questions and solutions to problems are arrived at using interpersonal skills such as negotiation, debate, and critical reflection. In CMC, such dynamic processes are both a means and an end in themselves.

On-line communities also mirror real communities in the sense that they are defined by common interests and common sets of moral values. Most computer conferences have rules of conduct which may or may not be formally codified, but demand the responsible participation of their members if they are to function properly. In this sense, CMC can provide a context in which students learn the dynamics of responsibility, a sense of justice and right relationship.

The World Wide Web

The Web is fast becoming the information metaphor of our time. The publication and consumption of information is moving away from traditional paper documents to hypermedia documents. Historically, information has been presented in a linear, sequential form usually in a single medium. Nowadays, information may be presented in many different ways, in a multitude of media and organised in various structures. The term 'hypertext' was coined to mean non-linear arrangements of text, and essentially has come to mean sets of links from a computer screen to information in a database allowing the interrelation of texts. Hypermedia is the extension of this idea to include multimedia resources. It covers computer based material with links that allow the user non-sequential access to text, pictures, sound, animation and video. The next generation of 'word' processor applications are likely to be based on the hypermedia model, producing documents in Internet-ready form. This kind of technology has made it possible for anyone to become an 'information provider', a publisher of documents to a world wide audience over the Web.

It is increasingly likely that future generations of students will be encouraged to publish their work in this way, and even create their own websites. The Web is also redefining what it means to be a learner: handling knowledge with this technology is about browsing or 'surfing'. Surfing the Web involves a complex interplay of being driven by, and exploiting, the power of hyper-connected pages. We will analyse the values of Web technology in terms of what it means to be both an information provider and an information browser. These values are expressed both in the content of the pages themselves and in the connections made between pages. In other words, there are values inherent in the associations made between items of information within and between websites, values which are most subtly absorbed through the process of surfing itself.

Even a cursory investigation of Web 'culture' reveals the highly prized value of 'free speech', taken to mean that information providers have the right to publish material of any sort without regulation. It might also be taken as a logical consequence of this position that Web browsers have the right to access such material without restriction. Web technology presses the ethical tension between the values of personal freedom and corporate responsibility.

Unlike the communities created by CMC, the Web is not directly concerned with the dynamics of interpersonal relations, but with the most efficient way of serving information upon demand. Information providers may produce material which may be of a culturally sensitive or even subversive nature (such as pornography, and terrorist, racist or anti-Semitic entries). Given that material on the Web is, on the whole, indiscriminately made available to all, it may be argued that the freedom to provide information must be weighed against a sense of social responsibility for what one actually publishes.

Responsibility for handling information, however, extends to both provider and browser alike. Many people will exploit the apparent anonymity of surfing to access information which they might otherwise have avoided. Teachers might, therefore, consider using the Web as a way to illustrate and explore the power of information, and the ethical issues faced by publishers and public alike.

As an educational tool, the Web also has much to commend it as a means for enhancing skills in the area of personal research. Students can learn to value the broad corpus of human interest and knowledge as a field for exploration and discovery. The metaphor of 'surfing' points to the business of knowledge acquisition, and understanding, as a journey which values all the unpredictability and unexpectedness of human experience. The serendipitous nature of knowledge has been, after all, the mode of many great human discoveries, and it is through experiences such as these that a contribution can be made to a student's 'spiritual' development: offering a sense of awe and wonder, the stimulation of imagination, and a context for self-reflection.

The activity of surfing can also have the benefit of developing a variety of information handling skills, from simple data gathering to sorting, judging and sifting of relevant materials. The very nature of hyperlinked documents means that the student can more easily get a feel for the interconnection of information. The ability to draw upon material published from all over the world can contribute to the development of global perspectives among our students. Indeed, exploring subject matter provided by people from different places around the world can soon bring an appreciation of the socio-cultural location of knowledge.

It can also be argued that the experience of surfing the Web has the power to trivialise as well as maximise the value of information: the capacity to access information being matched only by the capacity to discard it without proper reflection. Surfing could disguise a failure or unwillingness to confront issues and experiences which are challenging, and perhaps painful. Bringing this concern into the context of interpersonal relations, the thoughts, opinions and expressions of other people should be valued by giving them time and proper attention. People are always to be valued, even if Web pages are not. Exercises whereby students constructed a critique of entries which they had discovered, debated the points of view and constructed their own understanding of the issues would provide a rich arena for social, moral, spiritual and cultural debate.

The computer as a tool

The most common uses of ICT in the classroom are those where the computer is used as a tool, a generic term covering the use of applications such as word processors and databases. Uses of such applications can create problems in terms of the spiritual, moral, social and cultural curriculum, but they can also be fertile ground for exploring many of the issues. The educator can perform a valuable role in alerting the student to what may be lost by the indiscriminate use of the tool.

The primary concern is that computer tools are not value free and the use of a particular computer tool may implicitly force the user into certain modes of thought or analysis. The word processor with its myriad of options can give a spurious importance to presentation over content. The use of an automatic grammar checker can impose limitations on personal style. The creation of a database can be an objectifying process where subject matter is categorised and classified as objects in terms of a few characteristics rather than being dealt with in holistic terms, thereby losing something of their essence in the process. The use of a spreadsheet to model a real life situation requires a simplification of the reality into a more easily manageable form, hence losing some of the richness of detail of the original and sacrificing some of the interrelationships between the parts of the whole. The use of large information sources such as are available on CD-ROM can lead to a tendency to present great quantities of information indiscriminately, confusing quantity with quality.

Another concern is that the use of such tools distance the user from the task and presuppose an objective stance to the material. The depersonalisation of the processes could lead to supposedly cold, purely logical but poorly informed decisions being arrived at without the spiritual, moral, social and cultural dimensions for pupils coming into the picture.

However, as we have said already, from the existentialist perspective the manipulation and communication of information can never be purely objective. Students should be alerted to the possible dangers and limitations of thoughtless use of the computer tools. They should be taught that the user of computer tools is not driven remorselessly into one mode of use, but is free to choose appropriate courses of action in the light of their own experience and requirements. An antidote to the seeming restrictions of a given tool is the increasing possibilities for the customisation of the ICT to reflect the needs and preferences of the user. The use of the word processor to prepare a document allows for repeated redrafting and editing if these processes are valued. The creation of a database should necessitate some thought about what data to include and how to record it, in the light of what information it is hoped the database will provide. Thus the experienced, enlightened database user should always be aware of what is left out and make allowances for this. The point of modelling, whether with a spreadsheet or otherwise, is to attempt to make sense of a complex situation by simplifying it, but the insights gained must always be referred back to the full original to see how valid they are. When faced with boundless information on a topic from a CD-ROM, the task is to decide what is important or salient to the point at issue, and to present what really matters (being aware that that itself will be determined by the prevailing socio-cultural situation).

The use of ICT for these tasks allows for the eventual finished product to be repeatedly refined much more easily than has previously been possible. Pupils can use the computer tools to go beyond the mechanics of the tasks and explore the meanings of the activity they are engaged in. They can allow the product that is to be created to emerge as a sculptor or a painter might, when using their particular tools on their raw material. What might have been termed pupils' errors or mistakes can now be viewed not as failures terminating the enterprise, but as intermediate steps on the route to eventual success. Errors are of benefit, as they focus attention on what is not yet finished, and in redrafting or correcting the pupils learn from their mistakes.

When we discuss the use of the computer as a tool we should not think in terms of a logician with a cold processing device, but more in terms of a musician with an instrument or a craftsman with his tools. The user of the tool is not driven to a single outcome but can explore many nuances and subtleties of tone, and the full range of the spiritual, moral, social and cultural curriculum can be brought into the discussion.

Computer tutoring systems

The development of computer tutoring technology has tended to move away from the behaviourist models found in most early systems to employ cognitive theory in its design and implementation, with its emphasis on problem-solving through experimentation. At its simplest level, such a system will interactively prompt and guide a student through a problem to attain a certain solution through a specific procedure. More sophisticated intelligent systems will be open to alternative solutions and have a dynamic learner-model capable of responding to the different needs of individual students – providing the appropriate level of student-centred and context-sensitive feedback as and when it is needed. There is always the risk, however, that no matter how intelligent a computer-tutor is, the student will be depersonalised through being reduced to fit such a learner-model.

Tutoring systems can be evaluated with respect to the relative amount of student versus computer direction in the learning process. On the one hand, highly directive systems can stifle creativity and lateral thinking, by focusing on specific goals and solutions. On the other hand, where the priority becomes maximising the student-initiative while minimising tutorial input, there would seem to be an implicit valuing of the student as problem-solver, dependent upon an ever diminishing amount of external help.

These computer tutoring technologies, typically classified as Integrated Learning Systems, serve to reinforce the generally individualistic and mostly solipsistic approach found in much computer based learning. In reality, people are more likely to find themselves in contexts of corporate problem-solving where a collective diversity of specialised skills is valued. It is important, therefore, that where computer tutoring technology tends to be over individualistic, it should be supplemented by other forms of socialised learning.

Existentially, recognition and acceptance of our limitations is an important part of the learning process – and this is not to be construed in terms of failure or deficiency, but as a consequence of our humanity. On an interpersonal level, the corporate nature of discovery, learning, and problem-solving has an irreducible and even transcendent value – the whole is greater than the sum of its parts. So, the use of ICT is to be affirmed where it can provide a stimulus, or context, for such interaction to take place.

On a more general note, we need to be aware of the possibility that cognitive approaches to learning might suggest that life can be viewed as a set of problems to be solved, where there are always 'right answers' to be had, and the truth of a matter is always available. Insofar as many of our life situations are problematic, the problem-solving approach would seem to be infinitely valuable. For most people, however, life experience demonstrates that 'right answers' are usually elusive. Similarly, life often seems more ambiguous than perspicuous, and meaning is often only to be had in retrospect rather than through foresight. ICT will help equip our students for such a life only if they take a critical approach to its various manifestations.

Conclusion

We finish by returning to the two questions we posed at the beginning:

– *'To what extent does ICT help to shape the students' spiritual, moral, social and cultural values?'*
The students' exposure to ICT comes from the use of ICT applications in diverse areas of the curriculum. The ICT is interrelated with the areas of the curriculum and inseparable from them, so the power of ICT to shape the world views and value systems of students comes from its ubiquity as a learning resource.

– *'How is this function of ICT to be evaluated and directed?'*
We make no apology for the somewhat abstract approach taken in this chapter. It is our hope that subject specialists will find the educator-computer-student model we have outlined, and the evaluative method we have illustrated, helpful for reflecting upon the use of ICT in their own fields. It is important to remember that the diversity of these technologies demands a holistic approach to the use of ICT across the curriculum. In any given application different dimensions of spiritual, moral, social and cultural education will come to prominence and our model cuts across them all. Furthermore, the need to evaluate the use of ICT in teaching and learning applies to both educator and student alike – the value laden nature of information, communication, and technology is our common concern.

Further reading

Bonnett, M. (1997) 'Computers in the classroom: some values issues', in McFarlane, A. (ed.) *Information Technology and Authentic Learning*. London: Routledge.
A useful introduction to many of the issues we have discussed, but with a somewhat staid and dated point of view.

Meadows, P. (1995) 'The Gospel in Cyberspace', *Epworth Review* **22**(2), 53–73.
A discussion of the moral, ethical and spiritual questions surrounding the concept and use of cyberspace and virtual reality.

Porter, D. (ed.) (1997) *Internet Culture*. London: Routledge.
A collection of essays addressing the relationship between Internet technologies and questions of society and culture.

Index